Microsoft Excel 7.0a for Windows® 95

Timothy J. O'Leary
Linda I. O'Leary

Copyright © 1996 by McGraw-Hill, Inc. All rights reserved. Printed in the United States of America. Except as permitted under the United States Copyright Act of 1976, no part of this publication may be reproduced or distributed in any form or by any means, or stored in a database or retrieval system, without prior written permission of the publisher.

5 6 7 8 9 0 BAN BAN 9 0 9 8 7

ISBN 0-07-049110-0

Library of Congress Catalog Card Number 95-82267

Information has been obtained by The McGraw-Hill Companies, Inc. from sources believed to be reliable. However, because of the possibility of human or mechanical error by our sources, The McGraw-Hill Companies, Inc., or others, The McGraw-Hill Companies, Inc. does not guarantee the accuracy, adequacy, or completeness of any information and is not responsible for any errors or omissions or the results obtained from use of such information.

Contents

Spreadsheet Overview SS5
Definition of Electronic Spreadsheets   SS5
Advantages of Using an Electronic Spreadsheet   SS6
Electronic Spreadsheet Terminology   SS7
Case Study for Labs 1–6   SS7
Before You Begin   SS8
Microsoft Office Shortcut Bar   SS9

Lab 1 Creating a Worksheet: Part 1   SS10
Part 1 SS12
Loading Excel for Windows 95   SS12
Examining the Excel Window   SS12
Examining the Worksheet   SS14
Using Toolbars   SS15
Moving Around the Worksheet   SS16
Scrolling the Worksheet   SS17
Designing Worksheets   SS19
Entering Data   SS20
Clearing an Entry   SS22
Editing an Entry   SS23
Entering Long Text Entries   SS25
Entering Numbers   SS27
Closing and Opening a Workbook   SS28
Part 2 SS32
Copying Data   SS32
Review of Copying Methods   SS36
Entering Formulas   SS37
Recalculating the Worksheet   SS38
Changing Cell Alignment   SS39
Documenting a Workbook   SS41
Saving a Workbook   SS42
Printing a Workbook   SS44
Exiting Excel   SS45
Lab Review   SS45
　Key Terms   SS45
　Command Summary   SS46
　Matching   SS46
　Fill-In Questions   SS47
　Discussion Questions   SS48
Hands-On Practice Exercises   SS48
　Step by Step   SS48
　On Your Own   SS50
Concept Summary   SS52

Lab 2 Creating a Worksheet: Part 2   SS54
Part 1 SS55
Entering Formulas Using Point Mode   SS55
Copying Formulas   SS57
Entering Functions   SS59
Clearing Cell Contents   SS63
Using Function Wizard   SS64
Using Absolute References   SS65
Adding Cell Notes   SS67
Adjusting Column Widths   SS69
Using Undo   SS71
Zooming the Worksheet   SS71
Formatting Numbers   SS72
Applying Styles   SS75
Part 2 SS77
Inserting Rows   SS77
Moving Cell Contents   SS78
Centering Across Columns   SS79
Changing Fonts and Font Styles   SS79
Copying a Sheet   SS82
Naming Sheets   SS84
Using AutoFill   SS85
Linking Worksheets   SS86
Previewing a Workbook   SS88
Lab Review   SS91
　Key Terms   SS91
　Command Summary   SS92
　Matching   SS93
　Fill-In Questions   SS93
　Discussion Questions   SS93
Hands-On Practice Exercises   SS93
　Step by Step   SS93
　On Your Own   SS96
Concept Summary   SS98

Lab 3 Managing a Large Worksheet   SS100
Part 1 SS101
Splitting Windows   SS101
Freezing Panes   SS105
Viewing Multiple Windows   SS107
Using What-If Analysis   SS109
Using Solver   SS111
Moving a Sheet   SS115

Opening a Second Workbook   SS115
Spell-Checking the Worksheet   SS116
Linking Workbooks   SS118
Part 2   SS122
Using Goal Seek   SS122
Adding Color and Borders   SS125
Moving Toolbars   SS127
Adding Text Boxes   SS128
Using Predefined Headers and Footers   SS131
Changing Page Orientation   SS132
Creating Custom Headers and Footers   SS133
Lab Review   SS136
   Key Terms   SS136
   Command Summary   SS136
   Matching   SS137
   Fill-In Questions   SS137
Hands-On Practice Exercises   SS137
   Step by Step   SS137
   On Your Own   SS141
Concept Summary   SS142

Lab 4   Creating Charts   SS144

Part 1   SS145
Using Autoformats   SS145
About Charts   SS148
Selecting the Data to Chart   SS150
Using ChartWizard   SS153
Sizing a Chart   SS157
Changing the Type of Chart   SS157
Creating a Chart with Multiple Data Series   SS158
Activating a Chart   SS160
Part 2   SS163
Moving the Legend   SS163
Adding Patterns   SS163
Adding a Text Box   SS165
Adding Arrows   SS167
Creating a Combination Chart   SS167
Adding Data Labels   SS171
Creating a Pie Chart   SS172
Changing Worksheet Data   SS175
Printing Charts   SS175
Lab Review   SS177
   Key Terms   SS177
   Command Summary   SS177
   Matching   SS178
   Fill-In Questions   SS178
   Discussion Questions   SS178
Hands-On Practice Exercises   SS178
   Step by Step   SS178
   On Your Own   SS180
Concept Summary   SS182

Lab 5   Creating Templates   SS184

Naming a Range   SS185
Using the IF Function   SS190
Using Paste Special   SS194
Protecting a Sheet   SS195
Creating a Template File   SS198
Lab Review   SS201
   Key Terms   SS201
   Command Summary   SS202
   Matching   SS202
   Fill-In Questions   SS202
   Discussion Questions   SS202
Hands-On Practice Exercises   SS203
   Step by Step   SS203
   On Your Own   SS204
Concept Summary   SS205

Lab 6   Sharing Data Between Applications   SS206

Pasting Between Applications   SS207
Linking a Chart to a Word Document   SS211
Updating a Linked Object   SS213
Embedding Objects   SS216
Updating an Embedded Object   SS218
Deciding When to Use Linking or Embedding   SS221
Lab Review   SS221
   Key Terms   SS221
   Command Summary   SS221
   Matching   SS222
Hands-On Practice Exercises   SS222
   Step by Step   SS222
   On Your Own   SS224
Concept Summary   SS225

Case Project   SS227
Part 1   SS227
Part 2   SS228
Part 3   SS229

Glossary of Key Terms   SS230

Command Summary   SS235

Windows 95 Review   SS239

Index   SS249

SPREADSHEET

Spreadsheet Overview

In contrast to a word processor, which manipulates text, an electronic spreadsheet manipulates numerical data. The first electronic spreadsheet software program, VisiCalc, was offered on the market in 1979. Since then the electronic spreadsheet program has evolved into a powerful business tool that has revolutionized the business world.

Definition of Electronic Spreadsheets

The electronic spreadsheet, or worksheet, is an automated version of the accountant's ledger. Like the accountant's ledger, it consists of rows and columns of numerical data. Unlike the accountant's ledger, which is created on paper using a pencil and a calculator, the electronic spreadsheet is created using a computer system and an electronic spreadsheet application software program.

The electronic spreadsheet eliminates the paper, pencil, and eraser. With a few keystrokes, the user can quickly change, correct, and update the data. Even more impressive is the spreadsheet's ability to perform calculations from very simple sums to the most complex financial and mathematical formulas. The calculator is replaced by the electronic spreadsheet. Analysis of data in the spreadsheet has become a routine business procedure. Once requiring hours of labor and/or costly accountants' fees, data analysis is now available almost instantly using electronic spreadsheets.

Nearly any job that uses rows and columns of numbers can be performed using an electronic spreadsheet. Typical uses of electronic spreadsheets are for budgets and financial planning in both business and personal situations.

Advantages of Using an Electronic Spreadsheet

An electronic spreadsheet application helps you create well-designed spreadsheets that produce accurate results. The application not only makes it faster to create the spreadsheet, but produces a professional-appearing result. The advantages are in the ability of the spreadsheet program to quickly edit and format data, perform calculations, create graphs, and print the spreadsheet.

The data entered in an electronic spreadsheet can be edited and revised using the program commands. Numeric or text data is entered into the worksheet in a location called a cell. These entries can then be erased, moved, copied, or edited. Formulas can be entered that perform calculations using data contained in specified cells. The results of the calculations are displayed in the cell containing the formula.

The design and appearance of the spreadsheet can be enhanced in many ways. There are several commands that control the format or display of a numeric entry in a cell. For instance, numeric entries can be displayed with dollar signs or with a set number of decimal places. Text or label entries in a cell can be displayed centered or left- or right-aligned to improve the spreadsheet's appearance. Columns and rows can be inserted and deleted. The cell width can be changed to accommodate entries of varying lengths.

Many spreadsheet programs let you further enhance the appearance of the spreadsheet by changing the type style and size. You can emphasize different parts of the spreadsheet by using bold or italics and adding underlines, borders, boxes, drop shadows, and shading around selected cells. The ability to see these styles and format changes on the screen as they will appear when printed is called WYSIWYG ("what you see is what you get").

You have the ability to play with the values in the worksheet, to see the effect of changing specific values on the worksheet. This is called what-if or sensitivity analysis. Questions that once were too expensive to ask or took too long to answer can now be answered almost instantly and with little cost. Planning that was once partially based on instinct has been replaced to a great extent with facts. However, any financial planning resulting from the data in a worksheet is only as accurate as that data and the logic behind the calculations.

Most electronic spreadsheets also have the ability to produce a visual display of the data in the form of graphs or charts. As the values in the worksheet change, a graph referencing those values automatically reflects the new values. These graphs are a tool for visualizing the effects of changing values in a worksheet. Thus they are analytic graphs. Many spreadsheet programs let you include a graph with the spreadsheet data. This way you can display and print it with the data it represents. You can also enhance the appearance of a graph by using different type styles and sizes, adding three-dimensional effects, and including text and objects such as lines and arrows.

Another feature of many spreadsheet programs is the ability to open and use multiple spreadsheet files at the same time. Additionally, you can create multiple spreadsheets within a file, called 3-D spreadsheets. Even more important is the ability to create formulas that link one spreadsheet file to another file or that link one spreadsheet in a file to another spreadsheet in the same file. This linking capability lets you change data in one file and automatically update the linked data in another file.

Electronic Spreadsheet Terminology

Alignment: The position of an entry in a cell to the left, centered, or right in the cell space.

Cell: The space created by the intersection of a horizontal row and a vertical column. It can contain a label (text), value (number), or formula.

Columns: The vertical blocks of cells in the spreadsheet identified by letters.

Copy: A feature that duplicates the contents of a cell or range of cells to another location in the worksheet.

File linking: A spreadsheet feature that creates a connection between two files in order to share data.

Format: The styles applied to a cell that control how entries in the spreadsheet are displayed (currency, percent, number of decimal places, and so on).

Formula: An entry that performs a calculation.

Function: A built-in or preprogrammed formula.

Graph: The visual representation of ranges of data in the worksheet. Also called a chart. Some graph types are line, bar, stacked-bar, and pie.

Label: An entry that consists of text and numeric characters.

Move: A feature that relocates the contents of a cell or cells to another area in the worksheet.

Rows: The horizontal blocks of cells in the worksheet identified by numbers.

Value: An entry that is a number or the result of a formula or function.

What-if analysis: A process of evaluating the effects of changing one or more values in formulas to help in decision making and planning.

WYSIWYG: The "what you see is what you get" feature that lets you see onscreen the format and text enhancement features as they will appear when printed.

Case Study for Labs 1–6

As a recent college graduate, you have accepted your first job as a management trainee for The Sports Company. The program requires that you work in several areas of the company. In this series of labs, you are working in a retail store as an assistant to the store manager.

In Labs 1 and 2 you will create an operating budget for the retail store. You will learn how to use the worksheet program to enter descriptive text, numbers, formulas, and functions. You will also learn how to format the worksheet to improve its appearance. Finally, you will open and work with multiple worksheet files and create a workbook to organize related files.

Lab 3 demonstrates how to freeze row and column titles and split windows to manage large worksheets. It also shows you how to use the operating budget worksheet to perform what-if analysis. Finally, in this lab you learn how to link workbook files.

In Lab 4 you decide you want to analyze the sales data by sport at the store. To better visualize the changes in sales over time, you learn how to create several charts of the data.

In Lab 5 you will create a worksheet template to be used to track the monthly new charge card enrollments and employee bonuses. While working on this project, you learn about the IF function, naming ranges, and using worksheet protection.

Lab 6 demonstrates how an Excel chart can be incorporated into a Word document. The differences between linking and embedding are demonstrated.

Before You Begin

To the Student

The following assumptions have been made:

- The Microsoft Excel 7.0a program has been properly installed on the hard disk of your computer system, and the default program settings are in effect.

- The data disk contains the data files in the root directory that are needed to complete the series of Excel 7.0a labs and practice exercises. These files are supplied by your instructor.

- You have completed the Windows 95 Labs or you are already familiar with how to use Windows 95.

To the Instructor

The following assumptions about the setup of the Excel 7.0a program have been made:

- When the worksheet window is maximized, the number of rows and columns that are displayed varies with the computer system display settings established in Windows. These labs assume a standard VGA display setting, which displays columns A through I and rows 1 through 18. The text and figures reflect this setup.

- The Standard and Formatting toolbars are displayed whenever a worksheet is opened.

- The Quick Preview on-line tutorial is not on.

- The TipWizard is not on.

- The Solver application has been installed.

- The Ignore Other Applications setting is on and the Prompt for Summary Info setting is off. These options are in the General folder of the Options dialog box in the Tools menu.

Microsoft Office Shortcut Bar

The Microsoft Office Shortcut Bar (shown below) may be displayed automatically on the Windows 95 desktop. Commonly, it appears in the upper right section of the desktop; however, it may appear in other locations, depending upon your setup. The Shortcut Bar on your screen may display different buttons. This is because the Shortcut Bar can be customized to display other toolbar buttons.

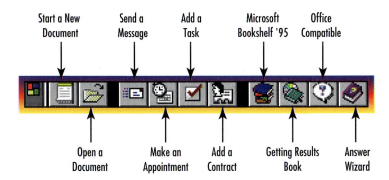

The Office Shortcut Bar makes it easy to open existing documents or to create new documents using one of the Microsoft Office applications. It can also be used to send e-mail, add a task to a to-do list, schedule appointments using Schedule+, or access Office Help.

Creating a Worksheet: Part 1

Unlike most tools, the computer is a multipurpose tool. Its purpose is to improve your efficiency and accuracy and to help solve problems. Because it can run many different types of software programs, it is a tool that can create a wide variety of products and solve a wide variety of problems.

> **COMPETENCIES**
>
> After completing this lab, you will know how to:
>
> 1. Load Excel for Windows 95.
> 2. Use toolbars.
> 3. Move around the worksheet.
> 4. Design a worksheet.
> 5. Enter data.
> 6. Delete and edit cell entries.
> 7. Open and close workbooks.
> 8. Copy data.
> 9. Enter formulas.
> 10. Recalculate a worksheet.
> 11. Change cell alignment.
> 12. Document, save, and print a workbook.
> 13. Exit the Excel program.

Each application program your computer runs has a specific purpose. For example, word processors help you produce text-based documents, and drawing programs produce graphic art. The software tool you will learn about in this series of labs is the spreadsheet application, Excel. Its purpose is to store, manipulate, and display numeric data.

Concept Overview

The following concepts will be introduced in this lab:

1. Worksheet Design	A well-designed worksheet produces accurate results, and is clearly understood, adaptable, and efficient.
2. Types of Entries	Cell entries can be text or numbers.
3. Select Cells	Selecting highlights the cell or cells that will be affected by your next action.
4. Cut, Copy, and Paste Cell Contents	The contents of worksheet cells can be deleted, moved, or copied to new locations in the worksheet.
5. Range	A range is two or more contiguous or noncontiguous cells on a worksheet.
6. Formulas	A formula is an entry that performs a calculation. The result is displayed in the worksheet cell.
7. Automatic Recalculation	Excel automatically recalculates formulas whenever a change occurs in a referenced cell.
8. Format	Formats control how information is displayed in a cell and are used to improve the appearance of the worksheet data.
9. Alignment	Alignment settings allow you to change the horizontal and vertical placement and the orientation of an entry in a cell.
10. Dates	Excel automatically recognizes certain types of data input, such as dates and times, and formats the entry as appropriate.
11. Save Files	To create a permanent copy of your workbook, you save the document as a file on a disk.
12. Excel Filenames	An Excel filename follows the same filename rules as other Windows 95 products. It is automatically saved with the filename extension .XLS.

CASE STUDY

The Sports Company is a chain of sporting goods shops located in large metropolitan areas across the United States. The stores are warehouse oriented, discounting the retail price of most items 15 percent. They stock sporting goods products for the major sports: team sports, racquet sports, aerobics, golf, and winter sports.

As a recent college graduate, you have accepted your first job in a management training program for The Sports Company. The training program emphasis is on computer applications in the area of retail management. The program requires that you work in several areas of the company, beginning in a retail store as an assistant to the store manager.

During the next six labs, you will create and use several worksheets using the Microsoft Excel 7.0a program. In this lab you will create a store budget. You will learn how to enter descriptive row and column headings, enter numbers and formulas, copy data, and print the worksheet.

SPREADSHEET

Part 1

Loading Excel for Windows 95

If necessary, turn on your computer and put your data disk in drive A (or the appropriate drive for your system). The Windows 95 desktop screen should be displayed.

To start Excel 7.0a for Windows 95,

Choose: Start/<u>P</u>rograms

> If a shortcut to Excel button is displayed on your desktop, you can double click on the button to start the program.

The Microsoft Excel 7.0 program should appear in the program list.

Choose: Microsoft Excel

> If the Microsoft Office suite is on your system and the Office Shortcut bar is displayed, you can load Excel by clicking the Open New Document button, selecting Blank Workbook, and choosing OK.

A title screen is briefly displayed while the computer loads the Excel program into memory. After a few moments, your screen should be similar to Figure 1-1.

If necessary, maximize the Excel application window.

> Refer to the Sizing Windows section in the Windows 95 Review for information on this feature.

Examining the Excel Window

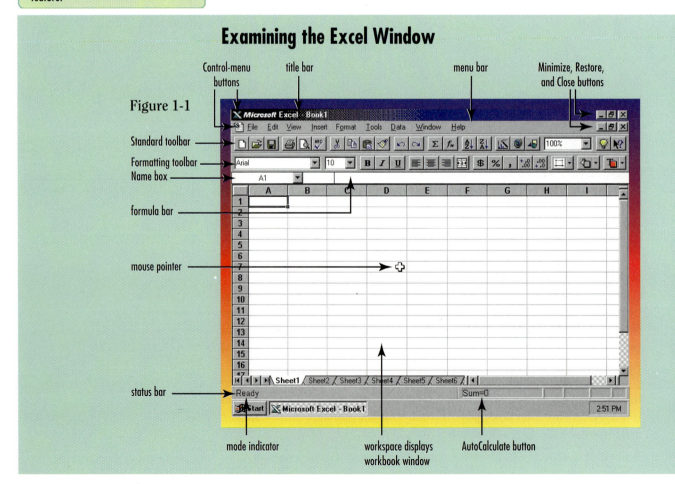

Figure 1-1

Figure 1-1 is the **Excel application window**. As you can see, many of the Excel window features are common to the Windows 95 environment. Among those features are a title bar, menu bar, control menus, Minimize and Restore buttons, icons, document windows, and mouse compatibility. You can move and size Excel windows, select commands, use Help, and switch between files and programs just as in Windows and other Windows-based applications. Your knowledge of how to use Windows makes using Excel much easier. The Excel window includes all these features, plus some additional features that are specific to Excel.

The largest area of the Excel window is the **workspace**. The workspace is where different windows are displayed. Currently there is only one window open, and it occupies the entire workspace. The window displays a workbook. A **workbook** is an Excel file that stores the information you enter using the program. Excel calls a window that displays a workbook a **workbook window**. You can have several workbooks open at once, each displayed in their own workbook window in the workspace. You will learn about the different parts of the workbook window shortly.

The Excel window title bar displays the program name, Microsoft Excel, followed by the file name Book1, the default name of the file displayed in the workbook window. The left end of the title bar contains the Excel application window Control-menu icon, and the right end displays the Minimize, Restore, and Close buttons. They perform the same functions and operate in the same way as in Windows 95.

> If the title bar does not display the file name, the workbook window is not maximized. Maximize the workbook window by clicking on the workbook window Maximize button.

The menu bar below the title bar displays the Excel program menu. The left end of the menu bar displays the workbook window Control-menu icon, and the right end displays the workbook window Minimize, Restore, and Close buttons.

The two toolbars below the menu bar contain buttons that are mouse shortcuts for many of the menu items. The upper toolbar is the **Standard toolbar**, and the bottom is the **Formatting toolbar**. There are 13 different toolbars in Excel. The toolbars operate just like Windows 95 toolbars. You will learn more about Excel toolbars shortly.

Below the toolbars is the formula bar. The **formula bar** displays entries as they are made and edited in the workbook window. The **Name box**, located at the left end of the formula bar, provides information about this selected item.

The status bar at the bottom of the Excel window displays information about various Excel settings. The left side of the status bar displays the current mode or state the Excel program is in. The current mode is Ready. When "Ready" is displayed, you can move around the workbook, enter data, use the function keys, or choose a command. As you are using the program, the status bar will display the current mode. The modes will be discussed as they appear throughout the labs. The button that currently displays "Sum=0" is the **AutoCalculate button**. It displays the sum of selected data in the worksheet. You will learn more about this feature shortly.

The mouse pointer probably appears as a or on your screen. As in Windows 95, the mouse pointer changes shape depending upon the task you are performing or where the pointer is located on the window.

> Refer to the Mouse section in the Windows 95 Review for information on this feature.

SPREADSHEET

Now that you have examined the Excel Window, you can examine the parts of the worksheet.

Examining the Worksheet

A workbook can contain six different types of sheets. A **sheet** is used to display different types of information, such as financial data or charts. Whenever you open a new workbook, it displays a worksheet. A **worksheet** is a rectangular grid of **rows** and **columns** used to enter data. It is always part of a workbook and is the primary type of sheet you will use in Excel. The parts of the worksheet are shown in Figure 1-2 below.

> The default workbook opens with 16 worksheets. The number of sheets in a workbook is limited only by the available memory on your computer.

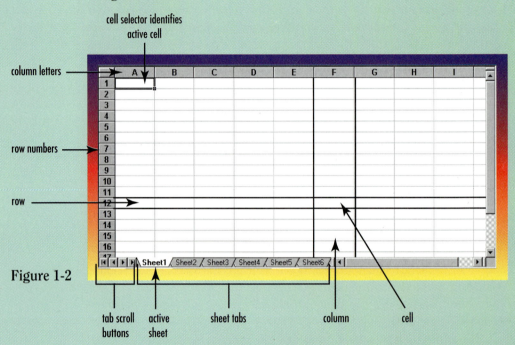

Figure 1-2

The **row numbers** along the left side and the **column letters** across the top of the window identify each worksheet row and column. The intersection of a row and column creates a **cell**. Notice the highlighted cell on your screen. The heavy border around this cell, called the **cell selector**, identifies the active cell. The **active cell** is the cell your next entry or procedure affects. The Name box displays the reference of the active cell. The **reference** consists of the column letter and row number. The reference of the active cell is A1 (see Figure 1-1).

Each sheet in a workbook is named. The default names are Sheet1, Sheet2, and so on, displayed on **sheet tabs** at the bottom of the workbook window. The name of the **active sheet** appears bold and is the sheet you can work in. The currently displayed worksheet in the workspace, Sheet1, is the active sheet.

The sheet tab area also contains **tab scroll buttons**, which are used to scroll tabs right or left when there are more worksheet tabs than there is available space. You will learn about these features throughout the labs.

Using Toolbars

By default the Standard toolbar and the Formatting toolbar, shown below, are automatically displayed.

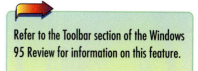

Refer to the Toolbar section of the Windows 95 Review for information on this feature.

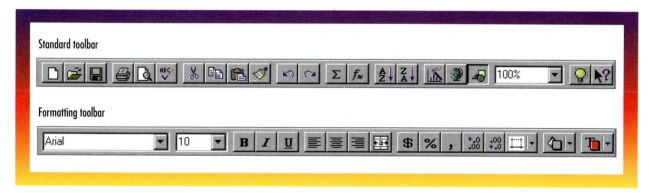

The Standard toolbar contains buttons that are used to complete the most frequently used menu commands. The Formatting toolbar contains buttons that are used to change the format or design of the worksheet. Many of the buttons are the same as those you have seen in toolbars in other Windows 95 applications. Many, however, are specific to the Excel 7.0 application.

To quickly identify the toolbar buttons, point to each button in both toolbars to display the button name in the Tooltip and a description in the status bar.

The last button on the Standard toolbar is the Help button. It is used to get Help on any command or window element.

Mouse use is assumed throughout. Marginal notes will discuss keyboard tips as appropriate.

Click: Help

The mouse pointer appears as a ▸?. Now by clicking on any command or window element, you can get Help information directly related to the item you are pointing to.

Click on the 💡 button and read the Screen Tip that appears in the box. To clear the Screen Tip, click anywhere or press Esc.

As you learned from the Screen Tip, the TipWizard button turns the TipWizard toolbar on and off. To turn it on,

Click: TipWizard

SPREADSHEET

Your screen should be similar to Figure 1-3.

Figure 1-3

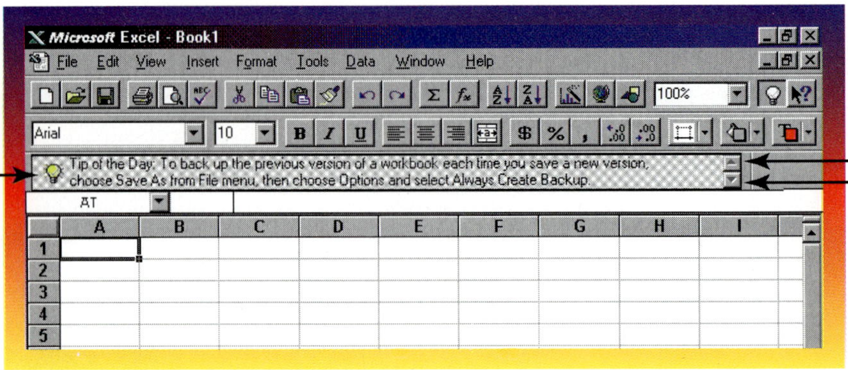

TipWizard toolbar
scroll arrows

The TipWizard toolbar appears below the Formatting toolbar. It displays the Tip of the Day when first opened. As you use Excel, the TipWizard toolbar will display a tip about the task you are performing if there is a more efficient or alternative method of performing the task. It also stores all tips that have been displayed since you started the program.

Although many of the toolbars open automatically as different tasks are performed, you can also open toolbars whenever you want using the toolbar Shortcut menu.

To open the toolbar Shortcut menu, right-click on the toolbar.

The menu displays the list of toolbars. Clicking on a toolbar from the list will display it onscreen. Likewise, clicking on a checked toolbar will remove the toolbar from the screen. You do not need to display any other toolbars.

Clear the Shortcut menu.

Moving Around the Worksheet

Either the mouse or the keyboard can be used to move the cell selector from one cell to another in the worksheet. To move using a mouse, simply point to the cell you want to move to and click the mouse button.

Click: cell B3

The cell selector is in cell B3, making this cell the active or selected cell. The Name box reflects the new location of the cell selector in the worksheet by displaying the reference, B3 (column B, row 3).

Depending upon what you are doing, using the mouse to move may not be as convenient as using the keyboard. The directional keys are used to move the cell selector around the worksheet. To use the keyboard to move to cell E7,

Press: → (3 times)
Press: ↓ (4 times)

> To reset TipWizard to display tips that may have already been seen, click 💡 while holding down Ctrl.

> The menu equivalent is View/Toolbars.

> You can use the directional keys in the numeric keypad or, if you have an extended keyboard, you can use the separate directional keypad area.

> If you are using the numeric keypad area, make sure the Num Lock feature is off. "NUM" is displayed in the status bar when it is on.

Your screen should be similar to Figure 1-4.

Name box displays reference of active cell

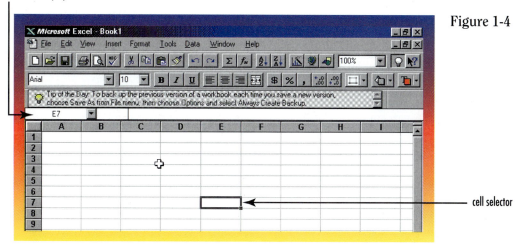

Figure 1-4

cell selector

The cell selector is now in cell E7, making this cell the active cell.
To return quickly to the upper left corner, cell A1, of the worksheet,

Press: Ctrl + Home

Wherever you are in the worksheet, pressing Ctrl + Home will move the cell selector to the upper left corner of the worksheet.

The worksheet is much larger than the part you are viewing in the window.

The worksheet actually extends many columns to the right and many rows down. An Excel worksheet has 256 columns and 16,384 rows.

To move down one full window on the worksheet, press Page Down.

The window is positioned over rows 15 through 29 of the worksheet. Columns A through I have remained the same.

Move to cell A1.

Scrolling the Worksheet

Either the mouse or the keyboard can be used to quickly move through or scroll the worksheet to see an area that is not currently in view. Again, both methods are useful, depending upon what you are doing.

> You cannot move the cell selector above row 1 or to the left of column A.

> Page Up moves up a window on the worksheet.

In addition, the keys shown in the table below can be used to move around the worksheet. For example, if you hold down the arrow keys, the [Alt] + [Page Down] or [Alt] + [Page Up] keys, or the [Page Up] or [Page Down] keys, you can quickly scroll through the worksheet. As you scroll the worksheet using the keyboard, the cell selector moves to the new location.

Keys	Action
Arrow keys ([↑][↓][→][←])	Moves cell selector one cell in direction of arrow
[Alt] + [Page Down]	Moves cell selector right one full window
[Alt] + [Page Up]	Moves cell selector left one full window
[Page Down]	Moves cell selector down one full window
[Page Up]	Moves cell selector up one full window
[Ctrl] + [Home]	Moves cell selector to cell in upper left corner of worksheet
[End] [→]	Moves cell selector to last used cell in row
[End] [↓]	Moves cell selector to last used cell in column

Practice moving the cell selector around the worksheet using each of the keys presented in the table above.

Another way to move around the worksheet is to use the scroll bars. When you use this method, the cell selector does not move until you click on a cell that is visible in the window.

Mouse	Action
Click cell	Moves cell selector to selected cell
Click scroll arrow	Scrolls worksheet one row/column in direction of arrow
Click above/below scroll box	Scrolls worksheet one full window up/down
Click right/left scroll box	Scrolls worksheet one full window right/left
Drag scroll box	Scrolls worksheet multiple windows up/down or right/left

Practice moving the cell selector around the worksheet using each of the mouse procedures presented in the table above.

When you are ready to go on,

Move to: A1

You can use the mouse or the keyboard with most of the exercises in these labs. As you use both the mouse and the keyboard, you will find that it is more efficient to use one or the other in specific situations.

Designing Worksheets

Now that you are familiar with the parts of the worksheet, you will begin creating the budget for the first six months for The Sports Company. The first step to creating a worksheet is to develop the worksheet design. A well-designed worksheet produces accurate results, is clearly understandable by the users, is easily adapted to changing needs, and is efficient in terms of its ease of use.

Concept 1: Worksheet Design

A well-designed worksheet produces accurate results, and is clearly understood, adaptable, and efficient. To achieve a well-designed worksheet, a worksheet plan must be developed. There are four steps in this planning process.

1. **Specify purpose.** As your first step, you must decide exactly what you want the worksheet to do. This means clearly identifying the data that will be input and the output that is desired.
2. **Design and build.** You can design the worksheet on paper or directly in Excel for Windows. Your design should include a worksheet title and row and column headings that identify the input and output. Sample data is used to help generate the formulas needed to produce the output.
3. **Test.** Once your design is complete, you are ready to test the worksheet for errors. Several sets of real or sample data are used as the input, and the resulting output is verified. The input data should include a full range of possible values for each data item to ensure the worksheet can function successfully under all possible conditions.
4. **Document.** Well-designed worksheets typically are documented within the worksheet. Documentation is important to ensure that whoever uses the worksheet will be able to clearly understand its objectives and procedures.

As the complexity of the worksheet increases, the importance of following the design process increases. Even for simple worksheets like the one you will create in this lab, the design process is important.

After reviewing past budgets and consulting with the store manager, you have designed the basic layout for the six-month budget for the retail store as shown in Figure 1-5.

Figure 1-5

	A	B	C	D	E	F	G	H	I
1									
2				1998 First Half Budget					
3									
4		JAN	FEB	MAR	APR	MAY	JUN	TOTAL	
5	SALES								
6	Clothing	$ 140,000	$ 125,000	$ 175,000	$ 210,000	$ 185,000	$ 185,000	$1,020,000	
7	Hard Goods	$ 94,000	$ 85,000	$ 120,000	$ 145,000	$ 125,000	$ 125,000	$ 694,000	
8	Total Sales	$ 234,000	$ 210,000	$ 295,000	$ 355,000	$ 310,000	$ 310,000	$1,714,000	
9									
10	EXPENSES								
11	Advertising	$ 9,360	$ 8,400	$ 11,800	$ 14,200	$ 12,400	$ 12,400	$ 68,560	
12	Cost of Goods	$ 135,720	$ 121,800	$ 171,100	$ 205,900	$ 179,800	$ 179,800	$ 994,120	
13	Salary	$ 32,000	$ 32,000	$ 32,000	$ 32,000	$ 32,000	$ 32,000	$ 192,000	
14	Lease	$ 19,000	$ 19,000	$ 19,000	$ 19,000	$ 19,000	$ 19,000	$ 114,000	
15	Miscellaneous	$ 16,000	$ 16,000	$ 16,000	$ 16,000	$ 16,000	$ 16,000	$ 96,000	
16	Overhead	$ 22,000	$ 22,000	$ 22,000	$ 22,000	$ 22,000	$ 22,000	$ 132,000	
17	Total Expenses	$ 234,080	$ 219,200	$ 271,900	$ 309,100	$ 281,200	$ 281,200	$1,596,680	

You will have created this worksheet by the end of Lab 2.

SPREADSHEET

Entering Data

The information or data you enter in a cell can be text, numbers, or formulas. First you will enter the worksheet headings. Row and column **headings** are entries that are used to create the structure of the worksheet and describe other worksheet entries. Generally, headings are text entries.

> **Concept 2: Types of Entries**
>
> **Text** entries can contain a combination of letters, numbers, and any other special characters. **Number** entries can include only the digits 0 to 9, and any of the special characters, + - ( ) , . / $ % E e. Number entries are used in calculations. An entry that begins with an equal sign (=) is a formula. Formula entries perform calculations using numbers or data contained in other cells. The resulting value is a **variable** value because it can change if the data it depends on changes. In contrast, a number entry is a **constant** value. It does not begin with an equal sign and does not change unless you change it directly by typing in another entry.

To create the structure for this worksheet, you will begin by entering the column headings. The column headings in this worksheet consist of the six months (January through June) and a total (sum of entries over six months) located in columns B through H (see Figure 1-5). To enter data in a worksheet, you must first select the cell where you want the entry displayed.

Refer to the Selecting section of the Windows 95 Review for more information.

> **Concept 3: Select Cells**
>
> Before you can carry out most commands or tasks in Microsoft Excel, you must select (highlight) the cells you want to work with. The selected cells will then be affected by the next command or action you perform. The active cell is always the selected cell and is surrounded by the cell selector.

The column heading for January will be entered in cell B2.

Move to: B2
Type: J

Your screen should be similar to Figure 1-6.

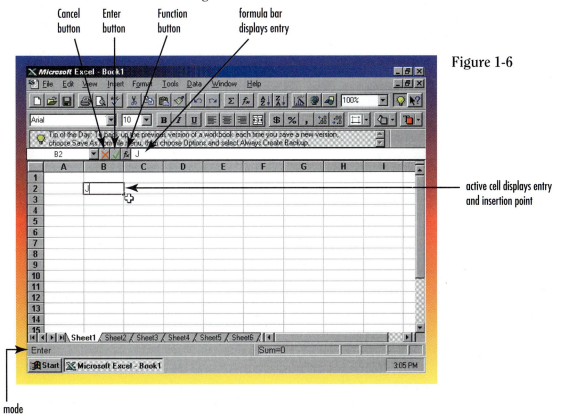

Figure 1-6

Several changes have occurred in the window. As you type, the entry is displayed both in the active cell and in the formula bar. An insertion point appears in the active cell and marks your location in the entry. Three new buttons, Cancel, Enter, and Function, appear in the formula bar. They can be used by the mouse to complete your entry, cancel it, or select a function (a predefined formula).

Notice also that the mode displayed in the status bar has changed from "Ready" to "Enter." This notifies you that the current mode of operation in the worksheet is entering data. To continue entering the heading,

Type: anuary

The cell and the formula bar should display "January."

Although the entry is displayed in both the active cell and the formula bar, it has not yet been completed. The ←Enter key or Enter button is used to complete your entry and enter it into the cell. If you press Esc or choose the Cancel button, the entry is cleared and nothing appears in the cell.

Since your hands are already on the keyboard, it is quicker to press ←Enter than it is to use the mouse to click. To actually enter the text into cell B2,

Press: ←Enter

> Refer to the Insertion Point section of the Windows 95 Review for information about this feature.

> You will learn about functions in Lab 2.

> If you made an error while typing the entry, use Backspace to erase the characters back to the error. Then retype the entry correctly.

Lab 1: Creating a Worksheet: Part 1

Your screen should be similar to Figure 1-7.

Figure 1-7

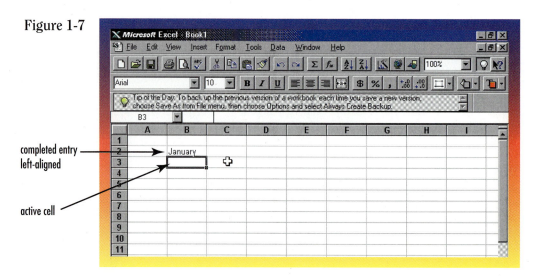

completed entry left-aligned

active cell

The cell selector moves down to cell B3. When you press ←Enter, the cell selector automatically moves down one cell.

The entry "January" is displayed in cell B2, and the mode has returned to "Ready." Notice that the entry is positioned to the left side of the cell space. The positioning of cell entries in the cell space is called alignment. By default text entries are displayed left-aligned. You will learn more about this feature later in the lab.

> Pressing ⇧Shift + ←Enter to complete an entry will move the cell selector up a cell.

Move to: B2

Because the cell selector is positioned on a cell containing an entry, the contents of the cell are also displayed in the formula bar.

Clearing an Entry

After looking at the entry, you decide you want the column headings to be in row 3 rather than in row 2. This will leave more space above the column headings for a worksheet title.

The Delete key can be used to clear the contents from a cell. To remove the entry from cell B2, with the cell selector on the entry to be removed,

> The menu equivalent is Edit/Clear/Contents. Clear Contents is also an option on the Shortcut menu.

Press: Delete

The cell entry is no longer displayed in the cell or in the formula bar. To enter the label in cell B3,

Move to: B3
Type: January
Press: ←Enter

Editing an Entry

You would like to change the heading from January to JAN. An entry in a cell can be entirely changed in the Ready mode or partially changed or edited in the Edit mode. To use the Ready mode, you move the cell selector to the cell you want to change and retype the entry the way you want it to appear. As soon as a new character is entered, the existing entry is cleared.

Generally, however, if you need to change only a part of an entry, it is quicker to use the Edit mode. To change to Edit mode, double-click on the cell whose contents you want to edit.

Pressing the [F2] key will also change to Edit mode.

Double-click: B3

The status bar shows the new mode of operation is Edit. The insertion point appears in the entry, and the mouse pointer changes to an I-beam I when positioned on the cell. The mouse pointer can now be used to move the insertion point in the entry by positioning the I-beam and clicking.

The mouse pointer must be ✥ when you double-click on the cell. Double-clicking on a blank cell changes the mode to Enter.

In addition, in the Edit mode, the following keys can be used to move the insertion point:

Key	Action
[Home]	Moves insertion point to beginning of entry
[End]	Moves insertion point to end of entry
[→]	Moves insertion point one character right
[←]	Moves insertion point one character left

If the insertion point is not at the end of the entry, move it there.

To edit an entry, you can use the [Delete] key to erase characters at the insertion point and the [Backspace] key to erase characters to left of insertion point. To remove the last four characters of the entry,

Press: [Backspace] **(4 times)**

Then, to move to the beginning of the entry,

Press: [Home]

Next you will change the entry to all uppercase characters. To turn on [Caps Lock],

Press: [Caps Lock]

The [Caps Lock] key affects only the letter keys. To produce the characters above the number or punctuation keys, you must use the [⇧Shift] key.

Notice that the keyboard mode indicator "CAPS" appears in the status bar to tell you that the feature is on.

The letters "a" and "n" need to be changed to uppercase. To move to the "a,"

Press: [→]

SPREADSHEET

Lab 1: Creating a Worksheet: Part 1

To write over the existing letters with uppercase characters,

Press: [Insert]

Your screen should be similar to Figure 1-8.

Figure 1-8

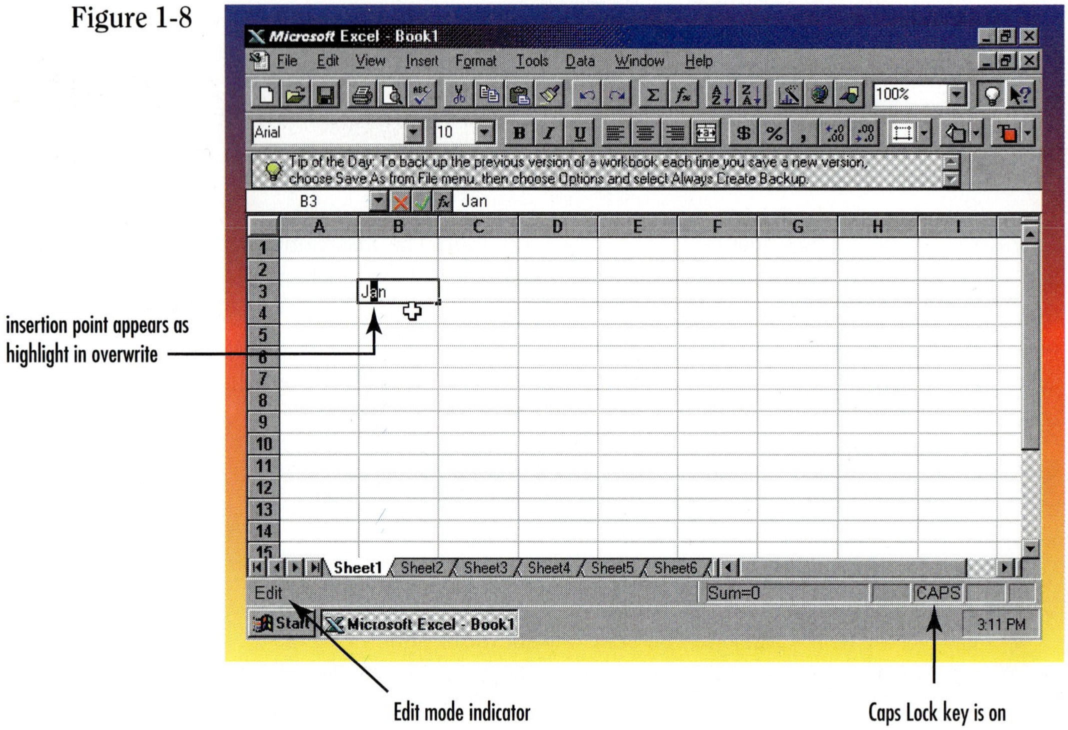

insertion point appears as highlight in overwrite

Edit mode indicator

Caps Lock key is on

The [Insert] key acts as a toggle to switch between inserting and overwriting text. The insertion point changes to a blinking highlight when overwrite is on. Overwrite is automatically turned off when you leave Edit mode or if you press [Insert] again.

Type: AN
Press: [←Enter]

The new heading JAN is entered into cell B3, replacing January. As you can see, editing will be particularly useful with long or complicated entries.
   To turn off [Caps Lock],

Press: [Caps Lock]

Next you will enter the month heading for February in cell C3.

Move to: C3
Type: February
Press: [←Enter]

Using the Edit mode, you will change February to FEB.

Move to: C3

Turn on Edit mode.
To change the heading to all capital letters,

> Double-click C3 or press [F2] EDIT.

Press: [Home]
Press: [→]
Press: [Caps Lock]
Type: EB

To erase all the letters after the insertion point,

Press: [Ctrl] + [Delete]
Press: [←Enter]

You are now ready to enter the heading for March into cell D3.

Move to: D3
Type: MAR
Press: [→]
or
Click: E3

Moving the cell selector to any other cell will both complete the entry and move the cell selector. The CAPS status indicator is still displayed, showing that the [Caps Lock] key is still on.

Complete the column headings by entering APR, MAY, JUN, and TOTAL in cells E3 through H3. When you are done, turn off [Caps Lock].

Notice that the TipWizard message has changed. It tells you about another way to enter months. You will learn about this feature in Lab 2.

> The ▲ and ▼ TipWizard scroll buttons are used to view tips that have been displayed since starting Excel.

Entering Long Text Entries

Above the column headings, in row 2, you want to enter a title for the worksheet.

Move to: C2
Type: 1998 First Half Budget
Press: [←Enter]

Your screen should be similar to Figure 1-9.

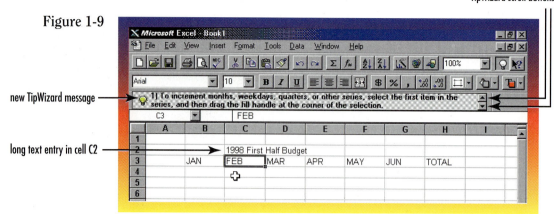

Figure 1-9

- new TipWizard message
- long text entry in cell C2
- TipWizard scroll buttons

Notice that the worksheet title is longer than the nine spaces in cell C2. When a text entry is longer than the cell's column width, Excel will display as much of the entry as it can. If the cell to the right is empty, the whole entry will be displayed. If the cell to the right contains an entry, the overlapping part of the entry is not displayed.

Next the row headings need to be entered into the worksheet. The row headings in column A and what they represent are shown below:

Heading	Represents
SALES	Category head for all items that are a result of sales
Clothing	Income from clothing sales
Hard Goods	Income from equipment, machines, and miscellaneous sales
Total Sales	Sum of clothing and hard goods sales
EXPENSES	Category head for all items that are a result of expenses
Advertising	Monthly advertising costs (4 percent of total sales)
Cost of Goods	Cost of items sold (58 percent of total sales)
Salary	Personnel expenses
Lease	Monthly lease expense
Miscellaneous	Monthly expenses for phone, electricity, water, trash removal, and so on
Overhead	Monthly payment to corporate headquarters
Total Expenses	Sum of advertising, cost of goods, salary, lease, miscellaneous, and overhead expenses
INCOME	Total Sales minus Total Expenses

You will enter the SALES category row headings beginning in cell A4.

Move to: A4
Type: SALES
Press: ←Enter

Complete the row headings for the SALES portion of the worksheet by entering the following headings in the indicated cells:

Cell	Heading
A5	Clothing
A6	Hard Goods
A7	Total Sales

Entering Numbers

Next you will enter the expected clothing sales numbers for January through June into cells B5 through G5. As you learned earlier, number entries can include the digits 0 to 9 and any of these special characters: + - ( ) , . / $ % E e. When entering numbers, it is not necessary to type the comma to separate thousand or the currency ($) symbol. You will learn about adding these symbols later.

Move to: B5

To enter the expected clothing sales for January,

Type: 140000
Press: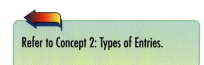

Your screen should be similar to Figure 1-10.

> Remember to press ←Enter or an arrow key to complete the last entry.

> Refer to Concept 2: Types of Entries.

> You can use the number keys above the alphabetic keys or the numeric keypad area to enter numbers. If you use the numeric keypad, the Num Lock key must be on.

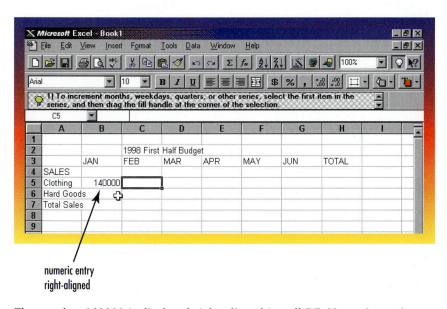

numeric entry right-aligned

Figure 1-10

The number 140000 is displayed right-aligned in cell B5. Numeric entries are displayed right-aligned by default.

In the same manner, enter the clothing sales numbers for February through June (left) and the hard goods sales for the six months in row 6 (right), using the numbers shown below in the specified cells:

Cell	Number		Cell	Number
C5	125000		B6	94000
D5	200000		C6	85000
E5	210000		D6	120000
F5	185000		E6	145000
G5	185000		F6	125000
			G6	125000

When you are done, your screen should be similar to Figure 1-11.

Figure 1-11

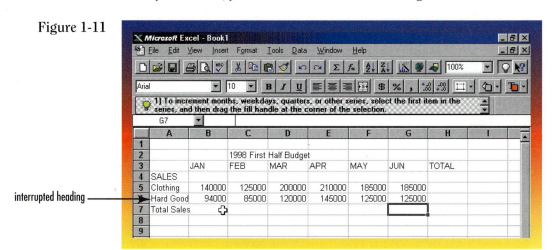

interrupted heading

Notice that the entry in cell A6 is no longer completely displayed. It is a long text entry, and because the cell to the right now contains an entry, the overlapping part of the entry is not displayed. The new entry in cell B6 causes the display of the heading to be interrupted.

Move to: A6

The formula bar displays the complete entry; only the display of the heading in cell A6 has been interrupted. In Lab 2 you will learn how to change the width of a column so the entire entry can be displayed.

Closing and Opening a Workbook

The rest of the row headings and several of the expense numbers for the month of January have already been entered and saved in a file called JANUARY DATA on your data disk. Before opening this workbook file, you will close the current workbook using the Close command on the File menu.

Choose: **File**

> Refer to the Menus section in the Windows 95 Review for information on this feature.

Your screen should be similar to Figure 1-12.

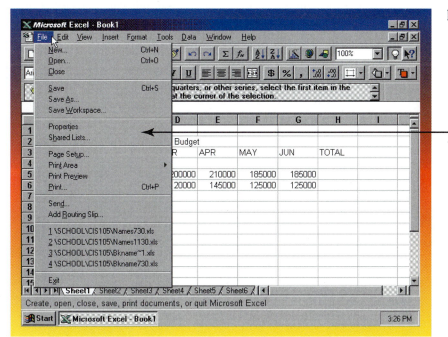

Figure 1-12

File drop-down menu

The File drop-down menu of commands is displayed. In addition to the commands you would expect to see in the File menu, such as Save and Exit, there are several commands that are specific to Excel. The horizontal line, within the drop-down menu divides the commands into related groups.

To close the workbook,

Choose: **Close**

> You could also click ⊠ to close the workbook file.

A dialog box is displayed asking if you want to save the contents of the current workbook to disk. Since the file you will open next contains the same information, you do not need to save it. To indicate you do not want to save this workbook,

> If you want to save your work, choose Yes. Then follow the directions on page SS42 to save the workbook as LAB 1 BUDGET to the drive containing your data disk.

Choose: **No**

The workbook window is cleared from memory, and the Excel window displays an empty workspace. Only two menus appear in the menu bar because there is no workbook open.

You are now ready to open the file named JANUARY DATA.

Put your data disk in the A drive (or the appropriate drive for your system).

As in all Windows 95 applications, the Open command on the File menu is used to open files. In addition, the toolbar shortcut can be used instead of the menu command.

Note: Throughout the Excel labs, command sequences will appear following the word "Choose." The command letters to type will be underlined and in boldface type. If a toolbar shortcut is available, it will appear following the word "Click" instead of the command, and a marginal note will display the equivalent command and keyboard shortcut.

> The menu equivalent is **File/Open** or [Ctrl] + O.

Click: **Open**

The dialog box on your screen should be similar to Figure 1-13.

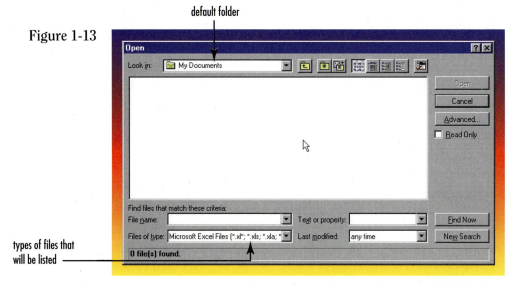

Figure 1-13

The Open dialog box is used to specify the name and location of the file to open. The Look In drop-down list box displays the default folder as the location where the program is looking for files. If necessary, you will need to change where Excel is looking for files to the drive containing your data disk.

> Refer to the Dialog Box section of the Windows 95 Review for information on this feature.

Select: **Look in**

> If your drive is already correctly specified in the Look In list box, skip this step.

The drop-down list displays the available drives on your system.

Select: 3½ Floppy (A:) **(or the drive containing your data disk)**

> If an error message is displayed, check that your disk is properly inserted in the drive and that the disk-drive door is completely closed. Then choose Retry.

Now the large list box displays the names of the Excel files on your data disk. The file you want to open is JANUARY DATA. The filename extension .XLS identifies this file as an Excel workbook file. If there are other files on your data disk that have different filename extensions, they are not listed. This is because the File of

> Refer to the Naming Files section of the Windows 95 Review for information on this feature.

Type list box shows the currently selected type is Excel files with the specified file extension of .XLS.

Select: **JANUARY DATA**

To complete the command,

Choose: **Open**

> If necessary, scroll the list box until the filename JANUARY DATA is visible. If the filename is not displayed, ask your instructor for help.

> You could also type the location and name of the file you want to open in the File Name text box.

The new workbook file is loaded and displayed in the workbook window. Your screen should be similar to Figure 1-14.

> You can double-click on the filename to both select it and choose Open.

Figure 1-14

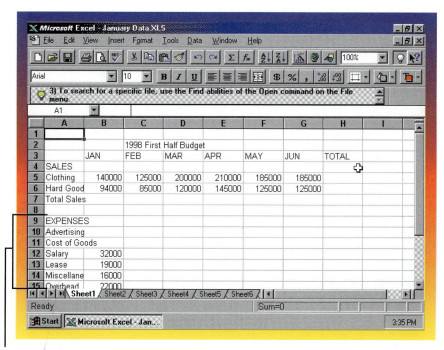

Expenses row headings

The opened workbook, JANUARY DATA, contains the expense row headings and numbers for salary, lease, miscellaneous, and overhead for the month of January.

To see the rest of the headings in the workbook,

Move to: **A18**

Note: If you are stopping at the end of Part 1, follow the instructions on page SS45 to exit the program. When you begin Part 2, load Excel and open the JANUARY DATA file.

Part 2

Copying Data

Next you want to enter the estimated expenses for salary, lease, miscellaneous, and overhead for February through June. They are the same as the January expense numbers.

When you entered the sales numbers for January through June, you entered them individually into each cell because the numbers changed from month to month. However, the number in cell B12 is the same number that needs to be entered in cells C12 through G12. You could type the same amount into each month, or you can copy the number in B12 into the other cells.

> **Concept 4: Cut, Copy, and Paste Cell Contents**
>
> The contents of worksheet cells can be deleted (cut) and inserted (pasted) in a new location in the worksheet. They can also be duplicated (copied) and pasted. When you cut or copy cell contents, the contents are stored in the Clipboard. Then when they are pasted to the new location, the Clipboard contents are copied into the selected cells. Be careful when pasting because any existing entries in the new location will be replaced by the contents of the Clipboard.

Refer to the Cut, Copy, and Paste section of the Windows 95 Review for information on these features.

There are several methods you can use to copy entries in a worksheet. One method is to use the Copy and Paste commands on the Edit menu. To use the Copy command, you first must select the cell or cells containing the data to be copied. The selected cell or cells are called the **source**.

To copy the value in cell B12,

Move to: B12

The active cell is the selected cell that will be affected by your next action. To copy the contents of the selected cell,

Click: **Copy**

The menu equivalent is Edit/Copy and the shortcut key is Ctrl + C. Copy is also an option on the Shortcut menu.

Your screen should be similar to Figure 1-15.

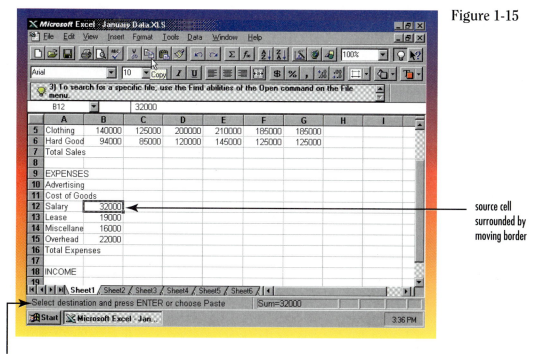

Figure 1-15

source cell surrounded by moving border

status bar instructions

Cell B12 is surrounded by a moving border, and the contents of the cell have been copied to the Clipboard. The instructions displayed in the status bar tell you to select a **destination** or the location where you want the contents copied. To specify cell C12 as the destination,

Move to: C12

Cell C12 is the active cell and the selected cell. Following the directions in the status bar, to insert the contents of the Clipboard into the destination,

Click: **Paste**

The menu equivalent is **E**dit/**P**aste and the shortcut key is Ctrl + V. Paste is also an option on the Shortcut menu.

The number 32000 is entered into cell C12. The number is also still in the Clipboard, so you could paste it again into another location. Not until you copy another selection or exit the program will the Clipboard contents change.

To complete the data for the Salary row, you could continue to select a cell and paste the contents of Clipboard into them one at a time. Instead, however, it is much faster to select multiple cells and paste the contents to all cells in the selection at once. A selection consisting of two or more cells is a range.

Concept 5: Range

A **range** is two or more cells on a worksheet. A range can be contiguous or noncontiguous. A contiguous range is a rectangular block of adjoining cells. In the example shown below, the shaded areas show examples of valid and invalid contiguous ranges. A noncontiguous range is two or more selected cells that are not adjoining. If all the valid ranges in the example below were selected at the same time, they would be a noncontiguous range.

You can also hold down ⇧Shift and use the directional keys to select a range.

To complete the data for the Salary row, you want to copy the Clipboard contents to the range of cells D12 through G12. To select a range, drag the mouse from one corner of the range to the other.

Select cells D12 to G12.

Your screen should be similar to Figure 1-16.

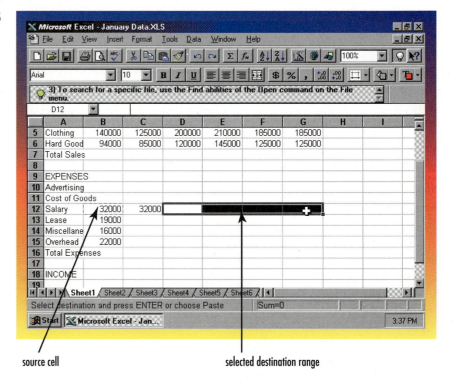

Figure 1-16

source cell

selected destination range

Copying Data **ss35**

The entire destination range is surrounded by a heavy border. The active cell is white while the other cells are black. The source cell is still surrounded by the moving border.

To copy the Clipboard contents,

Click: Paste

> The destination does not have to be adjacent to the source.

The value 32000 is copied into each cell of the range. Also notice that the AutoCalculate button in the status bar shows the total of the values in the selected range. This feature allows you to quickly check the sum of values in a range. The destination range is still highlighted. It will clear as soon as you select another cell.

> While the moving border is still displayed, you can also simply press ←Enter to paste again.

> You can display the average or count of numbers in a selection by choosing from the AutoCalculate button's Shortcut menu.

Next you will copy the January lease expense to cells C7 through G7. Another way to copy is to use the Fill command on the Edit menu. This command requires that the destination range be in the same row or column as the source cell or range. In addition, the range must be selected before the command is used and must include both the source and the destination.

Select cells B13 through G13.

Choose: E**d**it/**F**ill

The first four Fill submenu options are used to specify in which direction to fill from the source cell. In this case, you are filling to the right.

Choose: **R**ight

> The shortcut Ctrl + R could be used to fill right instead of selecting from the menu.

The selected range of cells to the right of the active cell is filled with the same value as in the active cell. The Fill command does not copy the source to the Clipboard; therefore, you cannot paste the source multiple times.

Finally, the numbers for the miscellaneous and overhead expenses (cells B14 and B15) need to be copied to February through June (C14 through G15). A shortcut for the Fill command is to drag the **fill handle**, the black box in the lower right corner of the selection.

Select the source range B14 through B15. Move the mouse pointer to the fill handle.

When the mouse is positioned over the fill handle, it changes to +, indicating you can drag to select a range to be filled.

With the mouse pointer as +, drag the mouse until cells B14 through G15 are selected. Release the mouse button.

SPREADSHEET

Your screen should be similar to Figure 1-17.

Figure 1-17

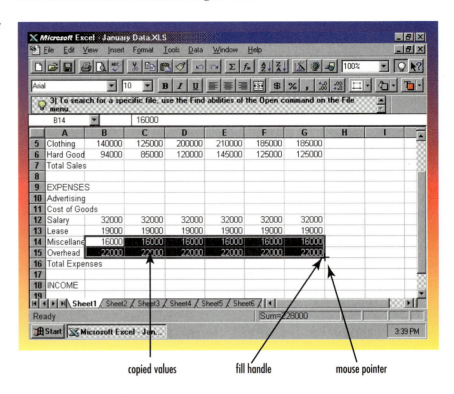

The contents of the selected range have been copied to the destination. You can use the fill handle only if the destination range is adjacent to the selected range.

Review of Copying Methods

To review, you have learned two methods to copy an entry:

1. Use the Copy and Paste commands: Edit/Copy (Ctrl + C) or and Edit/Paste (Ctrl + V) or.

2. Use the Edit/Fill command: Right, Left, Up, or Down or drag the fill handle.

When you use the Copy command, the contents are copied to the Clipboard and can be copied to any location in the worksheet, another workbook, or another application. When you use Edit/Fill or drag the fill handle, the destination must be in the same row or column as the source and the source is not copied to the Clipboard.

Entering Formulas

The remaining entries that need to be made in the worksheet are formula entries.

> **Concept 6: Formulas**
>
> A **formula** is an entry that performs a calculation. The result of the calculation is displayed in the cell containing the formula. A formula always begins with an = (equal) sign, which defines it as a numeric entry. Formulas use the following arithmetic operators to specify the type of numeric operation to perform:
>
> | + | for addition |
> |---|---|
> | − | for subtraction |
> | / | for division |
> | * | for multiplication |
> | ^ | for exponentiation |
>
> In a formula that contains more than one operator, Excel performs the calculation in a specific order of precedence. First exponentiations are performed, then multiplications and divisions, and finally additions and subtractions. This order can be overridden by enclosing the operation you want performed first in parentheses. Excel evaluates operations in parentheses working from the innermost set of parentheses out. For example, in the formula =5*4−3, Excel first multiplies 5 times 4 to get 20, and then subtracts 3, for a total of 17. If you enter the formula as =5*(4−3), Excel first subtracts 3 from 4 because the operation is enclosed in parentheses. Then Excel multiplies the result, 1, by 5, for a final result of 5. If two or more operators have the same order of precedence, calculations are performed in order from left to right.
>
> The values on which a numeric formula performs a calculation are called **operands**. Numbers or cell references can be operands in a formula. Usually cell references are used, and when the numeric entries in the referenced cell(s) change, the result of the formula is automatically recalculated.

The first formula you will enter will calculate the total clothing sales for January through June. The cells containing the sales numbers for January through June are cells B5 through G5. A formula is entered in the cell where you want the calculated value to be displayed.

Move to: H5

Next, to indicate that the type of entry is a formula,

Type: =

The formula is entered next following the = sign. The formula will sum the numbers in cells B5 through G5. You will use cell references in the formula as the operands and the + arithmetic operator to specify addition. To enter the formula to sum the numbers in these cells,

Type: B5+C5+D5+E5+F5+G5
Press: ⏎Enter
Move to: H5

> Cell references can be typed in either uppercase or lowercase letters. Spaces between parts of the formula are optional.

> If you enter a formula incorrectly, Excel will display an error message box. Clear the message box by choosing OK. Then Excel will change to the Edit mode to allow you to correct the entry.

Your screen should be similar to Figure 1-18.

Figure 1-18

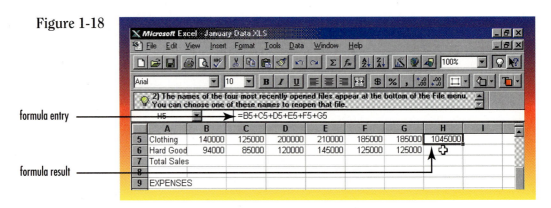

formula entry
formula result

The result of the formula, 1045000, is displayed in cell H5 and the formula is displayed in the formula bar.

You will learn more about formula entries in the next lab, when you will complete the worksheet by entering the formulas to calculate the cost of goods, total sales, total expenses, and income in the worksheet.

Recalculating the Worksheet

After considering the sales estimates for the six months, you decide that the estimated clothing sales for March are too high, and you want to reduce this number from 200000 to 175000. To change this entry,

Move to: D5
Type: 175000
Press: ⏎Enter

The total in cell H5 has been automatically recalculated, and the number displayed is now 1020000.

Concept 7: Automatic Recalculation

The **automatic recalculation** of a formula whenever a number in a referenced cell in the formula changes is one of the most powerful features of electronic worksheets. Only those formulas directly affected by a change in the data are recalculated. This is called **minimal recalculation**. Without this feature, in large worksheets it could take several minutes to recalculate all formulas each time a number was changed in the worksheet. The minimal recalculation feature decreases the recalculation time by only recalculating dependent formulas.

Changing Cell Alignment

Now that many of the worksheet values are entered, you want to improve the appearance of the worksheet by changing the format of the column headings.

> **Concept 8: Format**
>
> **Formats** control how information is displayed in a cell and include such features as font (different type styles and sizes), color, patterns, borders, and number formats such as commas and dollar signs. Applying different formats greatly improves both the appearance and readability of the data in a worksheet.

You decide the column headings would look better if they were right-aligned in their cell spaces. Then they would appear over the numbers in the column. Alignment is a basic format setting that is used in most worksheets.

> **Concept 9: Alignment**
>
> **Alignment** settings allow you to change the horizontal and vertical placement and the orientation of an entry in a cell. Horizontal placement allows you to left-, center-, or right-align text and number entries in the cell space. Vertical placement allows you to specify whether the cell contents are displayed at the top, centered, or at the bottom of the vertical cell space. Orientation changes the character placement of the entry to sideways, vertical, or horizontal. Examples of the basic alignment settings are shown below.
>
> | | A | B | C | D | E | F | G | H | I |
> |---|---|---|---|---|---|---|---|---|---|
> | 1 | | | **Alignment** | | | | | | |
> | 2 | | | | | | | | | |
> | 3 | Horizontal | | | | | Vertical | | | |
> | 4 | Left | Center | Right | Fill | | | | | |
> | 5 | | | | | | Top | Bottom | Center | Justify |
> | 6 | Text | Text | Text | TextText | | | | | |
> | 7 | | | | | | Text | Text | Text | Alignment of Text |
> | 8 | Orientation | | | | | | | | |
> | 9 | | | | | | | | | |
> | 10 | Text | T e x t | Text | Text | | | | | |
> | 11 | | | | | | | | | |
> | 12 | | | | | | | | | |
>
> The default horizontal alignment is left for a text entry and right for a number entry. Vertical alignment is bottom for both types of entries.

First you will change the column heading in cell B3 to right-aligned using the Format menu.

Move to: B3
Choose: F**o**rmat/C**e**lls

> The shortcut key is Ctrl + 1. Format Cells is also an option on the Shortcut menu.

SPREADSHEET

The dialog box on your screen should be similar to Figure 1-19.

Figure 1-19

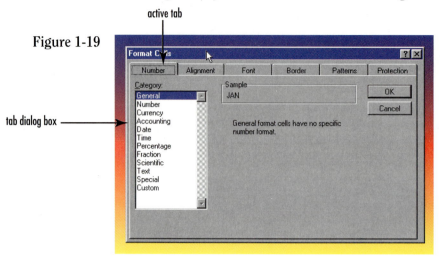

The Format Cells tab dialog box contains six tabs that are used to change the appearance of the worksheet. The Alignment tab contains the options to change the alignment of a selection.

> Refer to the discussion of tab dialog boxes in the Dialog Box section of the Windows 95 Review for information on this feature.

Select: Alignment tab

The Alignment tab shows the default horizontal alignment setting is General. This setting left-aligns text entries and right-aligns number entries. To change the horizontal alignment of the entry to right-aligned,

Select: Right
Choose: OK

Your screen should be similar to Figure 1-20.

Figure 1-20

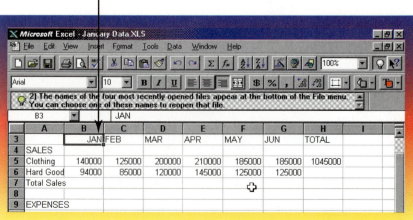

JAN is now right-aligned in the cell.

You can quickly align a range of cells by selecting the range and then choosing the command. A quick way to select a contiguous range of filled cells is to hold down ⇧Shift and double-click on the edge of the active cell in the direction in which you want the range expanded. For example, to select the contiguous range to the right of the active cell you would double-click the right border.

Move to cell C3 and use this method to select cells C3 through H3.

The three buttons in the Formatting toolbar that can be used to align entries are ▤ Align Left, ▤ Center, and ▤ Align Right. To right-align the entries in the selected range,

> If you do not hold down ⇧Shift while double-clicking on a border, the cell selector moves to the last used cell in the direction indicated.

Click: **Align Right**

All the column headings are right-aligned in the cell spaces.

Documenting a Workbook

In the next lab you will complete the worksheet by entering the formulas to calculate the advertising, cost of goods, total sales, total expenses, and income.

Enter your first initial and last name in cell A1. Enter the current date in cell A2 in the format mm/dd/yy (for example, 10/10/97).

> Pressing Ctrl +; will automatically enter the current date in the active cell.

Notice that Excel displays the date right-aligned, indicating it has interpreted the date as a number.

> **Concept 10: Dates**
>
> Excel automatically recognizes certain types of data input, such as dates and times, and formats the entry as appropriate. It stores all dates as serial numbers with each day numbered from the beginning of the century; the date serial number 1 corresponds to the date January 1, 1900, and the integer 65380 is December 31, 2078. The integers are assigned consecutively beginning with 1 and ending with 65,380. They are called **date numbers**. Conversion of the date to a serial number allows dates to be used in calculations.

If you had preceded the date entry with =, Excel would have interpreted it as a formula and a calculation of division would have been performed on the numbers.

Now you are ready to save the changes you have made to the workbook file to your data disk. Before doing this, you want to document the workbook. Each workbook includes summary information that is associated with the file.

Choose: **File/Properties**

The Properties tab dialog box displays information about the file.

Select each tab and look at the recorded information.

The Summary tab is used to specify information you want associated with the file. This information helps you locate the workbook file you want to use as well as indicates the objectives and use of the workbook.

Select: Summary tab

The Summary tab contains text boxes that allow you to enter a title, subject, author, keywords, and comments about the workbook file. First you will enter a title for the workbook that is more descriptive of the contents of the workbook. In the Title text box,

Type: The Sports Company 1998 Budget

Next you will enter a brief description of this workbook. In the Subject text box,

Type: First 6-month Budget

> The Author text box may be blank or show your school or some other name. Clear the existing contents first if necessary.

To enter your name as the creator, in the Author text box,

Type: [your name]
Choose: OK

> You could also add more detailed information about the workbook in the Comments text box.

Saving a Workbook

You are now ready to save the active workbook in a file on your data disk.

Concept 11: Save Files

While working on a document, your changes are stored in memory. Not until you **save** the document as a file on a disk are you safe from losing your work due to a power failure or other mishap. Two commands found on the File menu of all Windows programs can be used to save a file: Save and Save As. The Save command saves a document using the same path and filename by replacing the contents of the existing disk file with the changes you have made. The Save As command allows you to select the path and provide a different filename. This command lets you save both an original version of a document and a revised document as two separate files. When you save a file for the first time, either command can be used. Although many programs create automatic backup files if your work is accidentally interrupted, it is still a good idea to save your work frequently.

You will use the Save As command and save the changes you have made to the JANUARY DATA file using a different filename.

Choose: File/Save As

Your screen should be similar to Figure 1-21.

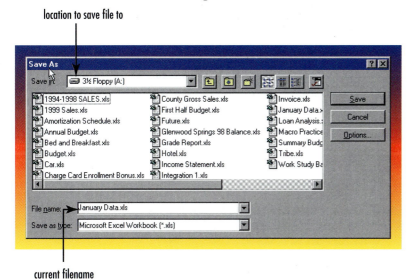

Figure 1-21

The Save As dialog box is used to specify the location to save the file to and the filename. The Save In list box displays the location of the current file as the location where the new file will be saved.

If the Save In location is not correct, select the appropriate location from the drop-down list.

The filename of the file you opened, JANUARY DATA, is displayed in the File Name text box. You would like to save the worksheet with the filename SIX MONTH BUDGET.

Concept 12: Excel Filenames

An Excel filename follows the same filename rules as other Windows 95 products. It is automatically saved with the filename extension .XLS, which identifies it as a workbook file. Excel uses several different file extensions for different types of files that are created using the program.

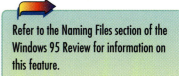

Refer to the Naming Files section of the Windows 95 Review for information on this feature.

To enter a new name in the text box,

Type: **SIX MONTH BUDGET**
Choose: **S**ave

The new filename is displayed in the worksheet window title bar. The worksheet data that was on your screen and in the computer's memory is now saved on your data disk in a new file called SIX MONTH BUDGET.

Always save your active workbook before closing a file or leaving the Excel program. As a safeguard against losing your work if you forget to save the workbook changes, Excel will remind you to save them before closing the file or exiting the program.

SPREADSHEET

Printing a Workbook

If you have printer capability, you can print a copy of the worksheet.

If necessary, turn the printer on and check to see that it is on-line. If your printer uses continuous form-feed paper, adjust the paper so that the perforation is just above the printer scale (behind the ribbon).

To print the worksheet,

Choose: **File/Print**

> The shortcut key is Ctrl + P.

The dialog box on your screen should be similar to Figure 1-22.

Figure 1-22

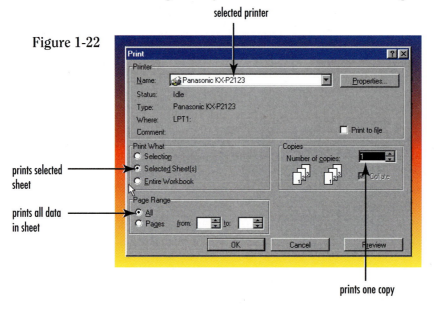

The Print dialog box is used to specify your print settings. The default settings print one copy of all pages of the selected sheet. You will learn about the print settings in the next lab. The default settings are satisfactory for now. The name of the printer displayed in the Printer information line of the dialog box should be your printer.

If you need to select a different printer, open the Name drop-down list in the Printer section and select the appropriate printer.

To print the sheet,

Choose: **OK**

> If you do not need to change the default print settings, you can click 🖨 to print the worksheet.

Your printer should be printing out the worksheet. Your printed output should look like Figure 1-23. By default Excel prints the sheet name at the top of the page as a header, and the page number at the bottom of the page as a footer.

Lab Review **ss45**

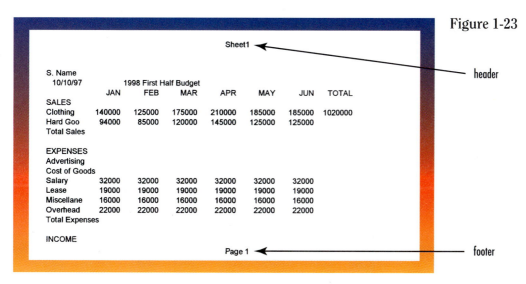

Figure 1-23

— header

— footer

Exiting Excel

Before exiting, you will turn off the TipWizard toolbar. The button is also used to hide the TipWizard toolbar when it is displayed.

> If TipWizard is displayed when you exit the program, it will be displayed when the program is reloaded.

Click: **TipWizard**

If you want to quit or exit the Excel program at this time,

Click:

> The menu equivalent is File/Exit.

You have exited from the Excel program, and the Windows 95 desktop is displayed.

LAB REVIEW

Key Terms

active cell (SS14)	fill handle (SS35)	row number (SS14)
alignment (SS39)	format (SS39)	save (SS42)
active sheet (SS14)	Formatting toolbar (SS13)	sheet (SS14)
AutoCalculate button (SS13)	formula (SS37)	sheet tab (SS14)
automatic recalculation (SS38)	formula bar (SS13)	source (SS32)
cell (SS14)	heading (SS20)	Standard toolbar (SS13)
cell selector (SS14)	minimal recalculation (SS38)	tab scroll button (SS14)
column (SS14)	Name box (SS13)	text (SS20)
column letter (SS14)	number (SS20)	variable (SS20)
constant (SS20)	operand (SS37)	workbook (SS13)
date number (SS41)	range (SS34)	workbook window (SS13)
destination (SS33)	reference (SS14)	worksheet (SS14)
Excel application window (SS13)	row (SS14)	workspace (SS13)

SPREADSHEET

Command Summary

Command	Shortcut	Toolbar	Action
File/**O**pen <filename>	Ctrl + O	📂	Opens an existing workbook file
File/**C**lose			Closes open workbook file
File/**S**ave <filename>	Ctrl + S	💾	Saves current file on disk using same file name
File/**S**ave **A**s <filename>			Saves current file on disk using a new file name
File/Propert**i**es			Displays information about a file
File/**P**rint	Ctrl + P	🖨	Prints a sheet
File/E**x**it		✖	Exits Excel
Edit/**C**opy	Ctrl + C	📋	Copies selected data to Clipboard
Edit/**P**aste	Ctrl + V	📋	Pastes selected data from Clipboard
Edit/**F**ill			Fills selected cells with contents of source cell
Edit/**G**o To	Ctrl + G		Moves to specified cell
Format/C**e**lls/Alignment		≡ ≡ ≡	Aligns data left, center, or right in cell space

Matching

1. source   _____   **a.** right-aligns cell entry
2. *   _____   **b.** moves cell selector to upper left corner of worksheet
3. ≡   _____   **c.** the cell you copy from
4. Ctrl + Home   _____   **d.** two or more worksheet cells
5. .XLS   _____   **e.** a cell reference
6. F2   _____   **f.** displays current cell entry
7. =C19+A21   _____   **g.** an arithmetic operator
8. range   _____   **h.** accesses Edit mode
9. D11   _____   **i.** a formula summing two cells
10. formula bar   _____   **j.** Excel workbook filename extension

Fill-In Questions

1. In the following worksheet, several items are identified by letters. Enter the correct term for each item in the spaces that follow.

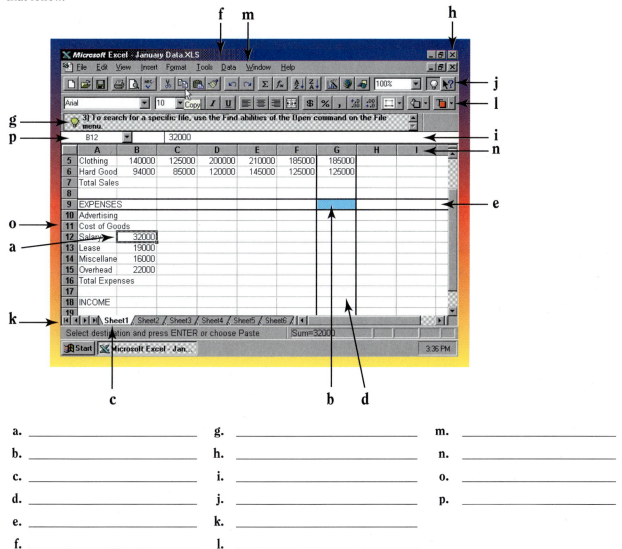

a. _____   g. _____   m. _____
b. _____   h. _____   n. _____
c. _____   i. _____   o. _____
d. _____   j. _____   p. _____
e. _____   k. _____
f. _____   l. _____

ss48 Lab 1: Creating a Worksheet: Part 1

2. Complete the following statements by filling in the blanks with the correct terms.

   a. The _____ occupies the center of the Excel window and can display multiple windows.

   b. The worksheet displays a rectangular grid of _____ and _____.

   c. A _____ consists of two or more contiguous or noncontiguous worksheet cells.

   d. The intersection of a row and column creates a(n)_____.

   e. _____ are text entries that are used to create the structure of the worksheet.

   f. By default, text entries are _____-aligned and number entries are _____-aligned.

   g. A(n) _____ consists of the column letter and row number used to identify a cell.

   h. A(n) _____ is an entry that performs a calculation.

   i. _____ is the recalculation of only those formulas in the worksheet that are directly affected by a change of data.

   j. _____ control how information is displayed in a cell.

Discussion Questions

1. Discuss why it is important to design a worksheet before you begin entering actual data into it.

2. What types of entries are used in worksheets? Discuss the uses of each type of entry.

3. Discuss how formulas are created. Why are they the power behind worksheets?

4. Discuss the formatting features presented in the lab. Why are they important to the look of the worksheet?

Hands-On Practice Exercises

For all exercises, go to cell A1 before you save the workbook. That way, the next time you open the workbook, the cell selector will be at the top of the worksheet.

Step by Step

Rating System
★ Easy
★★ Moderate
★★★ Difficult

1. Open the workbook file BED AND BREAKFAST on your data disk. Scott and Toni have researched several bed and breakfast inns for a family trip to New England. This worksheet lists the inns they are considering and occupancy rates for single and double rooms with private or shared baths. Follow the directions below to modify the worksheet.

   a. Change the first word in the title to uppercase.

   b. Correct the names of the inns so that only the first letter of each word is in uppercase. Similarly, correct the names of the cities and make sure they are all left-aligned.

   c. Center cells E3 through H3 and cell E4, and make sure all worksheet numbers are right-aligned.

   d. Copy the state abbreviation "Conn" in cell D5 to cells D6 through D8. Copy the word "Bath" from cell E4 to the three adjacent cells to the right. Cells F4 through H4 should now contain the text entries "Bath." What else was copied with the text?

   e. Enter the state name "Maine" in cell D14. What happened after you typed the first three letters? Use the Answer Wizard in the Help menu to obtain information on this feature. Ask the question: How do I repeat entries in a column? Choose Search, and display the How do I topic, "Quickly fill in repeated entries in a column." Read the topic and close the Help window when you are finished.

   f. Enter your name and the current date on separate rows below the worksheet.

Your corrected worksheet will look like the worksheet below.

	A	B	C	D	E	F	G	H
1	NEW ENGLAND BED AND BREAKFASTS							
2					Single Rates		Double Rates	
3					Private Bath	Shared Bath	Private Bath	Shared Bath
4	Name		City	State				
5	Mystic Mansion		Mystic	Conn	90	80	95	85
6	Colonial Inn		Hartford	Conn	65	55	85	70
7	Windsor Farms		Windsor	Conn	75	65	85	75
8	Litchfield House		Winsted	Conn	85	75	95	85
9	Harbor House		Nantucket	Mass	68	58	88	78
10	Quincy Cottage		Boston	Mass	95	85	125	115
11	Hanging Lantern Inn		Cambridge	Mass	70	80	90	85
12	Yankee Inn		Kennebunk	Maine	78	52	94	64
13	Blue Heron Inn		Biddeford	Maine	95	70	105	80
14	Bay View Inn		Portland	Maine	85	65	100	80
15								
16			Average Rates					
17			Low Rates					
18			High Rates					

g. Move to cell A1. Use the Properties dialog box to document the workbook. Save and replace the workbook file BED AND BREAKFAST. Print the worksheet.

You will complete this exercise as Practice Exercise 1 in Lab 2.

2. You are the owner of The Cookie Jar, a shop that sells gourmet cookies by the pound. You are interested in tracking first quarter sales for each type of cookie.

a. Create the worksheet as shown below.

	A	B	C	D	E	F	G
1	The Cookie Jar						
2							
3	Type			Jan	Feb	Mar	Total
4	Chocolate Chip			1800	1825	1835	
5	Chocolate Chip w/ Nuts			1430	1425	1390	
6	White Chocolate Macadamia			1220	1250	1295	
7	Butterscotch			750	775	800	
8	Peanut Butter			1000	1050	975	
9	Oatmeal Raisin			450	375	415	
10	Gingerbread			530	535	500	
11	Total						
12							

b. Right-align the month and total headings in row 3.

c. Calculate a total for chocolate chip cookies only. You will learn how to copy this formula down the column in the next lab.

d. Enter your name and the current date on separate rows below the worksheet.

e. Move to A1. Use the Properties dialog box to document the workbook. Save the workbook as COOKIE JAR. Print the worksheet.

You will complete this exercise as Practice Exercise 2 in Lab 2.

3. Laura is changing her eating habits to include foods that obtain no more than 30 percent of their calories from fat. She has listed several of her favorite "diet" snack foods and decides to calculate the percent of fat for each one. Complete the following steps to help Laura with her task.

a. Create the worksheet as shown below.

	A	B	C	D	E	F
1	Food			Fat Grams	Calories	% Fat
2	Bagel			1	240	
3	Lite Cream Cheese			5	60	
4	Peanut Butter (25% Less Fat)			13	190	
5	Saltine Crackers			1.5	60	
6	Lite Pop Corn			2	40	
7	Cholesterol Free Potato Chips			6	130	
8	Lite Frozen Fudge Pops			1.2	35	
9	Pretzels			1	110	
10						

Next, you want to enter a formula to calculate the percent of fat. Each gram of fat contains nine calories. To calculate the percent of fat, multiply fat grams by nine and divide that product by the number of calories.

b. In cell F2, enter the formula =D2*9/E2 to calculate the percent of fat for bagels. Then calculate the percent of fat for lite cream cheese. Are bagels and lite cream cheese a good snack for Laura?

c. Right-align the headings in columns E and F.

d. Enter your name and the current date on separate rows below the worksheet.

e. Move to A1. Use the Properties dialog box to document the workbook. Save the workbook as FAT GRAMS. Print the worksheet.

You will continue this exercise as Practice Exercise 3 in Lab 2.

4. Open the workbook file INVOICE on your data disk. You are an employee of The Office Center, a discount office super store. You recently sold computer equipment to a new computer training facility. Follow the directions below to complete the transaction with the customer.

  a. Replace The Office Center address with your address information, and enter the current date in the appropriate cell.
  b. Make changes you feel are necessary to improve the appearance of the invoice.
  c. Enter a formula to calculate a total for the Pentium computers only. You will learn how to copy this formula down the column in the next lab.
  d. Enter your name below the worksheet.

Your modified worksheet will look something like the worksheet below.

	A	B	C	D	E	F	G	H	I
1	The Office Center						Invoice #	11001	
2	Street Address						Date:	[Current Date]	
3	City, State, and Zip Code								
4									
5	Customer:	Lionel Computer Training							
6		123 Main St.							
7		Greenwich, CT 06830							
8									
9	Qty	Description			Price	Total			
10	15	Pentium-75 MHz Computers			1975	29625			
11	15	Ergonomic Mice			34.95				
12	15	Mouse Pads			4.75				
13	3	Laser Printers			850				
14	5	Power Strips			30				
15	15	Desk Chairs			95.99				
16	6	Tables			300				
17					Subtotal:				
18					State Tax:				
19					Total:				

  e. Move to cell A1. Use the Properties dialog box to document the workbook. Save and replace the workbook file INVOICE. Print the worksheet.

You will continue this exercise as Practice Exercise 4 in Lab 2.

On Your Own

5. Open the file INCOME STATEMENT on your data disk. Custom Manufacturing Company is drawing up a budgeted income statement for the next year. Sales amounts reflect past trends. Cost of goods sold is traditionally 60 percent of sales, variable costs are 15 percent of sales, and fixed costs are budgeted at $1,500 a month for the first half of the year. Other calculations are performed as follows:

> Gross Profit = Sales − Cost of Goods Sold
> Contribution Margin = Gross Profit − Variable Costs
> Income = Contribution Margin − Fixed Costs
> Income Tax Expense = 40% of Income Before Taxes
> Net Income = Income Before Taxes − Income Tax Expense

Use the above information to calculate net income for the month of January only. Appropriately align the month and total headings in row 5. Enter your name and the current date on separate rows below the worksheet. Document the worksheet and save it as INCOME STATEMENT. Print the worksheet.

Your modified worksheet will look something like the worksheet below.

	A	B	C	D	E	F	G	H	I
1	Custom Manufacturing Company								
2	Budgeted Income Statement								
3	For the Year Ending December 31, 1997								
4									
5			Jan	Feb	Mar	Apr	May	Jun	Total
6	Sales		80000	65000	80000	100000	120000	125000	
7	Cost of Goods Sold		48000						
8	Gross Profit		32000						
9	Variable Costs		12000						
10	Contribution Margin		20000						
11	Fixed Costs		1500						
12	Income Before Taxes		18500						
13	Income Tax Expense		7400						
14	Net Income		11100						
15									

You will continue this exercise as Practice Exercise 5 in Lab 2.

6. Obtain an IRS Form 1040EZ. Use Excel to create a worksheet for an IRS Form 1040EZ. Enter formulas to perform the necessary calculations. Change the values you entered to see how the refund or amount you owe is affected by increases and decreases to total wages and other amounts you adjust. Move to A1. Use the Properties dialog box to document the workbook. Save the workbook file as IRS FORM 1040EZ, and print the worksheet.

You will continue this exercise as Practice Exercise 7 in Lab 2.

Concept Summary

Creating a Worksheet: Part 1

Worksheet Design
A well-designed worksheet produces accurate results, and is clearly understood, adaptable, and efficient.

Types of Entries
Cell entries can be text or numbers.

Select Cells
Selecting highlights the cell or cells that will be affected by your next action.

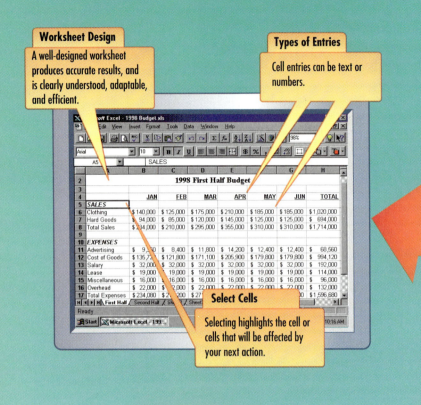

Concepts

Worksheet Design
Types of Entries
Select Cells

Cut, Copy, and Paste Cell Contents
Range

Formulas
Automatic Recalculation

Format
Alignment
Dates

Save Files
Excel Filenames

Formulas
A formula is an entry that performs a calculation.

Automatic Recalculation
Excel automatically recalculates formulas whenever a change occurs in a referenced cell.

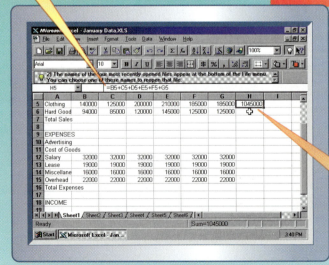

ss52

Cut, Copy, and Paste Cell Contents

The contents of worksheet cells can be deleted, moved, or copied to new locations in the worksheet.

Range

A range is two or more contiguous or noncontiguous cells on a worksheet.

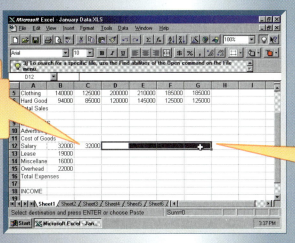

Dates

Excel automatically recognizes certain types of data input, such as dates and times, and formats the entry as appropriate.

Format

Formats control how information is displayed in a cell and are used to improve the appearance of the worksheet data.

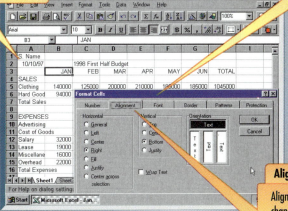

Alignment

Alignment settings allow you to change the horizontal and vertical placement and the orientation of an entry in a cell.

Save Files

To create a permanent copy of your workbook, you save the document as a file on a disk.

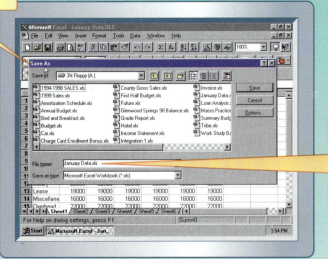

Excel Filenames

An Excel filename follows the same filename rules as other Windows 95 products. It is automatically saved with the filename extension .XLS.

Creating a Worksheet: Part 2

Computers make life easier. The programs they run eliminate a lot, but not all, of the drudgery for you. With all software programs, you still need to do the planning and designing. You also need to enter the information. But they make life easier by helping with all phases of the process.

COMPETENCIES

After completing this lab, you will know how to:

1. Enter formulas using Point mode.
2. Copy formulas.
3. Enter functions.
4. Clear cell contents.
5. Use absolute references.
6. Add cell notes.
7. Change column widths.
8. Use Undo.
9. Zoom the worksheet.
10. Format numbers.
11. Apply styles.
12. Insert and delete rows and columns.
13. Move and center cell contents.
14. Change fonts and font styles.
15. Copy and name sheets.
16. Use AutoFill.
17. Link worksheets.
18. Preview a workbook.

In this lab you will learn about many features in Excel that make life easier. As you learn about these features, think what it would be like to do the same task by hand. How long would it take? Would it be as accurate or as attractive? Your appreciation grows as you learn more about what the application can do for you.

Concept Overview

The following concepts will be introduced in this lab:

1. Relative Reference	A relative reference is a cell or range reference in a formula whose location is interpreted by Excel as relative to the cell that contains the formula.
2. Functions	Excel includes many built-in formulas, called functions, that perform certain types of calculations automatically.
3. Absolute Reference	An absolute reference is a cell or range reference in a formula whose location does not change when the formula is copied.
4. Column Width	The size or width of a column controls how much information can be displayed in a cell.
5. Number Formats	Number formats affect how numbers look onscreen and when printed.
6. Insert and Delete Cells, Rows, and Columns	Individual cells or entire rows or columns can be inserted and deleted from a worksheet.
7. Fonts	Fonts consist of typefaces, point size, and styles that can be applied to characters to improve their appearance.
8. Sheet Names	Each sheet in a workbook can be assigned a name to identify the contents of the sheet.
9. AutoFill	The AutoFill feature makes entering long or complicated headings easier by logically repeating and extending the series.
10. Link Worksheets	A 3-D reference formula creates a link between worksheets in a workbook, allowing you to use data from other worksheets and to calculate new values based on this data.

CASE STUDY

During Lab 1 you defined the row and column headings for The Sports Company budget worksheet. You entered the expected sales figures and many of the expected expenses. You also learned how to copy numbers and to enter a formula.

In Lab 2 you will continue to build the worksheet. In Part 1 you will enter the formulas to calculate the advertising, cost of goods sold, total expenses, and income. The physical appearance of the worksheet will be improved. You will do this by adjusting column widths, inserting and deleting rows and columns, formatting numbers, and changing font sizes and styles.

Finally, in Part 2 you will create another worksheet for the second half of the year budget analysis.

Part 1

Entering Formulas Using Point Mode

Load Excel 7.0 for Windows 95. Put your data disk in drive A (or the appropriate drive for your system).

To continue to build the budget worksheet, open the workbook file FIRST HALF BUDGET. This file is on your data disk. If necessary, maximize the workbook window.

Your screen should be similar to Figure 2-1.

Figure 2-1

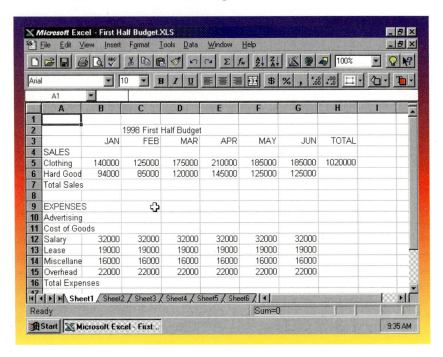

This worksheet should be the same as the worksheet you created in Lab 1 and saved as SIX MONTH BUDGET on your data disk.

To finish the worksheet, you need to enter the formulas to calculate total sales, advertising, cost of goods, total expenses, and total income. First you will enter the formula to calculate total sales. This formula will sum the numbers for clothing and hard goods sales in cells B5 and B6.

Move to: B7
Type: =

Rather than typing the cell references into the formula, you will enter them by selecting the worksheet cells. To tell Excel to add the number in cell B5,

Click: B5

> You can also use the directional keys to move to the cell.

Your screen should be similar to Figure 2-2.

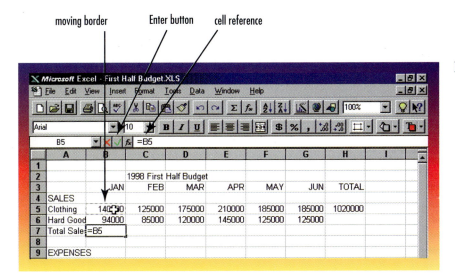

Figure 2-2

Cell B5 is surrounded by a moving border. Notice also that the status bar displays the current mode as Point. This tells you the program is allowing you to select cells by highlighting them. The cell reference, B5, is entered following the = sign. To continue the formula,

Type: +

Then, to enter the reference for the cell containing the January hard goods sales, B6,

Click: B6

Now the entry in cell B7 is "=B5+B6." Because your hands are not on the keyboard, it is faster to click ✓ than to press ⏎Enter to complete the entry.

Click: ✓ (Enter button on formula bar)

The calculated total sales number of 234000 is displayed in cell B7. Also notice that clicking ✓ does not move the cell selector to another cell.

Copying Formulas

The formulas to calculate the February through June total sales (C7 through G7) can be entered next. Just like text and numeric entries, you can copy formulas from one cell to another.

Copy the formula in cell B7 to cells C7 through G7.

The calculated numbers are displayed in the specified cell range. To look at the formulas as they were copied into the cells,

> Refer to the Review of Copying Methods box on page SS36 in Lab 1 to review how to copy.

Move to: C7

Your screen should be similar to Figure 2-3.

Figure 2-3

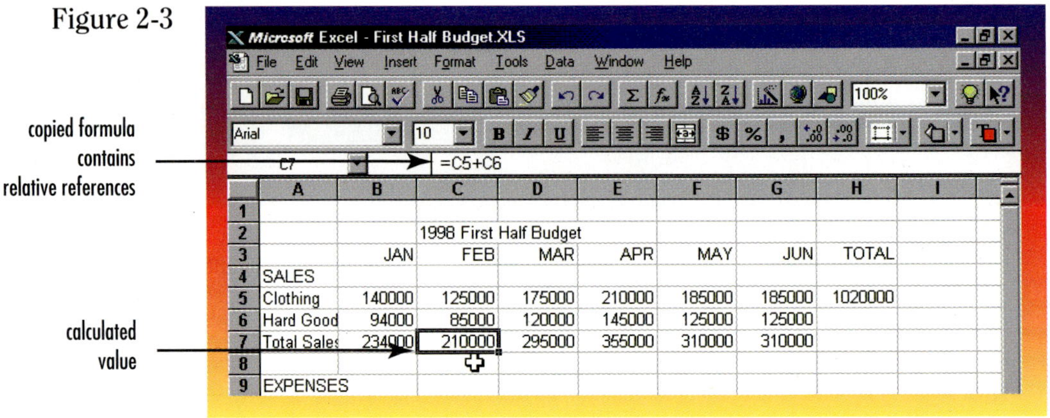

copied formula contains relative references → =C5+C6

calculated value → (C7: 210000)

	A	B	C	D	E	F	G	H
1								
2			1998 First Half Budget					
3			JAN	FEB	MAR	APR	MAY	JUN	TOTAL
4	SALES							
5	Clothing	140000	125000	175000	210000	185000	185000	1020000
6	Hard Good	94000	85000	120000	145000	125000	125000	
7	Total Sales	234000	210000	295000	355000	310000	310000	
8								
9	EXPENSES							

The number 210000 is displayed in the cell. The formula displayed in the formula bar is =C5+C6. The formula to calculate the February total sales is not an exact duplicate of the formula used to calculate the January total sales (=B5+B6). Instead the cells referenced in the formula have been changed to reflect the new location of the formula in column C. This is because the references in the formula are relative references.

Concept 1: Relative Reference

A **relative reference** is a cell or range reference in a formula whose location is interpreted by Excel as relative to the cell that contains the formula. When a formula is copied, the referenced cells in the formula automatically adjust to reflect the new location so the relative relationship between the referenced cell and the new location is maintained. Because relative references automatically adjust for the new location, the relative references in a copied formula refer to different cells than the references in the original formula. The relationship between these cells and the cell that contains the copy of the formula is the same as the relationship between the cells referred to in the original formula and the cell that contains the formula itself.

Move to: **D7**

Notice that the formula in the formula bar has changed again to reflect the new column location, and it appropriately calculates the number based on the March sales.

Next you will enter the formulas to calculate the advertising and cost of goods sold. These numbers are estimated by using a formula to calculate the number as a percent of total sales. As a general rule, The Sports Company calculates advertising expenses at 4 percent of sales and cost of goods expenses at 58 percent of sales. The formula to make these calculations for January takes the number in cell B7 and multiplies it by the percentage.

To make the process of entering and copying entries even easier, Excel has a feature that lets you enter data into a cell and copy it to a selected range at the

same time. You will use this feature to enter the formulas to calculate the advertising and cost of goods expenses for January through June.
> To calculate the advertising expenses first, select cells B10 through G10.

Next you enter the formula to calculate the January advertising expenses.

Type: **=B7*4%**

> Even when a range is selected, you can still point to specify cells in the formula.

To complete the entry and have it copied to the selected range,

Press: Ctrl + ←Enter

In the same manner, enter the formula =B7*58% to calculate the cost of goods sold for January through June.
> Your screen should be similar to Figure 2-4.

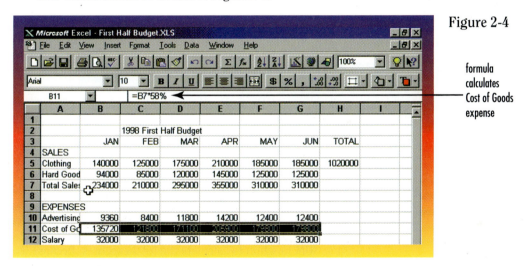

Figure 2-4

formula calculates Cost of Goods expense

The calculated numbers for advertising and for cost of goods are displayed in cells C10 through G11.

Entering Functions

Now that all the expenses have been entered into the worksheet, the total expenses can be calculated. The formula to calculate the total expenses for January needs to be entered in cell B16 and copied across the row through June.

Move to: **B16**

You could use a formula similar to the formula used to calculate the total sales (B7). The formula would be =B10+B11+B12+B13+B14+B15. However, it is faster and more accurate to use one of Excel's functions.

> **Concept 2: Functions**
>
> **Functions** are built-in formulas that perform certain types of calculations automatically. The **syntax** or rules of structure for entering all functions is:
>
> =Function name (argument1, argument2,...)
>
> Like formulas, functions begin with the = sign. This is followed by the function name. The function name identifies the type of calculation to be performed. Most functions require that you enter one or more arguments following the function name. An **argument** is the data the function uses to perform the calculation. The type of data the function requires depends upon the type of calculation being performed. Most commonly the argument consists of numbers or references to cells that contain numbers. The argument is enclosed in parentheses, and multiple arguments are separated by commas.
>
> Several very common functions and the results they calculate are shown below.
>
> | Function | Calculates |
> | --- | --- |
> | =SUM() | Total of arguments |
> | =AVERAGE() | Average of arguments |
> | =MAX() | Maximum value in argument |
> | =MIN() | Minimum value in argument |
> | =COUNT() | Tally of arguments that are numbers |

You will use the SUM function to calculate the total expenses. Because the SUM function is the most commonly used function, it has its own shortcut. To use the shortcut to calculate the total expenses for January,

> Pressing [Alt] + = is the keyboard shortcut for AutoSum.

Click: **AutoSum**

Your screen should be similar to Figure 2-5.

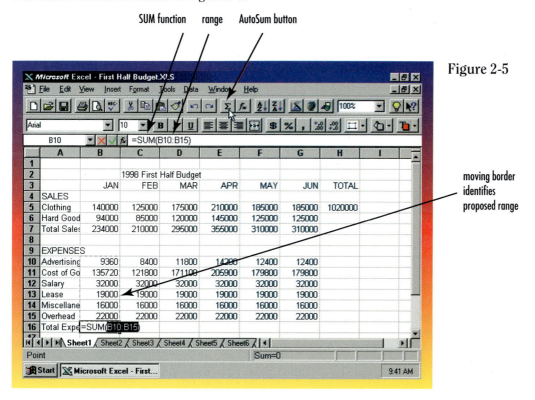

Figure 2-5

moving border identifies proposed range

The numbers above cell B16 are surrounded by a moving border. Excel automatically proposes a range based upon the data above or to the left of the active cell. The name of the function followed by the range argument enclosed in parentheses is displayed in the formula bar. Excel displays a range reference as the leftmost cell and rightmost cell in the range separated by a colon (B10:B15). To accept the proposed range and enter the function,

Click: **Enter**

> If you used the ←Enter key, move to B16.

The result calculated by the function, 234080, is displayed in cell B16.
   Look at the function displayed in the formula bar.
   Next you need to calculate the total expenses for February through June.
   Copy the function to cells C16 through G16.

Move to: **C16**

Your screen should be similar to Figure 2-6.

Figure 2-6

relative references used in copied function → =SUM(C10:C15)

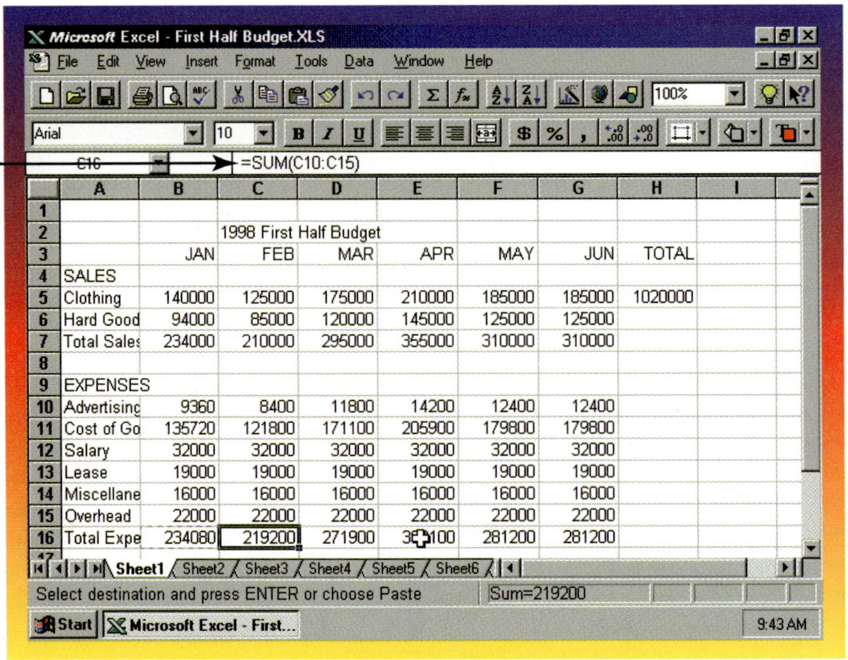

The result calculated by the function, 219200, is displayed in cell C16. Notice that the function displayed in the formula bar is =SUM(C10:C15). The function is copied relative to its new cell location because it contains relative references.

Now that the total expenses are calculated, the formula to calculate income can be entered. This number is the difference between sales and total expenses.

Select the range B18 through G18. Enter the formula =B7–B16 and press Ctrl + ←Enter .

The calculated income numbers are displayed in cells B18 through G18. The income numbers for January and February show a loss, while March through June show positive numbers. You are not concerned that the January and February income numbers are negative, because this is a projected budget to help the store manager make adjustments for the actual budget.

Finally, the total over the six months needs to be entered down column H.

Move to: H6

To enter the SUM function to total Hard Goods Sales,

Click: Σ AutoSum

Notice that the moving border is around cell H5 and not the row. Excel first checks for values above and then to the left of the active cell. If the values above are not the range you want to sum, you can edit the function by selecting another range.

> You can point to specify the cell references in the formula.

Select: B6 through G6
Press: ←Enter

Copy the function down the column to cell H18.

Clearing Cell Contents

Look at the contents of cells H8, H9, and H17. They display zeros.

Move to: H17

Your screen should be similar to Figure 2-7.

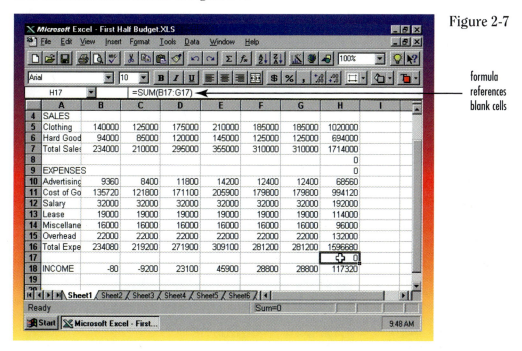

Figure 2-7

formula references blank cells

The formula bar displays the function to calculate the sum of cells B17 through G17. The formula was copied into a cell that references empty cells.

> Refer to Clearing an Entry on page SS22 in Lab 1 to review this feature.

Delete the formula from cell H17.

The formula is cleared from the cell, and consequently the number 0 is no longer displayed. Next you need to delete the contents of cells H8 and H9.

Select: H8 through H9

You can also clear cell contents using the fill handle.

Point to the fill handle of the selected range.

The mouse pointer changes to a black cross hair ✛.

Drag the mouse up until the entire selection is gray. Release the mouse button.

The contents of the selected cells are removed.

Using Function Wizard

Next you decide you want to add a new column showing the average values for the six months.

> Refer to Changing Cell Alignment on page SS39 in Lab 1 to review this feature.

Enter and right-align the heading "AVG" in cell I3.

Move to: I5

Another way to enter a function is use the Function Wizard feature. This feature simplifies entering functions by prompting you to select a function from a list and then helps you to enter the arguments correctly. To use the Function Wizard,

> The menu equivalent is Insert/Function and the shortcut key is ⇧Shift + F3.

Click: *fx* **Function Wizard**

Your screen should be similar to Figure 2-8.

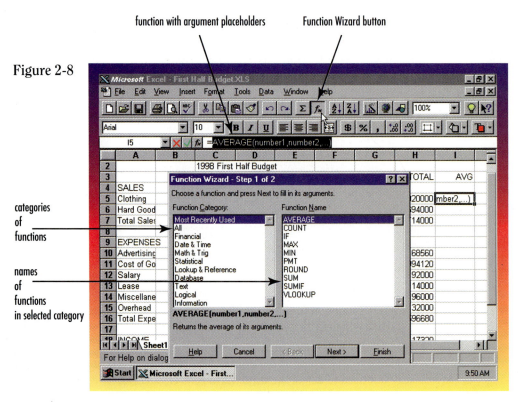

Figure 2-8

- function with argument placeholders
- Function Wizard button
- categories of functions
- names of functions in selected category

> The Most Recently Used category initially displays 10 of the most common functions.

You select the type of function you want to use from the Function Wizard-Step 1 of 2 dialog box. The Function Category list box displays the names of the function categories. The Function Name list box displays the names of the functions in the selected category. The currently selected category is Most Recently Used. This category displays the names of the last 10 functions used. Because the last function you used was SUM, the Function Name list box displays this function.

> If AVERAGE is not displayed in the list box, select it from the Statistical category.

If necessary, select the AVERAGE option in the Function Name list box.

The function and its argument placeholders are displayed in the formula bar. Since this is the function you want to use, to accept this selection and move to the next step,

Choose:

> You can press ←Enter to choose Next.

The Step 2 dialog box helps you correctly enter the arguments required for the selected function by telling you what information you need to provide. The Average function requires that you specify the numbers to average. The numbers or the cell references containing the numbers can be entered in the text box directly, or can be entered by selecting the cell or range from the worksheet. You will select the range B5 through G5 from the worksheet. This avoids the accidental entry of incorrect references.

If the Function Wizard dialog box covers row 5, move the window to another location.

>
> Refer to the Moving Windows section in the Windows 95 Review for more information on this feature.

Select: B5 through G5

The range is entered in the text box, and the actual values in the range are displayed in the box to the right. The function with the argument range is displayed in the formula bar. To complete the function,

>
> Keyboard users must type the range B5:G5 in the text box.

Choose:

The average of the clothing sales for the six months, 170000, is calculated and displayed in cell I5.

Copy the function down the column through row 18. Clear the function from any cells that reference blank cells.

By default numbers are displayed with as many decimal places as cell space allows and are rounded appropriately.

> If #DIV/0! appears in a cell, this is a warning that a number is being divided by zero.

Using Absolute References

Finally, you want to enter a formula to calculate what proportion the total clothing sales and total hardware sales for six months are of the total sales. You will display the proportion in the column to the right of the Average column.

Move to: J5

The formula to calculate the proportion for clothing is Total Clothing Sales/Total Sales.

Enter the formula =H5/H7 in cell J5.

The value 0.595099 is displayed in cell J5. This shows that the clothing sales are about 60 percent of total sales.

Next, to calculate the proportion that hardware sales is of total sales, you will copy the formula from J5 to J6. Another quick way to copy cell contents is to drag the cell border while holding down Ctrl. This method is most useful when the distance between cells is short and they are both visible in the window. It cannot be used if you are copying to a larger range than the source range.

> The mouse pointer appears as ⇲ to show that it will copy the cell contents.

Point to the border of cell J5. When the mouse pointer shape is ▸, hold down Ctrl, and drag the mouse pointer to cell J6.

Your screen should be similar to Figure 2-9.

Figure 2-9

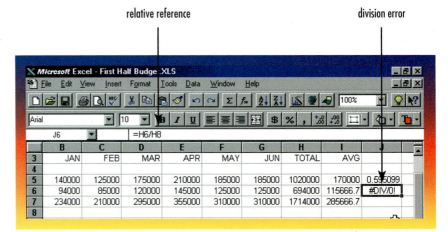

The proportion has been calculated, but there is something wrong. The cell displays "#DIV/0!." The formula bar shows that the formula in this cell is =H6/H8. This formula computes the proportion using the number in cell H8, a blank cell one row below the total number in cell H7. Since cell H8 is empty, #DIV/0! is displayed. When the formula was copied, the cell references adjusted relative to the new location of the formula in the worksheet.

The formula in J5 needs to be entered so that the row of the referenced cell, row 7, does not change to row 8 when the formula is copied. To do this, you will make the cell reference absolute.

Concept 3: Absolute Reference

An **absolute reference** is a cell or range reference in a formula whose location does not change when the formula is copied.

In an absolute reference, a $ (dollar sign) character precedes both the column letter and row number. When a formula containing an absolute cell reference is copied to another row and column location in the worksheet, the cell reference does not change. It is an exact duplicate of the cell reference in the original formula.

A cell reference can also be a **mixed reference**. In this type of reference either the column letter or the row number is preceded with the $. This makes only the row or column absolute. When a formula containing a mixed cell reference is copied to another row and column location in the worksheet, only the part of the cell reference that is not absolute changes relative to its new location in the worksheet. The table below shows examples of relative and absolute references and the results when a reference in cell C10 to cell B28 is copied to cell E13.

Cell Contents of C10	Copied to Cell E13	Type of Reference
$B$28	$B$28	Absolute reference
B$28	D$28	Mixed reference
$B28	$B31	Mixed reference
B28	D31	Relative reference

You can change a cell reference to absolute or mixed by typing in the dollar sign directly or by using the ABS (Absolute) key, F4 . To use the ABS key, the program must be in Edit mode.

Move to cell J5 and turn on Edit mode.

> Press F2 or double-click cell J5.

When using the ABS key, first position the insertion point on or immediately to the right of the cell reference you want to change.

If necessary, move the insertion point to the cell reference H7.

To change this cell reference to absolute,

Press: F4   **ABS**

The cell reference now displays $ characters before the column letter and row number ($H$7), making this cell reference absolute. If you continue to press F4 , the cell reference will cycle through all possible combinations of cell reference types. Leaving the cell reference absolute, as it is now, will stop the relative adjustment of the cell reference when you copy it again.

To accept the formula as displayed in the formula bar ($H$7),

Press: ←Enter

Copy the revised formula to cell J6.

Move to: **J6**

Your screen should be similar to Figure 2-10.

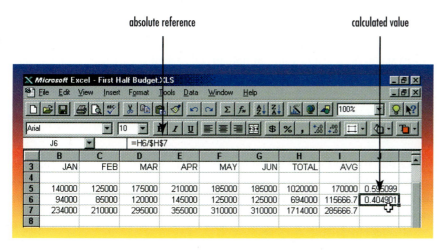

Figure 2-10

The calculated proportion is 0.404901, and the formula is H6/$H$7. Using an absolute cell reference easily solved the problem.

> A mixed reference of H$7 would also have solved the problem.

Adding Cell Notes

To clarify the meaning of the values, you decide to add cell notes to the two proportion value cells. Cell notes automatically appear whenever the mouse pointer rests on the cell. To add a note to clarify the hardware proportion value,

Lab 2: Creating a Worksheet: Part 2

Choose: **Insert/Note**

The cell reference of the active cell appears in the Cell text box of the dialog box. This is the cell that the note will be attached to. In the Text Note text box, you enter the text of the note.

Type: **Total hardware sales as a percent of total sales.**
Choose: **OK**

Notice that cell J6 displays a red box in the upper right corner. This indicates the cell contains a note.

To display the note, point to cell J6.
Your screen should be similar to Figure 2-11.

Figure 2-11

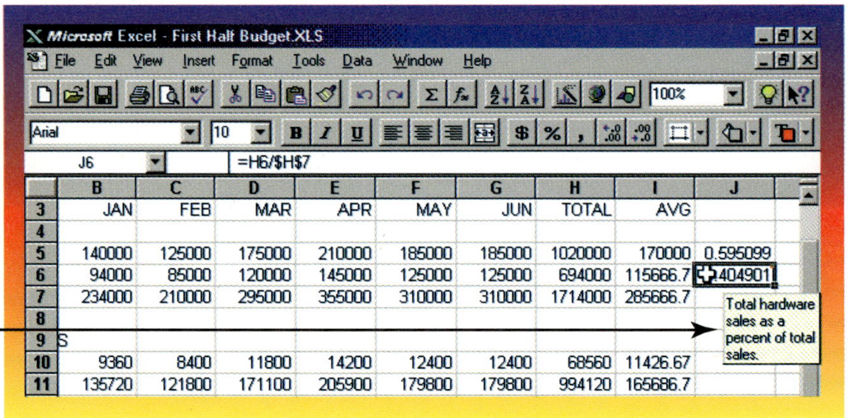

cell note

The note you entered is displayed in a small box below the cell.

Next you need to add a similar note to cell J5. Instead of creating an entirely new note, you will copy the note from cell J6 to J5 and then edit its contents. To do this,

Choose: **Insert/Note**

Notice that the Notes in Sheet list box displays a reference to the note you just created in cell J6. The note reference is highlighted, indicating it is selected, and the complete text for the selected note appears in the Text Note box. You need to indicate the cell to copy the selected note to.

Change the cell reference in the Cell text box to J5. Change the word "hardware" to "clothing" in the text in the Text Note box.

Choose: **Add**
Choose: **OK**

> The cell does not need to be active to display its cell note.

The note has been added to cell J5.
Display the note.

Adjusting Column Widths

Now that the worksheet data is complete, you want to improve its appearance by adjusting column widths, using underlining, and setting different number format styles.

After entering the numbers for January in column B, any long headings in column A were cut off or interrupted.

To move to column A,

Press: [Home]

To allow the long text entries in column A to be fully displayed, you can increase the column's width.

> **Concept 4: Column Width**
>
> The size or width of a column controls how much information can be displayed in a cell. An entry that is larger than the column width will be fully displayed if the cells to the right are blank. However, when the cells to the right contain data, the text is interrupted or numbers appear as # signs.
>
> When the worksheet is printed, it appears as it does currently on the screen. Therefore, you want to increase the column width to display the largest entry. Likewise, you can decrease the column width when the entries in a column are small.

The default column width setting in Excel is 8.43. This number represents the number of characters that can be displayed in a cell using the default font. The column width can be any number from 1 to 255.

The column width can be quickly adjusted by dragging the column divider line to the right of the column letter. Dragging it to the left decreases the column width, while dragging it to the right increases the width.

- Point to the column divider line to the right of the column letter A.
- The mouse pointer changes to ✥.
- Drag the mouse pointer to the right.

As you do, a temporary reference column line moves to the right and the Name box displays the width of the column.

- When the Name box displays 14.00, release the mouse button.

> You can also adjust the height of a row by dragging the row divider line.

> The menu equivalent is F**ormat**/**C**olumn/**W**idth.

Your screen should be similar to Figure 2-12.

Figure 2-12

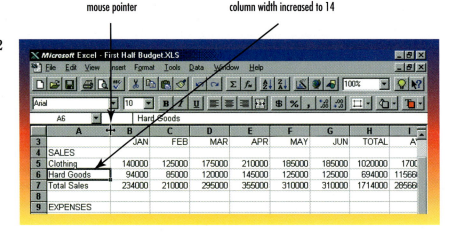

Next you want to see how the worksheet would look if you decreased the column widths of all the other columns in the worksheet. You can decrease the width of each column individually, but it would be faster to change the width of all the columns at once. First you need to select the columns you want to change.

Click on the column letter B.

The entire column to the last worksheet row is selected.

Drag the mouse to the right until columns B through J are selected.

Next you want to reduce the column width of all selected columns to 5.

Drag the right border of any column in the selected range to the left until the Name box displays 5.00. Release the mouse button.

To clear the selection,

Press: [Home]

> When you drag beyond the visible window, the window will scroll in the same direction.

Your screen should be similar to Figure 2-13.

Figure 2-13

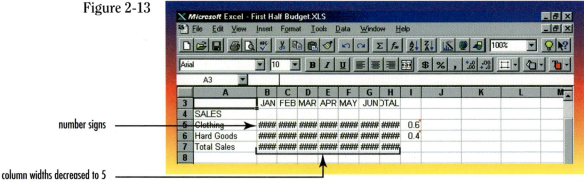

All the cells in the selected columns have changed to five characters. Notice that a series of number signs (#####) appears in most of the worksheet cells. Whenever the width of a cell is too small to display the entire number, number signs are displayed.

Using Undo

As you can see, this new column width is much too small. To cancel the most recent operation and restore the worksheet to how it was prior to your change,

Click: Undo

> Refer to the Undo section in the Windows 95 Review for information on this feature.

The effects of the column width command are reversed, and the columns are restored to the prior column width setting. The previously selected range is also highlighted again.

> The menu equivalent is **E**dit/**U**ndo Column Width and the shortcut key is Ctrl + Z.

Undo must be used before executing another command or making an entry that changes the worksheet. This is because Excel creates a backup copy of your existing worksheet in memory each time you make a change to the worksheet. When you use Undo, Excel redisplays the backup worksheet.

> The Redo button will reverse the action of Undo.

The Undo feature is primarily used to undo errors and is an important safeguard against mistakes that may take a lot of time to fix. When the Undo feature is selected, it reverses the most recent action performed. If the action cannot be undone, "Can't Undo" appears dimmed on the Edit menu.

> Immediately after you undo an action, the command changes to Redo to allow you to restore the action you just undid.

Clear the selection.

Zooming the Worksheet

Before adjusting the column widths any more, you want to improve the appearance of the numbers in columns B through J. However, this range is not entirely visible in the window. You can change how much information is displayed in the window to make it easier to navigate, view, and select the worksheet data.

Notice the "100%" displayed in the button at the right end of the Standard toolbar. This is the Zoom Control box, and it shows the current zoom percentage. This is the default sheet display percent setting, and it displays data onscreen as it will appear on the printed page. You can reduce or enlarge the amount of information displayed onscreen by changing the magnification from between 10 to 400 percent. Decreasing the percent displays more information, and increasing the percent displays less. To see how this works,

Click: Zoom Control

> The menu equivalent is **V**iew/**Z**oom.

The drop-down menu displays five preset percent options. The Selection option will automatically adjust the percentage to fit the selected range in the current window size.

Select: 75%

Your screen should be similar to Figure 2-14.

Figure 2-14

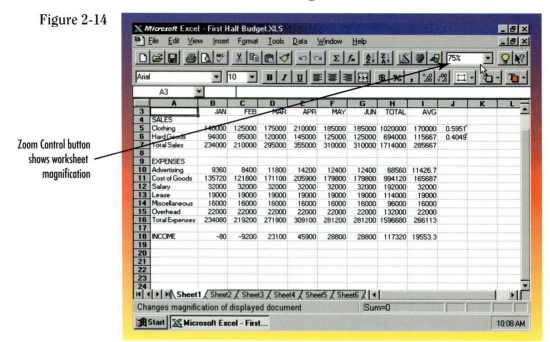

Zoom Control button shows worksheet magnification

Formatting Numbers

Now you can more easily select the range to change. You want to improve the appearance of the numbers in the worksheet by changing the format of the numbers.

Concept 5: Number Formats

Number formats affect how numbers look onscreen and when printed. They do not affect the way Excel stores or uses the values in calculations. The default format setting that controls how numbers are displayed in the worksheet is General. The General format setting automatically sets the number format to a Date, Time, Comma, Currency, Percent, or Scientific number format setting depending on the symbols you used when entering the data.

The table below shows samples of how Excel automatically formats a number based on how it appears when you enter it.

Entry	Format
10,000	Comma
$102.20	Currency with two decimal places
90%	Percent with zero decimal places
10/10/95	Long International Date
9:10	Time

If no symbol is used, Excel leaves the number unformatted. Unformatted numbers are displayed in the thousands without a separator such as a comma, with negative values preceded by a - (minus sign), and as many decimal place settings as cell space allows.

First you will change the number format of cells B5 through I18 to display dollar signs, commas, and decimal places.

A quick way to select a range is to click on the first cell of the range and then hold down ⇧Shift while clicking on the last cell of the range. This method is particularly useful when the range is large or if it is not entirely visible in the window.

Use this method to select the range B5 through I18.

To change the format of the selected cells to display as currency with dollar signs and two decimal places,

Choose: Format/Cells

> The keyboard shortcut is Ctrl + 1. Format Cells is also an option on the Shortcut menu.

The Number tab in the Format Cells tab dialog box contains the format options to change the display of values.

If necessary, select the Number tab.

The Category list box lists the names of the number formats. The default cell format setting is General.

Select: General

The dialog box on your screen should be similar to Figure 2-15.

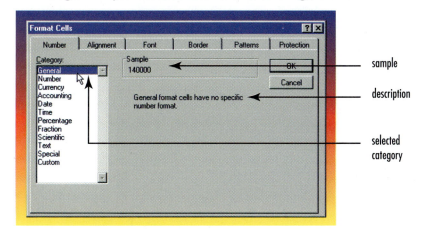

Figure 2-15

To the right of the list box a sample shows how numbers will appear using the selected category. In addition, below the Sample box a brief description of the selected format category is displayed.

Two categories display numbers as currency: Currency and Accounting.

Select: Currency

The Currency category includes options that allow you to specify the number of decimal places, how negative numbers appear, and the display of the dollar sign. These options are displayed to the right of the list box. The description of the Currency format now displayed below the list box indicates its use is primarily for displaying monetary values, and suggests using the Accounting format for other purposes. To see information on the Accounting format,

Select: **Accounting**

The primary difference with this format is that it aligns numbers at the decimal place and places the dollar sign in a column at the left edge of the cell space. In addition, it does not allow you to select different ways of displaying negative numbers, but displays them in black in parentheses.

In both formats, the display of the dollar sign is off by default. To turn it on,

Select: **Use $**

Notice that the sample now displays the $ symbol. The Accounting format makes it easier to read the numbers in a column. To use the Accounting format with two decimal places and the dollar sign,

Choose: **OK**

Your screen should be similar to Figure 2-16.

Figure 2-16

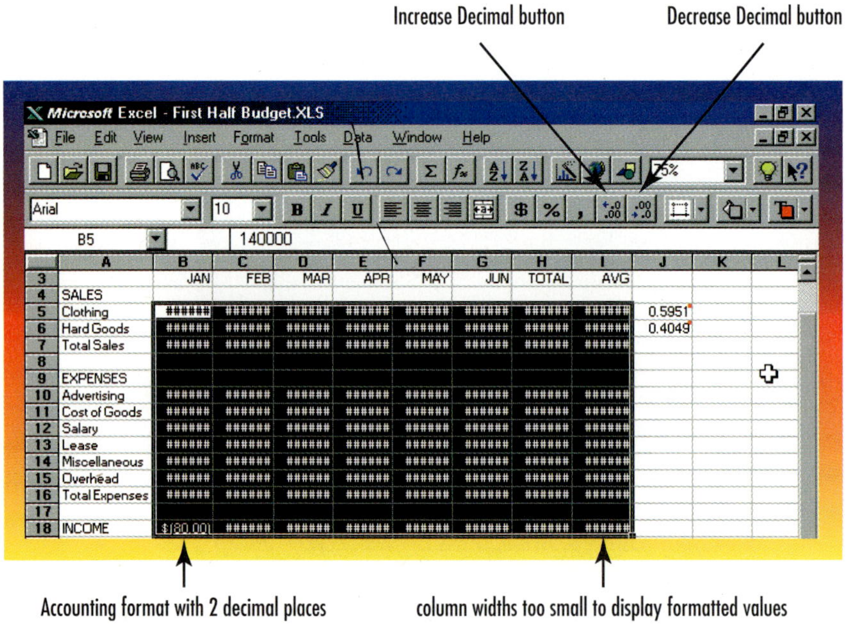

Increase Decimal button   *Decrease Decimal button*

Accounting format with 2 decimal places   *column widths too small to display formatted values*

The selected format is applied to the numbers in the selected range. However, most numbers cannot be displayed because the cell width is too small. The only displayed number is in cell B18, and as you can see, it displays a dollar sign and two decimal places. Because it is a negative number, it appears in parentheses.

Notice that the selected range is still active. This lets you continue to use the range and select other commands without having to redefine the range each time. You would like to see how the current format would look with zero decimal places. To do this, you could use the Format/Cells menu command and specify zero decimal places in the Accounting category. However, you can quickly decrease and increase decimal places using the and buttons on the Formatting toolbar. To decrease the number of decimal places from two to zero,

Click:  **Decrease Decimal (2 times)**

Several more values are now visible, but the column width is still too small. Now to fully display all the numbers, you will increase the width of columns B through I, the currently selected worksheet range. You will do this using the AutoFit feature. This feature automatically sets the column widths to the minimum necessary to display the contents of the selected cells.

Choose: **Format/Column/AutoFit Selection**

Your screen should be similar to Figure 2-17.

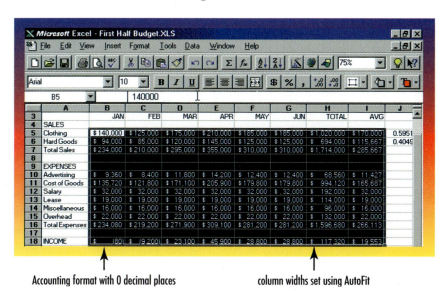

Figure 2-17

The width of columns B through I automatically increased to the minimum column width needed to fully display the numbers. The width of column A remained the same because it was not included in the selection.

Applying Styles

Next you want to format the two proportion values in cells J5 and J6 to a percent.

Select: **J5 and J6**

You could apply the Percent format using the Format/Cells menu command as you just did. However, Excel has several predefined format styles from which you can select. A **style** consists of a combination of formats that have been selected and named. You use styles to quickly apply a whole group of formats to a selection.

Choose: **Format/Style**

The dialog box on your screen should be similar to Figure 2-18.

Figure 2-18

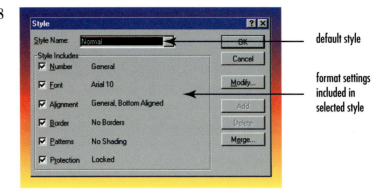

default style

format settings included in selected style

The Style Name list box displays the current style, Normal. Normal is the default style. It sets the number format to General and controls other format settings that are applied to all entries. The check boxes in the Style Includes area of the dialog box show the options that are included in this style and a description or sample.

To see the list of predefined styles, open the Style Name drop-down list box.

There are six predefined styles. Notice the two Currency styles. They will display dollar signs, commas, and two or zero decimal places, just as if you had selected these formats from the Format Cells dialog box.

To select the Percent style,

Select: **Percent**

The Number option is the only selected option. The sample shows this style will display whole numbers and a percent sign.

Choose: **OK**

Your screen should be similar to Figure 2-19.

numbers displayed in Percent style

Figure 2-19

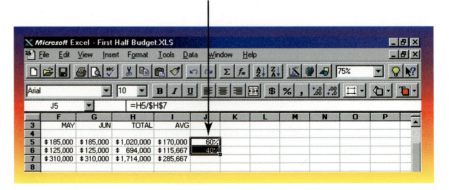

The numbers are displayed as whole numbers followed by a percent sign.

> To make the percentage more accurate, increase the decimal place setting to 2.

The proportion of clothing sales of total sales is 59.51 percent, and the proportion of hardware sales is 40.49 percent. Setting the cell format to Percent takes the value in the cell and multiplies it by 100. The decimal value is converted to a percent by moving the decimal point two places to the right and rounding the digits following the decimal to the nearest hundredth.

Press: Ctrl + Home

Note: If you are stopping at the end of Part 1, enter your name in cell A1, save the workbook file as 1998 FIRST HALF BUDGET, print the worksheet, and exit Excel. When you begin Part 2, open the file 1998 FIRST HALF BUDGET.

Part 2

Inserting Rows

The appearance of the worksheet is greatly improved already. However, it looks crowded and could be improved by inserting a blank row below the worksheet title as row 3.

> **Concept 6: Insert and Delete Cells, Rows, and Columns**
>
> Individual cells or entire rows or columns can be inserted and deleted from a worksheet. A cell is inserted by moving the contents of the active cell down or to the right. When inserting a row, the new row is added at the cell selector position, moving the current row and all others down. When a column is added, the current column and all other columns move to the right. The formats associated with surrounding cells are applied to the newly inserted cell, row, or column.
>
> You can also delete individual cells as well as entire columns and rows. When you delete the cell, column, or row, it is removed from the worksheet and the surrounding cells, columns, and rows shift to fill the space. Deleting cells is different from clearing cells. When you clear a cell, the cell contents, formats, or notes are erased, leaving a blank cell on the worksheet. Be very careful when you delete, however, because any information in the cell, column, or row will be erased.
>
> When you insert or delete cells, rows, or columns, all cell references in formulas and functions are automatically adjusted to their new locations. This keeps your formulas up to date. However, a worksheet formula containing a reference to a deleted cell displays a #REF! error message.

To insert a blank row into the worksheet, begin by moving the cell selector to the row where the new blank row will be inserted.

Move to: A3
Choose: Insert/Rows

> To delete a cell, row, or column, select it and choose **E**dit/**D**elete/Entire **R**ow or Entire **C**olumn.

> To insert a column, choose **I**nsert/**C**olumn.

> Insert and Delete are also on the Shortcut menu.

Your screen should be similar to Figure 2-20.

Figure 2-20

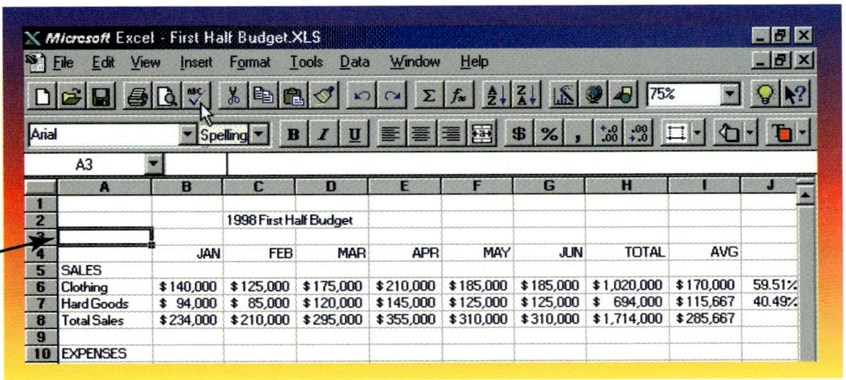

inserted blank row

A new blank row has been inserted into the worksheet at the cell selector location. Everything below row 3 has moved down one row.

Moving Cell Contents

Next you want the worksheet title centered over the worksheet data. The Alignment command on the Format/Cells menu lets you align text across a selection. But before using this feature, the text you want aligned must be in the leftmost cell of the range. To move the worksheet title in cell C2 to cell A2, you could cut and paste the contents, or you can drag the cell border to move the cell contents. Dragging is quickest and most useful when the distance between cells is short and they are visible within the window, whereas Cut and Paste are best for long distance moves.

Move to: C2

Point to the border of the cell. When the mouse pointer shape is ↖, drag the mouse pointer to cell A2.

As you drag, an outline of the cell appears to show its new location in the worksheet.

Release the mouse button.

The contents of cell C2 are copied into cell A2 and cleared from the original cell.

If you drag data to an area of the worksheet that already contains data, Excel replaces the existing data in the range with the new data. If this happens, you can use Undo to retrieve lost data. If you move cells containing formulas, the formulas are not adjusted relative to their new worksheet locations.

Centering Across Columns

Now you are ready to center the worksheet title over the worksheet. The text is centered from the leftmost cell across all selected blank cells to the right. You want to center the title across cells A2 through I2.

Select: A2 through I2

Click: Center Across Columns

> The menu equivalent is Format/Cells/Alignment/Center across selection.

The title now appears balanced over the worksheet columns. The actual text entry, however, is still in cell A2. To see this,

Move to: A2

Your screen should be similar to Figure 2-21.

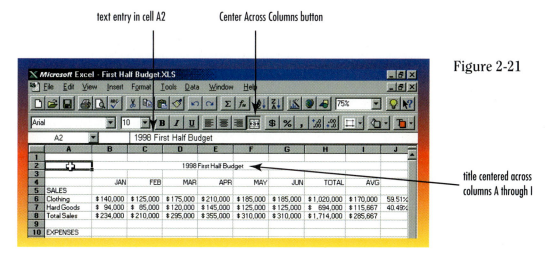

Figure 2-21

The formula bar displays the text entry of the active cell.

Changing Fonts and Font Styles

Finally, you want to improve the worksheet appearance by enhancing the appearance of the title. To do this you can change the title font settings.

Lab 2: Creating a Worksheet: Part 2

Concept 7: Fonts

Fonts consist of typefaces, size, and style. The **typeface** is the appearance and shape of characters. Some common typefaces are Roman and Courier. Size refers to the size of the printed characters and is commonly measured in points. A point is about 1/72 inch in height. A common point size is 12pt. This means the printed character is about 12/72 inch in height. Additionally, you can change the font style, such as bold, italics, and underlines, associated with a cell entry. The box below shows several examples of the same text in various typefaces, sizes, and styles.

Font Face	Font Size (12 pt/18 pt)	Font Style (Bold)
Arial	This is 12 pt./This is 18 pt.	**Bold 18 pt.**
Courier New	This is 12 pt./This is 18 pt.	**Bold 18 pt.**
Times New Roman	This is 12 pt./This is 18 pt.	**Bold 18 pt.**

The fonts on your computer system will be either printer or true type fonts. True type fonts appear onscreen as they will appear when printed. They are installed when Windows is installed. Printer fonts are supported by your printer and are displayed as close as possible to how they will appear onscreen, but may not match exactly when printed.

The Font and Font Size drop-down list boxes on the Formatting toolbar show the typeface and point size associated with the current cell. First you will change the typeface. The Font box shows that Arial is the font associated with the active cell. This is the default typeface.

> Open the Font drop-down list box.

The Font drop-down menu displays the available typefaces in alphabetical order. If a font is preceded with a 🖳, this means it is a font associated with your printer. Those preceded with 🆃 are true type fonts.

> The menu equivalent is F**o**rmat/**C**ells/**F**ont.

Select: 🆃 Times New Roman

The title appears in the selected typeface. Next you will increase the font size.

> Open the [10] Font Size drop-down list box.

The list of available font sizes is displayed. To increase the font size to 14,

Select: 14

Then to make the title darker, or bold,

Click: **B** Bold

Your screen should be similar to Figure 2-22.

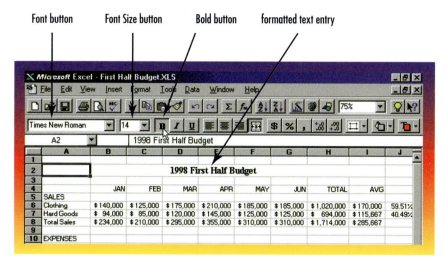

Figure 2-22

The title is in the typeface, size, and style you specified. Notice that the height of the row has increased to accommodate the larger character size of the heading in that row.

You also want to add bold, italics, and underlines to several other worksheet entries. First you want to change the row headings in cells A5, A10, and A19 to bold and italic.

Move to: A5
Click: **B** Bold, *I* Italic

> The keyboard shortcut for bold is Ctrl + B, and for italic is Ctrl + I.

You could repeat the same sequence for cells A10 and A19, but a quicker method is to copy the format from one cell to another using Format Painter on the Standard toolbar. To copy the format of the active cell,

Double-click: Format Painter

> A single click on allows you to copy to a single cell.

The mouse pointer appears as a . To apply the formatting,

Click: A10
Click: A19

The formatting is quickly added to each cell as it is selected. To turn off this feature,

Click: Format Painter

Finally, you want to bold and underline the column headings.

SPREADSHEET

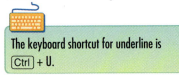

The keyboard shortcut for underline is [Ctrl] + U.

Select: B4 through I4

Click: **B** Bold, **U** Underline

Move to: A4

Your screen should be similar to Figure 2-23.

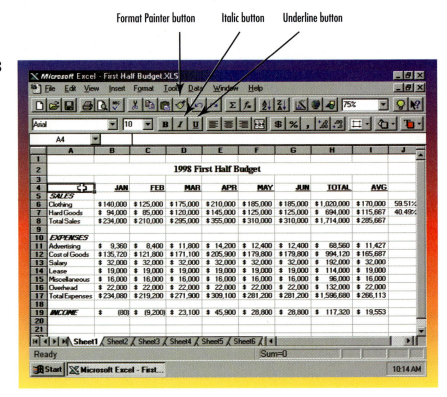

Figure 2-23

The six-month budget is now complete.

Return the magnification to 100%. Save the changes you have made to the workbook file as 1998 FIRST HALF BUDGET.

Copying a Sheet

Next you want to extend the worksheet to include the budget data for the last six months of the year. You can do this by adding the data to the active worksheet, or by using another worksheet to hold the data for the second six months. You will use a second worksheet.

By default Excel opens a workbook with 16 sheets. So far you have used only one sheet, Sheet1. To move between sheets, click on the sheet tab.

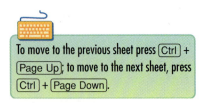

To move to the previous sheet press [Ctrl] + [Page Up]; to move to the next sheet, press [Ctrl] + [Page Down].

Click: Sheet2 tab

The blank worksheet, Sheet2, is the **active sheet** because it contains the cell selector and is the worksheet that will be affected by any actions. The name of the active sheet is always bold in the sheet tab. Sheet1, containing the budget for the first six months, is behind Sheet2.

To move from Sheet2 to Sheet1,

Click: Sheet1 tab

You want to copy the data from Sheet1 to another sheet in the workbook. To do this you could use the Copy and Paste commands. However, these commands will copy only the entries and formatting and not the column widths. To copy the entries, formatting, and column widths, you will copy the entire worksheet into a new sheet in the workbook.

To copy the entire sheet, you hold down Ctrl while dragging the sheet tab to where you want the new sheet inserted.

Hold down Ctrl and drag the mouse pointer from the Sheet1 tab to the Sheet2 tab.

The mouse pointer changes to a 🔲 as you drag the mouse from one tab to another. The + indicates that the sheet is being copied. The black triangle indicates where the copied sheet will be inserted.

Release the mouse button.

Your screen should be similar to Figure 2-24.

> You can move a sheet by dragging a sheet tab without holding down Ctrl.

> The menu equivalent is **E**dit/**M**ove or Copy Sheet.

> If the mouse pointer does not display +, this means the sheet is being moved, not copied. You must hold down Ctrl to create a copy.

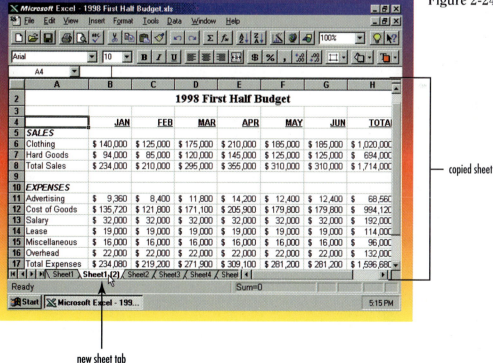

Figure 2-24

— copied sheet

new sheet tab

Excel renames the copy of the sheet Sheet1 (2) and inserts it before Sheet2. The new sheet is the active sheet and contains a duplicate of the first half budget in Sheet1.

> To create a new blank worksheet, use **I**nsert/**W**orksheet.

Naming Sheets

As more sheets are added to a workbook, remembering what information is in each sheet becomes more difficult. To help clarify the contents of the sheets, you will name the sheets.

Concept 8: Sheet Names

Each sheet in a workbook can be assigned a name to identify the contents of the sheet. The following guidelines should be followed when naming a sheet. A sheet name:

- Can be up to 31 characters
- Can be entered in uppercase or lowercase letters or a combination (it will appear as entered)
- Can contain any combination of letters, numbers, and spaces
- Cannot contain the following characters: : ? * / \
- Cannot be enclosed in square brackets ([ ])

You would like to name Sheet1 "First Half."

    Make Sheet1 active.

Double-click: **Sheet1 tab**

The Rename Sheet dialog box is displayed. To enter the new sheet name,

Type: **First Half**
Choose: **OK**

Your screen should be similar to Figure 2-25.

> The menu equivalent is Format/Sheet/Rename.

Figure 2-25

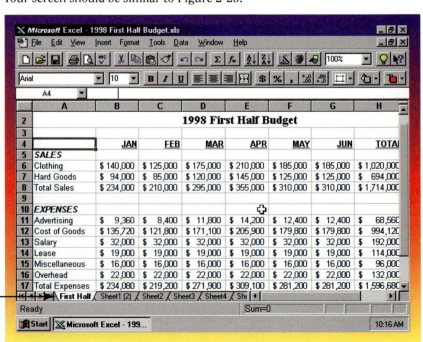

renamed Worksheet tab

Using AutoFill   **ss85**

The new name appears in the sheet tab.

Name the Sheet1 (2) worksheet tab "Second Half."

Using AutoFill

Now you can change the data in the new worksheet to reflect the data for the second half. First you need to change the title.

Change the title to "1998 Second Half Budget."

Now you need to change the month headings to July through December. You will use the AutoFill feature to enter the new month headings.

> **Concept 9: AutoFill**
>
> The AutoFill feature makes entering long or complicated headings easier by logically repeating and extending the series. AutoFill recognizes trends and automatically extends data and alphanumeric headings as far as you specify. For example, the entry Qtr1 would be extended to Qtr2, Qtr3, and so on, as far as you specify, beginning over again with Qtr1 again if appropriate.
>
> Dragging the fill handle activates the AutoFill feature. A starting value of a series may contain more than one item that can be incremented, such as JAN-98, in which both the month and year can increment. If you only want one value to increment, hold down the right mouse button as you drag the fill handle over the range. Release the mouse button and then click the appropriate command on the AutoFill shortcut menu to specify which value to increment. To fill in increasing order, drag down or to the right. To fill in decreasing order, drag up or to the left.
>
> When AutoFill extends the entries, it uses the same style as the original entry. For example, if you enter the heading for July as JUL (abbreviated with all letters uppercase) all the extended entries in the series will be abbreviated and uppercase.
>
> Other examples of time series are increments of days, weeks, or months that you specify, or it can include repeating sequences such as weekdays, month names, or quarters. A linear series increases or decreases values by a constant value, and a growth series multiplies values by a constant factor.

Enter the first month heading, JUL in cell B4.

The AutoFill feature will recognize this entry as the starting value of a series of months.

To automatically complete the month entries, drag the fill handle to extend the range from cell B4 through cell G4.

The column headings AUG through DEC are automatically entered into the selected cells. Next you need to change the sales numbers.

Enter the following numbers to update the budget for July through December clothing sales and hard goods sales.

> If a series is created when you drag the fill handle that you do not want incremented, select the original values again and hold down [Ctrl] as you drag the fill handle. The entries will be copied, not incremented.

> The menu equivalent is **E**dit/F**i**ll/**S**eries/Auto**F**ill.

Clothing		Hard Goods	
Cell	**Number**	**Cell**	**Number**
B6	200000	B7	135000
C6	180000	C7	120000
D6	172000	D7	115000
E6	175000	E7	118000
F6	160000	F7	110000
G6	390000	G7	280000

SPREADSHEET

Your screen should be similar to Figure 2-26.

Figure 2-26

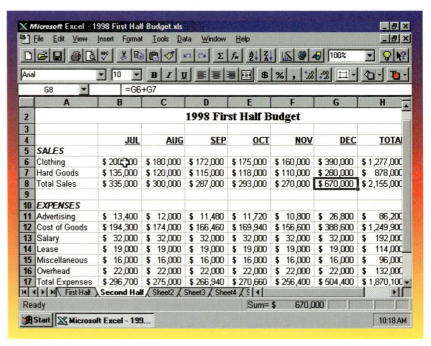

The worksheet has been recalculated and now contains the data for the second half.

Linking Worksheets

You also want to display a year-to-date income total in cell H21. The formula to make this calculation will sum the total income numbers from First Half cell E19 and Second Half cell E19. To reference data in another sheet in the same workbook, you create a link between cells in the worksheets through the use of a 3D reference.

Concept 10: Link Worksheets

A connection or **link** between cells in different worksheets of the same workbook allows you to use data from other sheets and to calculate new values based on this data. The link is created by entering a 3D reference in a formula. A **3D reference** is a reference to a cell or range of cells in another sheet or sheets in the same workbook.

A 3D reference to a cell or range in another sheet consists of the sheet name followed by an exclamation point and the cell or range reference: =Sheet1!H6   =SUM(Sheet1!H6:K8)

A 3D reference to a sheet range consists of the names of the beginning and ending sheets, separated by a colon. This is followed by an exclamation point and the cell or range reference. The cell or range reference is the same on each sheet in the specified sheet range: =SUM(Sheet1:Sheet4!H6)   =SUM(Sheet1:Sheet4!H6:K8)

Any changes in data that affect the cell or range in the 3D reference are automatically reflected in the result calculated by the formula containing the 3D reference.

You will enter the formula in cell H21 and a descriptive text entry in cell G21.

Enter and right-align the entry, Year-To-Date in cell G21.

When you right-aligned the text in cell G21, it moved to the left to be partially displayed in cell F21.

You will use the SUM function to enter the year-to-date formula in cell H21.

Move to: H21

Click: Σ AutoSum

The SUM function argument will consist of a 3D reference to cell H19 in the First and Second Half sheets. Although a 3D reference can be entered by typing it using the proper syntax, it is much easier to enter it by pointing to the cells on the sheets.

Click: H19

To extend the range to include the total value in cell H19 of the First Half sheet,

Press: ⇧Shift (and hold down)
Click: First Half tab

Release ⇧Shift.

Your screen should be similar to Figure 2-27.

Keyboard users must enter the 3D reference by typing it. The sheet names are included in single quotes: 'First Half:Second Half'!H19

To reference a range of sheets, select the cell or range in the beginning sheet and then hold down ⇧Shift and click on the sheet tab of the last sheet in the range to include the indicated call range on all sheets between and including the first and last sheet specified.

3D reference includes sheet range and cell reference

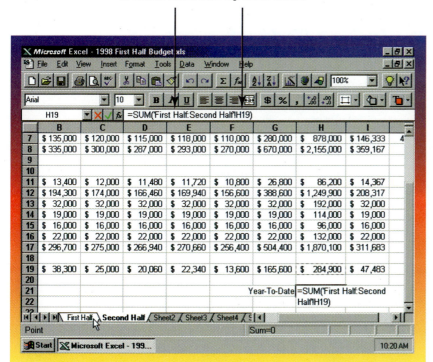

Figure 2-27

Excel automatically creates a 3D reference to cell H19 for the First Half worksheet.
To complete the function,

Press: ⏎Enter

The calculated number, 402220, appears in cell H21, and the function containing a 3D reference appears in the formula bar. The number does not display in Currency format because it is outside the range you selected when setting the cell format.

> Reminder: You can use Format Painter to copy the format.

Change the format of cell H21 to Accounting with zero decimal places.
Move to cell A1 of the First Half sheet.

Before saving and printing the worksheet, you want to update the workbook documentation to include your name.

Choose: File/Properties/Summary

Enter your name in the Author line and a description of the worksheet in the Subject line.

Choose: OK

Enter your first initial and last name in cell A1.

You also want to add the current date in the worksheet. Because the worksheet title is in cell A2, you will enter it in cell A3.

Enter the current date left-aligned in cell A3. Save the revised workbook as 1998 BUDGET.

Previewing a Workbook

Before printing, you may want to preview how the worksheets will appear on the printed page. To do this,

Choose: File/Print

If necessary, first select the correct printer for your computer.
To preview all sheets in the workbook,

Choose: Entire Workbook/ Preview

Your screen should be similar to Figure 2-28.

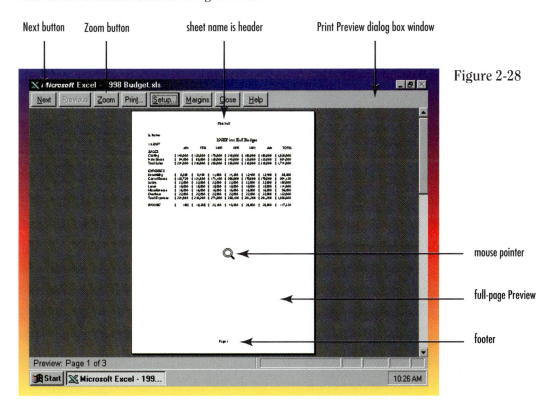

Figure 2-28

The Print Preview dialog box window displays the worksheet for the first six months as it will appear on the printed page. This is called the full-page view, but it is difficult to read. While previewing a worksheet, you can enlarge the display to a magnified view.

If necessary, move the mouse pointer onto the preview page.

The mouse pointer appears as a 🔍, indicating that you can switch between a full-page view and a a magnified view.

Click: the worksheet title

> The area you click on is the area that will be displayed in magnified view.

The worksheet is displayed in the actual size it will appear when printed.

Scroll the Preview window to see the rest of the worksheet.

Notice that by default Excel prints the sheet tab name in a header and the page number in a footer. To display the worksheet again in the full-page view,

Click: the worksheet

> The Zoom button can also be used to toggle between full-page view and magnified view.

The status bar shows the current page and total number of pages. To see the next page,

Choose:

The Average column and percent values for the First Half worksheet are displayed. You want these columns printed on the same page as the rest of the First Half budget. To return to the first page,

Choose: Previous

You will change the page setup to adjust the type size to fit the entire width of the worksheet on the page. You also want to display gridlines in the printed copy of the worksheet. To make these changes,

Choose: Setup...

The four tab folders are used to change how the worksheet is printed on a page.
   If necessary, open the Page tab.
The Fit To option will scale the print to fit the entire worksheet across one page of paper.

Select: Fit to

Next you will change the printed output to display gridlines.
   Open the Sheet tab.

Choose: Gridlines
Choose: OK

Your screen should be similar to Figure 2-29.

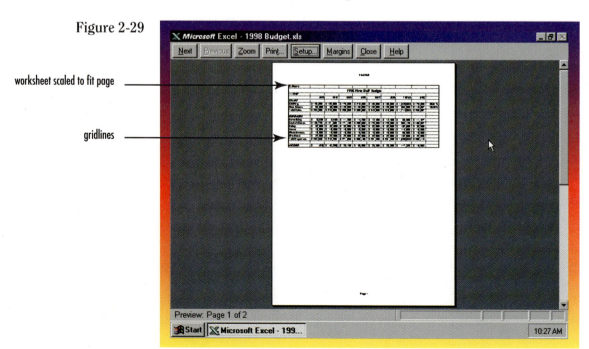

Figure 2-29

worksheet scaled to fit page

gridlines

The preview window is recreated. The entire worksheet width now fits on the page and the gridlines are displayed. To see how these setup changes affected the Second Half worksheet,

Choose:

None of the changes you made to the First Half worksheet are reflected in the Second Half worksheet. You will need to make all the same setup changes to this worksheet also.

Set the sheet to fit to a single page and turn on gridlines as you did for the First Half worksheet.

To print the workbook,

Choose: **Print**
Choose: **OK**

The printer should begin printing.

When you are ready, exit Excel, saving the workbook file using the same filename.

LAB REVIEW

Key Terms

absolute reference   (SS66)
active sheet (SS82)
argument   (SS60)
font   (SS80)
function   (SS60)
link (SS86)
mixed reference   (SS66)
relative reference   (SS58)
style   (SS75)
syntax   (SS60)
3D reference (SS86)
typeface   (SS80)

Command Summary

Command	Shortcut	Toolbar	Action
Edit/**U**ndo	Ctrl + Z	↶	Undoes last editing or formatting change
Edit/F**i**ll/**S**eries/Auto**F**ill			Automatically extends data and alphanumeric headings
Edit/**D**elete/Entire **R**ow			Deletes selected rows
Edit/**D**elete/Entire **C**olumn			Deletes selected columns
Edit/**M**ove or Copy Sheet			Moves or copies current sheet
View/**Z**oom		100% ▼	Changes magnification of window
Insert/**R**ows			Inserts a blank row
Insert/**C**olumns			Inserts a blank column
Insert/**W**orksheet			Inserts a new blank worksheet in the workbook.
Insert/**F**unction	⇧Shift + F3	f_x	Inserts a function
Insert/No**t**e			Inserts a note to a cell
F**o**rmat/C**e**lls	Ctrl + 1		Applies formats to selected cells
F**o**rmat/C**e**lls/Number/Currency			Applies Currency format to selection
F**o**rmat/C**e**lls/Number/Accounting			Applies Accounting format to selection
F**o**rmat/C**e**lls/Alignment/Center **a**cross selection		▦	Centers cell contents across selected cells
F**o**rmat/C**e**lls/Font			Changes font and attributes of cell contents
F**o**rmat/**C**olumn/**W**idth			Changes width of columns
F**o**rmat/**C**olumn/**A**utofit Selection			Changes column width to match widest cell entry
F**o**rmat/S**h**eet/**R**ename			Renames sheet
F**o**rmat/**S**tyle			Applies selected style to selection

Matching

1. General ____ a. function to add a series of numbers
2. F4 ____ b. a 3D reference
3. point ____ c. default magnification setting
4. 100% ____ d. indicates insufficient cell width to display numbers
5. AutoFill ____ e. method of entering a cell range or reference in a formula
6. style ____ f. recognizes trends and automatically extends data
7. SUM ____ g. centers across selection
8. Sheet1!H10 ____ h. a named group of format settings
9. ###### ____ i. in Edit mode, the ABS key
10. 100% ____ j. default cell format

Fill-In Questions

1. Complete the following statements by filling in the blanks with the correct terms.

   a. _____ are formulas that perform certain types of calculations automatically.
   b. To display more characters in a cell, you would increase the _____.
   c. When a formula is copied, and a cell reference does not adjust to the new location, the reference is _____.
   d. When text is displayed darker than other text in the worksheet, it is _____.
   e. A(n) _____ can be up to 31 characters long.
   f. When column widths are adjusted based on their contents, the _____ command is used.
   g. _____ appear when a cell width is too small to display the entire number in that cell.
   h. A(n) _____ character is used to make a reference absolute.
   i. A(n) _____ is the data the function uses to perform the calculation.
   j. _____ consist of typefaces and size.

Discussion Questions

1. How is the formula =F6+F7+F8 changed when it is copied from cell F10 to cell B16. How would the formula change if all the cell references where made absolute? How would the formula change if all the cell references where mixed references with the row number fixed?
2. Discuss the differences between relative, mixed and absolute cell references. Discuss how 3D references are used in a workbook.
3. What are the advantages of using a function instead of a formula to calculate a value?
4. Discuss the differences between the way numbers are displayed when the following formats are used: Currency, Accounting, Percent, and Date.

Hands-On Practice Exercises

Step by Step

Rating System
★ Easy
★★ Moderate
★★★ Difficult

★
1. To complete this problem, you must have completed Practice Exercise 1 in Lab 1. Open the workbook file BED AND BREAKFAST on your data disk. In this exercise, you will continue to modify the worksheet comparing prices of bed and breakfast inns in New England.

   a. Delete the contents of cell A1. Rename Sheet1 NEW ENGLAND BED AND BREAKFASTS so it will be displayed as a centered header on the printed page.
   b. Delete column B and change the width of columns A, B, and C to accommodate the widest entries.
   c. Format the numbers in columns D through G to display dollar signs and two decimals.

ss94 Lab 2: Creating a Worksheet: Part 2

d. Move the cell contents of cells A2 through G4 to cell A1.

e. Bold the contents of cells A1 through G3, and underline the row 3 headings.

f. Center the heading Single Rates across columns D and E, and center Double Rates across columns F and G. Increase the font size by two points for those two headings.

g. In cell D16, enter the formula =AVERAGE(D5:D14) to calculate the average rate for a single room with a private bath. Copy the formula to the three adjacent cells to the right. Use the Help Answer Wizard to look up the MIN and MAX functions, and calculate the low and high rates for the four occupancy categories.

h. Italicize the row headings Average Rates, Low Rates, and High Rates.

i. Replace the previous date with the current date and make sure it is left-aligned.

j. Save and replace the workbook file BED AND BREAKFAST. Preview, then print the worksheet with gridlines.

★★

2. To complete this problem, you must have completed Practice Exercise 2 in Lab 1. Open the workbook file COOKIE JAR on your data disk. In this exercise, you will continue to modify the quarterly sales worksheet for the gourmet cookie shop, The Cookie Jar.

a. Delete columns B and C and widen column A appropriately.

b. Format the sales numbers to display commas without dollar signs and two decimals.

c. Delete the formula that you used to calculate a total for chocolate chip cookies. Replace it with a SUM function, and copy the function down the column. Calculate totals for the three months, and sum the Total column. List three different ways you can total a column. Which do you think is the most efficient?

d. Make the necessary changes to column widths.

e. Center the worksheet title across the columns. Bold the title. Select a different font and increase the size to 14pt.

f. Bold and underline the column headings. Insert a blank row between the column headings and the chocolate chip cookie information.

g. Italicize the names of the cookies. Bold, italicize, and right-align the row heading Total.

h. Copy Sheet1 as Sheet1 (2) and insert it before Sheet2. Rename the Sheet1 tab 1ST QUARTER SALES and rename Sheet1 (2) 2ND QUARTER SALES.

i. Use the AutoFill feature to replace the months Jan through Mar with Apr through Jun on the 2ND QUARTER SALES sheet.

j. Enter the new April sales numbers as follows:

Type	Number
Chocolate Chip	1900
Chocolate Chip w/ Nuts	1425
White Chocolate Macadamia	1300
Butterscotch	750
Peanut Butter	1000
Oatmeal Raisin	350
Gingerbread	525

k. Aggressive advertising should account for a monthly 10 percent increase in sales. Enter formulas to calculate a 10 percent increase over previous month's sales for May and June (April Sales*1.10 and May Sales*1.10). Copy those formulas down the column.

l. Enter the heading "Projected Sales" over the May month heading. Bold the heading, and center it over the May and June columns.

m. Enter a heading "Projected Sales to Date Total" in cell B14 of the 2ND QUARTER SALES sheet. Bold and italicize the entry. In cell E14, calculate a total for the first six months by summing cells E12 on both sheets. Format the new entry to match the rest of the numbers in the workbook.

n. On both sheets, replace the previous date with the current date, and make sure the date is left-aligned.

o. Preview the workbook. Save and replace the workbook file COOKIE JAR. Print the workbook without gridlines.

You will complete this exercise as Practice Exercise 3 in Lab 4.

3. To complete this problem, you must have completed Practice Exercise 3 in Lab 1. Open the workbook file FAT GRAMS on your data disk. In this exercise, you will continue to modify the fat analysis worksheet.

   a. Eliminate columns B and C, and change the width of column A to accommodate the widest entry.
   b. Bold and underline the column headings and make any necessary adjustments to column width.
   c. Rename the Sheet1 tab FAT GRAM COUNTER so that it will be displayed as a centered header on the printed page.
   d. Insert a blank row between the column headings and the bagel information.
   e. By law, all prepared foods must contain nutrition facts, including calories and fat grams per serving. Go to the kitchen and look up the nutrition facts on some of your favorite snacks. Insert a few rows below the Pretzels row and use this information to add your snacks to the list. Copy the lite cream cheese fat formula down the column. What foods should Laura eliminate? What foods, if any, should you eliminate?
   f. Display one decimal place for all numbers in the Fat Grams column. Format the % Fat column to display a percent sign and two decimals.
   g. Add the following cell notes:
      Cell D4: Warning: "Lite" cream cheese is VERY high in fat!
      Cell D5: Stay away from the peanut butter!
   h. Replace the previous date with the current date, and make sure it is left-aligned.
   i. Save and replace the workbook file FAT GRAMS. Preview and then print the worksheet with gridlines.

You will complete this exercise as Practice Exercise 1 in Lab 3.

4. To complete this problem, you must have completed Practice Exercise 4 in Lab 1. Open the workbook file INVOICE on your data disk. In this exercise, you will continue to modify the invoice worksheet of computer equipment you sold to a new computer training facility.

   a. Use the formatting techniques you learned to improve the appearance of the invoice.
   b. Copy the total for the Pentium computers down the column and calculate a subtotal.
   c. Calculate the tax based on the tax rate in your state, and then calculate the total amount due.
   d. Format numbers using settings of your choice, and adjust column widths as needed.
   e. As you are ringing up the total for a customer, he decides he needs some diskettes. Insert a row between Tables and the Subtotal. Enter the following information:

Qty	Description	Price
1	**Formatted 2HD Diskettes 100 Pk**	49.95

   f. Calculate a total for the diskettes and edit the subtotal formula.
   g. Rename the Sheet1 tab INVOICE.
   h. Replace the previous date with the current date, and make any last-minute formatting changes you wish.
   i. Save and replace the workbook file INVOICE. Preview then print the worksheet.

You will complete this exercise as Practice Exercise 2 in Lab 5.

On Your Own

★★★

5. To complete this problem, you must have completed Practice Exercise 5 in Lab 1. Open the workbook file INCOME STATEMENT on your data disk. In this exercise, you will continue to modify the budget income worksheet for the Custom Manufacturing Company.

Copy the January formulas and the fixed cost entries to the months February through June. Calculate totals in column I.

Format the Sales and Net Income numbers to display dollar signs, commas, and two decimals. Change all other numbers to display commas and two decimals. Widen columns as needed.

Make changes you feel are necessary to improve the appearance of the invoice, such as font size, type and style changes, and centering the worksheet title.

You are interested in seeing how each month's net income compares to the total net income for the six months. Below the Net Income row, calculate the percent of total net income for each month. Format the new calculated values appropriately and add a row heading.

Replace the previous date with the current date, and make sure it is left-aligned. Save and replace the workbook file. Preview the worksheet and print it on one page.

You will continue this exercise as Practice Exercise 2 in Lab 3.

★★★

6. While attending college at night, Ilsa has a full-time day job. To better keep track of her weekly hours, she uses the time sheet shown below. Now that she has a computer, Ilsa will maintain her time sheet information using Excel. Follow the example below to create a time sheet. Hint: Use AutoFill to enter the days of the week.

	A	B	C	D	E
1	Time Sheet Of:	[Student's Name]			
2	Week Of:	[Starting Date]			
3		Total	Regular	Overtime	Adjusted
4	Day	Hours	Hours	Hours	Total Hours
5	Monday	10	8		
6	Tuesday	11	8		
7	Wednesday	8	8		
8	Thursday	9	8		
9	Friday	7	7		
10			Weekly Total:		
11					

Enter the formulas to calculate Overtime Hours and Adjusted Total Hours. Overtime Hours is the difference between Regular Hours and Total Hours multiplied by 1.5. The Adjusted Total Hours is the sum of Regular and Overtime Hours. Sum the Adjusted Total Hours to calculate a Weekly Total. (The Weekly Total should be equal to 48.) Enter last Monday's date as the Starting Date in B2. Use the formatting techniques you learned to improve the appearance of the time sheet.

Create a second time sheet in a new worksheet. Use last Friday's date as the Sheet1 name, and use this Friday's date as the Sheet1 (2) name. Enter different Total Hours and Regular Hours (8 is the maximum number for regular hours) in the new time sheet. Enter this Monday's date as the Starting Date in B2. Two rows below the weekly total amount, enter a formula to calculate the biweekly total as the sum of both weekly totals. Include an appropriate heading.

Document and save the workbook file as TIME SHEETS. Preview and print both worksheets without gridlines.

You will complete this exercise as Practice Exercise 1 in Lab 5.

7. To complete this problem, you must have completed Practice Exercise 6 in Lab 1. Open the workbook file IRS FORM 1040EZ on your data disk.

Make changes you feel are necessary to improve the appearance of the form. Rename the Sheet1 tab IRS FORM 1040EZ.

Use other sheets to create worksheets for additional IRS forms or schedules, and rename their sheet tabs accordingly.

Update the workbook documentation and save the workbook as IRS FORMS. Preview, then print the worksheet with gridlines.

Concept Summary

Creating a Worksheet: Part 2

Relative Reference
A relative reference is a cell or range reference in a formula whose location is interpreted by Excel as relative to the cell that contains the formula.

Absolute Reference
An absolute reference is a cell or range reference in a formula whose location does not change when the formula is copied.

Functions
Excel includes many built-in formulas, called functions, that perform certain types of calculations automatically.

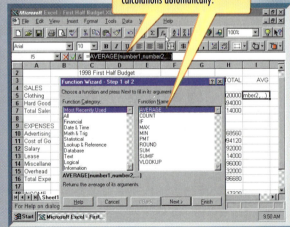

Column Width
The size or width of a column controls how much information can be displayed in a cell.

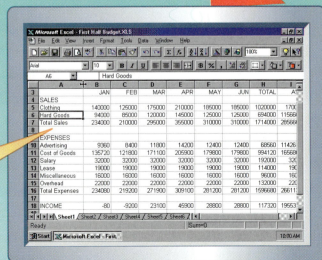

Insert and Delete Cells, Rows, and Columns

Individual cells or entire rows or columns can be inserted and deleted from a worksheet.

Fonts

Fonts consist of typefaces, point size, and styles that can be applied to characters to improve their appearance.

Number Formats

Number formats affect how numbers look onscreen and when printed.

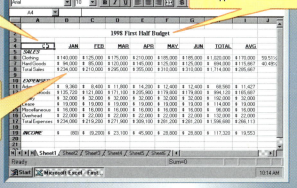

Concepts

- Relative Reference
- Absolute Reference
- Functions
- Column Width
- Inserte and Delete Cells, Rows, and Columns
- Number Formats
- Fonts
- Sheet Names
- AutoFill
- Link Worksheets

AutoFill

The AutoFill feature makes entering long or complicated headings easier by logically repeating and extending the series.

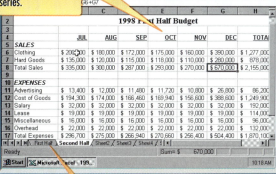

Sheet Names

Each sheet in a workbook can be assigned a name to identify the contents of the sheet.

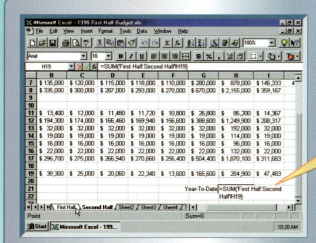

Link Worksheets

A 3-D reference formula creates a link between worksheets in a workbook, allowing you to use data from other worksheets and to calculate new values based on this data.

ss99

Managing a Large Worksheet

COMPETENCIES

After completing this lab, you will know how to:

1. Split windows.
2. Freeze panes.
3. View multiple windows.
4. Use what-if analysis.
5. Use Solver and Goal Seek.
6. Move sheets.
7. Open a second workbook.
8. Spell-check a worksheet.
9. Link workbooks.
10. Add borders, color, and cell shading.
11. Move toolbars.
12. Add text boxes.
13. Add headers and footers.
14. Change page orientation.

You have planned, entered, edited, and created a workbook that performs the basic tasks for which it was designed. The initial development of a workbook takes a lot of time. However, once you have set up the worksheet design and entered the data and formulas, you can then use the program to analyze the worksheet data and to make future projections.

As you have developed the workbook, it has grown in size and complexity. Now you are ready to learn about many of the Excel features that help you efficiently manage a large workbook. In addition, you will learn to use several of the built-in tools designed to help you analyze the data.

Splitting Windows **ss101**

Concept Overview

The following concepts will be introduced in this lab:

1. **Split Windows** — A sheet window can be split into sections called panes to make it easier to view different parts of the sheet at the same time.
2. **Freeze Panes** — To prevent scrolling of information in the top or left edge of a window, you can "freeze" the information in the left and topmost panes.
3. **What-If Analysis** — A technique used to evaluate the effects of changing selected factors in a worksheet.
4. **Solver** — The Solver is an Excel tool that answers what-if problems by determining the value of a cell by changing values in one or more cells in the worksheet.
5. **Spell Check** — A spell-checker program locates misspelled words, duplicate words, and capitalization irregularities and proposes the correct spelling.
6. **Link Workbooks** — A link creates a connection between workbook files that updates the linked data in the destination file whenever data in the source file changes.
7. **Goal Seek** — Goal Seek is an Excel tool that is used to find the value needed in one cell to attain a result you want in another cell.
8. **Objects** — Objects are many different types of elements that can be added to a workbook and that can be sized and moved.
9. **Headers and Footers** — Lines of text displayed below the top margin or above the bottom margin of each page are headers and footers.

CASE STUDY

You presented the completed first-half and second-half worksheets of the estimated operating budget to The Sports Company store manager. The manager has asked you to create a separate worksheet showing the annual budget and to include a line to calculate the profit margin for the store over the 12 months. At the end of 12 months, the profit margin should be 13 percent. Additionally, the manager wants you to create a summary worksheet showing only the total values for the year.

Part 1

Splitting Windows

Load Excel 7.0 for Windows. Your data disk should be in drive A (or the appropriate drive for your computer system).

Several of the changes requested by the manager have already been made and saved in the workbook file ANNUAL BUDGET on your data disk.

To see the revised and expanded budget, open the workbook file ANNUAL BUDGET.XLS. If necessary, maximize the application and workbook windows.

SPREADSHEET

Your screen should be similar to Figure 3-1.

Figure 3-1

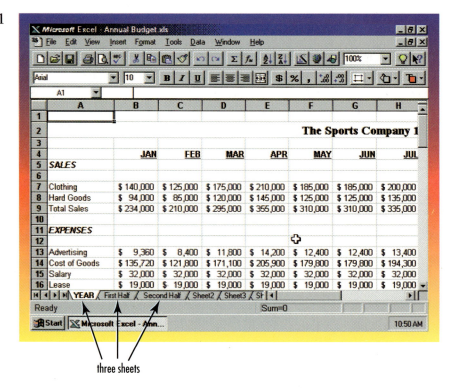

three sheets

The workbook file now contains three sheets: Year, First Half, and Second Half. The Year sheet contains the numbers for 12 months.

Most of the monthly values in the Year sheet are formulas that reference the appropriate cells in the First Half or Second Half sheets. To see an example of this,

Move to: B7

The formula in this cell is ='First Half'!B6.

The total formulas and the formula to calculate the income do not reference cells outside the Year worksheet.

Note: Although there are quicker ways to move to cells in the worksheet, use the arrow keys when directed. Your screen will then show the same rows and columns as the figures in the text.

The worksheet extends beyond the rows and columns you can see in the worksheet window. To bring the last row of data into view, using ↓,

Move to: B23

The row heading PROFIT MARGIN is now visible in the document window. You will enter the formula to calculate this number in the next section.

To see the rest of the worksheet to the right of column H, using →,

Move to: O23

The Total and Average columns and the numbers for the last six months are now visible, although it is difficult to know what the values represent because the row and column heading are not visible.

Move to: J17

The number in this cell is $16,000. Is this number a lease expense, an advertising expense, or a miscellaneous expense? Which month do the numbers in column J refer to? Without seeing the row and column headings, it is difficult for you to know. To view different areas of the same sheet at the same time, you can divide the window into panes.

> **Concept 1: Split Windows**
>
> A sheet window can be split into sections called **panes** to make it easier to view different parts of the sheet at the same time. The panes can consist of any number of columns or rows along the top or left edge of the window. You can divide the sheet into two panes either horizontally or vertically or four panes if you split the window both vertically and horizontally. Each pane can be scrolled independently to display different areas of the sheet. When split vertically, the panes scroll together when you scroll vertically, but scroll independently when you scroll horizontally. Horizontal panes scroll together when you scroll horizontally, but independently when you scroll vertically.
>
>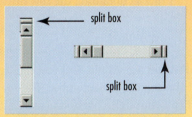
>
> A horizontal pane is created by dragging the split box, located at the top of the vertical scroll bar, downward to indicate the position where you want the horizontal split to appear. A vertical pane is created by dragging the split box at the right end of the horizontal scroll bar to the left to indicate the position of the vertical pane. Creating both a horizontal and vertical split divides the window into four panes. The Window/Split command can also be used to split the window into four panes at the active cell.

To display the column headings in the window at the same time as you are viewing data in cell J17, you will divide the window into two horizontal panes.

Point to: split box in the vertical scroll bar

When the pointer changes to ↕, this indicates you can create a split in the sheet. As you drag downward, a bar will be displayed to show where the split will appear when you stop dragging.

Drag down and position the bar at row 10.

> The menu equivalent is **W**indow/**S**plit.

There are now two horizontal panes with two separate scroll bars. Each pane can be scrolled independently. To scroll a pane, the cell selector must be positioned in the pane you want to scroll.

Click: J10 in the upper pane

Your screen should be similar to Figure 3-2.

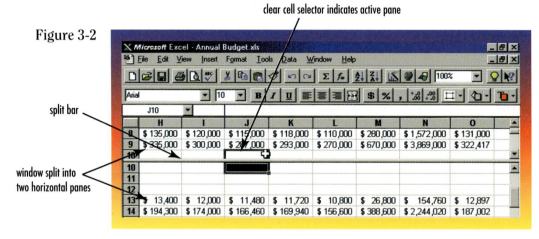

Figure 3-2

There are now two cell selectors visible. The clear cell selector is in the **active pane**, or the pane that will be affected by your movement vertically. The highlighted cell selector is in the pane that is not active. The cell selector moves in both panes, but only the active pane scrolls.

To scroll row 4 containing the row titles into view,

Press: ↑ (6 times)

The month titles are visible, and you can now see that the values in column J represent the month of September. The lower pane does not scroll when you move vertically through a horizontal pane, although the cell selector in the lower pane moves to the same location as in the upper pane. To see the row headings in column A,

Press: Home

You can now see that the numbers in row 17 represent miscellaneous expenses.
Although the row and column headings are visible again, you cannot see the numbers in columns I through O or below row 17, because both panes scrolled together as you moved horizontally through the sheet. Creating panes is helpful for viewing different areas of the same large sheet. However, you may find that as you scroll one pane, information you want to see moves out of view in another.
To clear the horizontal split from the window,

> The menu equivalent is **W**indow/Remove **S**plit.

Double-click: any part of the split bar

Freezing Panes

To stop the scrolling of information in panes, you can freeze the information displayed in the top and left panes of a window.

> **Concept 2: Freeze Panes**
>
> To prevent scrolling of information in the upper and left panes of a window, you can **freeze** the information in those panes. This is useful when you want to always be able to see the row and column titles in a sheet as you scroll to different areas.
>
> The Window/Freeze Panes command is used to freeze specified rows or columns (or both) on the window. To create two horizontal panes with the upper pane frozen, select the row below where you want the split to appear before choosing the command. To create two vertical panes with the left pane frozen, select the column to the right of where you want the split to appear first. If a column or row is not selected, the default is to create four panes at the active cell.

To keep the row and column headings visible in the window all the time while viewing the numbers in columns I through O and below row 19, you will freeze the worksheet headings in column A and row 4 in the window.

To do this, you will create four panes and freeze the headings in the upper and left panes.

Move to: B5
Choose: Window/**F**reeze Panes

Your screen should be similar to Figure 3-3.

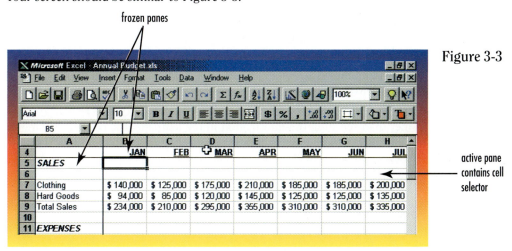

Figure 3-3

frozen panes

active pane contains cell selector

Now watch the movement of the columns in the window as you use → to,

Move to: O5

The pane to the left of the vertical split containing column A has remained fixed in the window while you scrolled the screen horizontally. Now columns J through

O are displayed while the headings in column A are still visible. This makes reading the worksheet much easier.

To quickly return to cell B5,

Press: Ctrl + Home

Pressing Ctrl + Home returns you to the upper left corner of the active pane, cell B5. You can move the cell selector into the other panes, but the rows and columns will remain fixed. For example,

Press: ↑

The cell selector is in the upper right pane, in cell B4. This is now the active pane.

Press: ↑ (2 times)

The cell selector is positioned in cell B2, although it is not visible and the rows did not scroll in the pane. This is because the rows in this pane are frozen. You can tell the location of the cell selector by looking at the cell reference in the reference area of the formula bar.

Press: ←

The cell selector is now in the upper left pane in cell A2.

Press: ↓ (3 times)

The cell selector is again visible on the screen and is positioned in the lower left pane in cell A5.

Press: →

Rather than scrolling the information in the left pane, the cell selector moves into the lower right pane. The lower left pane will not scroll because it is frozen.

Now, while the panes are frozen, you will enter the formula to calculate the profit margin in cell B23.

Move to: B23

The formula to calculate the monthly profit margin divides the monthly income by the monthly total sales.

Enter the formula =B21/B9 in cell B23.

The number 0.000342 is displayed in cell B23.

Change the display of this number to a percent with two decimal places.

The profit margin for January is now displayed as -0.03%. Next, you need to copy the formula across the row through the Total column. Because the column

> Use % to set the format to percent and ⁺⁰⁰ to increase decimal places.

headings are frozen in the upper pane, it will be easy to see which column is the Total column while you are specifying the destination range.

Copy the formula in cell B23 across the row through the Total column (N23).
Your screen should be similar to Figure 3-4.

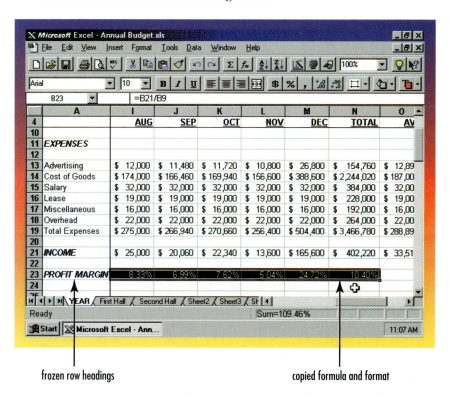

Figure 3-4

frozen row headings   copied formula and format

Notice that not only was the formula copied, but also the cell format. The total profit margin for the year displayed in cell N23 is 10.40 percent.

Press: Home

The cell selector should be back in cell B23, and the selection is cleared.
As you can see, freezing panes make it much easier to navigate in and use a large worksheet.

Viewing Multiple Windows

The manager wants the store to show a profit margin of 13 percent. Using the figures as budgeted for the year, the total profit margin of 10.40 percent is below this objective. After some consideration, you decide to reduce monthly salary expenses by scheduling fewer employees to work during slow periods to increase the total profit margin.

The total profit margin number is in cell N23 of the Year sheet. To see this value while you are substituting different monthly salary expenses in the First and Second Half sheets, you will open a second window in the workspace. This will allow you to view two sheets of the same workbook file on the screen at the same time. Viewing worksheet data in multiple windows makes it easier to enter, edit, and compare data in different parts of a sheet, in different sheets in a workbook, or in different workbook files.

Choose: Window/New Window

A new window containing the same information as the first window is displayed. You can tell it is a new window because the title bar displays the number 2 after the filename and the worksheet window does not display frozen panes. To view both windows in the workspace,

Choose: Window/Arrange/Tiled/OK

> Refer to the Arranging Windows section of the Windows 95 Review for information on this feature.

Your screen should be similar to Figure 3-5.

Figure 3-5

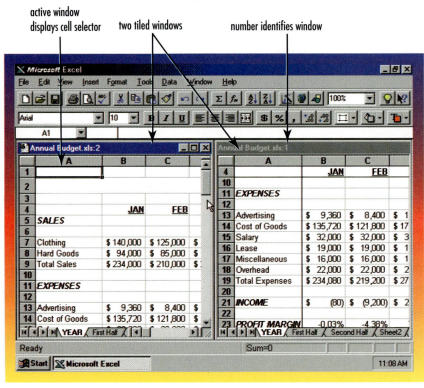

The new window (2) is displayed on the left side and is the active window. The Year sheet with the frozen panes is displayed in the original window (1) on the right side.

To display the First Half sheet in the active window,

Click: First Half tab

Using What-If Analysis

The process of evaluating what effect reducing the salary expenses will have on the total profit margin is called what-if analysis.

> **Concept 3: What-If Analysis**
>
> **What-if analysis** is a technique used to evaluate the effects of changing selected factors in a worksheet. This technique is a common accounting function that has been made much easier with the introduction of spreadsheet programs. By substituting different values in cells that are referenced by formulas, you can quickly see the effect of the changes when the formulas are recalculated.

You want to see the effect on the total profit margin of reducing salary expenses a set amount each month. First you want to see the effect of reducing the salary expenses to $30,000 per month.

Move to: B13
Type: 30000
Press: ←Enter

Now, by looking in cell B15 of the original window (1), you can see that the salary expense has been decreased to 30000. In addition, you can see that the change in this number has increased the January profit margin in cell B23 to .82 percent.

To see the effect on the total profit margin in column N of the Year sheet, you need to move to window 1. Simply clicking on the window makes it the active window.

Click on cell B23 of the Year sheet in window 1 to make it active.

Next you want to see how this change has affected the total profit margin; to quickly move to the last used cell in a row or column, you press End followed by a directional key to indicate the direction you want the cell selector to move.

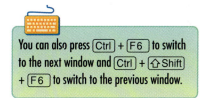

You can also press Ctrl + F6 to switch to the next window and Ctrl + ⇧Shift + F6 to switch to the previous window.

Press: End, →

Your screen should be similar to Figure 3-6.

Figure 3-6

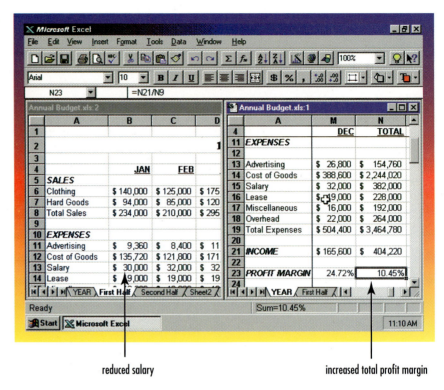

reduced salary   increased total profit margin

The cell selector moved to the last used cell in the row to the right and is positioned in cell N23. You can now see the total profit margin increased from 10.40 to 10.45 percent.

Press:

Now you can also see that the total and average salary numbers (N15 and O15) were recalculated, reflecting the change in the data.

Now you are ready to see what effect reducing the salary expenses to $30,000 for each month has on the total profit margin.

Make window 2 displaying the First Half sheet active. Copy the January salary number (B13) to the February through June salary cells (C13 through G13).

The Year worksheet displayed in window 1 has been recalculated, and the total profit margin, visible in the right pane of that window, has increased to 10.71 percent.

Next you need to copy the salary expense to the Second Half sheet.

If necessary, select the source range B13 through G13 in the First Half sheet.

Click: Copy

To highlight the destination range in the Second Half worksheet,

Click: Second Half tab
Move to: B13

> If the Second Half tab is not visible, use the tab scroll buttons to scroll it into view, or press Ctrl + Page Down.

To copy the salary expense,

Click: Paste

Your screen should be similar to Figure 3-7.

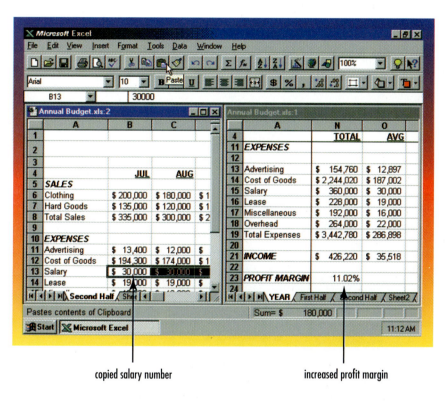

Figure 3-7

copied salary number   increased profit margin

The number $30,000 is copied into each cell in the Second Half worksheet. The total profit margin (N23) visible in the Year worksheet (window 1) has increased to 11.02 percent.

Using Solver

As you can see, it may take several guesses before you find the salary expense number that will increase the total profit margin to 13 percent. Each time you change the salary expense, you have to copy the values across the entire row and between sheets.

A quicker way to find the salary expense value is to use the Solver tool.

> Solver is an Excel add-on program that must be installed. If it is not on your system, skip to the end of this section (p.115) and follow the instructions to enter the value to attain a 13% total profit margin.

ss112   Lab 3: Managing a Large Worksheet

> **Concept 4: Solver**
>
> The Solver is an Excel tool that answers what-if problems by determining the value of a cell by changing values in one or more cells in the worksheet. Solver calculates a formula to achieve a given value by changing one of the variables that affect the formula. To do this Solver works backward from the result of a formula to find the numbers. The cells you select must be related through formulas on the worksheet. If not related, changing one will not change the other.

While using Solver, you do not need two windows.

Close the active window (2). Maximize the open workbook window and move to cell N23 of the Year sheet.

You want to use Solver to find the numbers that are needed in the referenced cells of the formula in cell N23 to make the solution to the formula 13 percent. To use Solver,

Choose: Tools/Solver

The dialog box on your screen should be similar to Figure 3-8.

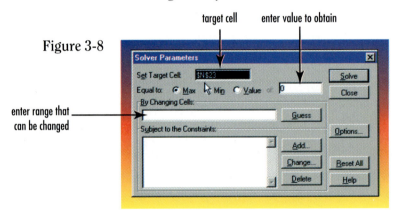

Figure 3-8

In the Solver Parameters dialog box, you need to supply three items of information. The cell reference of the cell containing the formula you want to solve is entered in the Set Target Cell text box. The cell reference of the current cell, N23, is already entered in this box. This is the correct location of the formula to be solved.

Second, the number you want as the result of the formula is entered in the Equal To text box. You can set the number to be a maximum, minimum, or an exact number. The maximum option sets the target cell to the highest possible number, while the minimum option sets the target cell for the lowest possible number. In this case, however, you are looking for a specific number. To specify an exact number,

Select: Value

In the Value Of text box to the right of the Value option,

Type: .13

The final item needed is the cells whose contents can be changed when the formula is computed. These are the adjustable cells. The cells to change are the range of cells B15 through M15 in the Year sheet.

Click: By Changing Cells text box

In the By Changing Cells text box, you can type the cell reference of the range or select the range from the sheet. To select the range, click on the sheet, then move to one corner cell of the range and drag to highlight the range.
Select the range B15 through M15.
The selected range is entered in the text box. To substitute values to meet the desired result,

> Reminder: You can move the dialog box if it covers the area of the worksheet you want to highlight.

Choose: Solve

The status bar displays the message "Setting Up Problem" while Solver finds the solution.
Your screen should be similar to Figure 3-9.

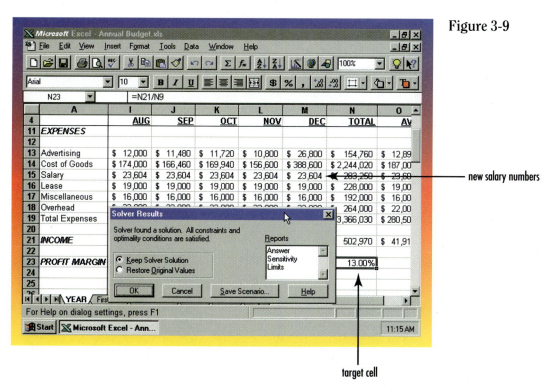

Figure 3-9

The Solver Results dialog box is displayed, and the worksheet is recalculated with the new numbers. The total profit margin is 13 percent if salary expenses are reduced to $23,604 per month. Solver quickly finds the number and enters it in cells B15 through M15. This was a lot quicker than making multiple guesses as to the correct value and changing it manually each time.

The Solver Results dialog box allows you to keep the Solver solution, restore original values, or create a report of the results. If you keep the Solver solution, Solver replaces the formulas in the cells with the new numbers. You do not want to replace the formulas with numbers, because then the Year sheet would not contain the same information as the First and Second Half worksheets. Rather than replace the contents, you will create a report of the solution.

Select: **Restore Original Values**

The three types of reports that can be created, Answer, Sensitivity, and Limits, are listed in the Reports list box. These reports are used to help you analyze how the new numbers affect the worksheet. To create a report of the Solver solution, from the Reports list box,

Select: **Answer**
Choose: **OK**

The message "Forming Answer Report" is displayed in the status bar. The Answer report is briefly displayed, and you are returned to the Year worksheet. The Year sheet now contains the original numbers. Notice that a new sheet tab named Answer Report 1 is inserted before the Year worksheet.

Make the Answer Report 1 sheet active.

Your screen should be similar to Figure 3-10.

Figure 3-10

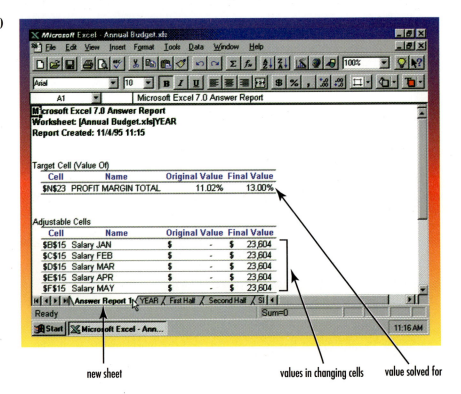

The report shows the original profit margin total of 11.02 percent and the final value of 13 percent. The Adjustable Cells table shows that by changing the numbers in cells B15 through M15 to $23,604, the profit margin becomes 13 percent. The Original Value column is blank because there are formulas in the Year worksheet and not numbers.

Enter 23604 for salary expense in the First and Second Half sheets. When you are done, make the Year sheet active.

The total profit margin (N23) should now be 13 percent.

Moving a Sheet

Next you want to move the Answer Report 1 sheet after the Second Half sheet.

To do this, make the Answer Report 1 sheet active. Drag the Answer Report 1 tab to the right end of the Second Half tab.

Notice the ▼ symbol above the sheet tab. This shows where the sheet will be inserted when you release the mouse button.

When the ▼ is displayed over the Second Half sheet, release the mouse button.

The Answer Report 1 worksheet is now stored after the Second Half sheet in the workbook.

Make the Year worksheet active.

> The menu equivalent is **E**dit/**M**ove or Copy Sheet

Opening a Second Workbook

Next you want to create a summary of the annual budget in a separate workbook file. The summary will contain the worksheet headings and the total numbers only. The headings for the summary worksheet budget have already been entered and saved for you in the workbook file named SUMMARY BUDGET.

Open the workbook file SUMMARY BUDGET.XLS.

Excel displays the SUMMARY BUDGET workbook file in a second window on top of the ANNUAL BUDGET workbook file window. There are now two active workbook files. The newly opened file is the **current workbook file**. It is the file that will be affected by changes and that contains the cell selector.

To view both files side by side, you will tile the windows.

Choose: Window/**A**rrange/**T**iled/OK

Your screen should be similar to Figure 3-11.

Figure 3-11

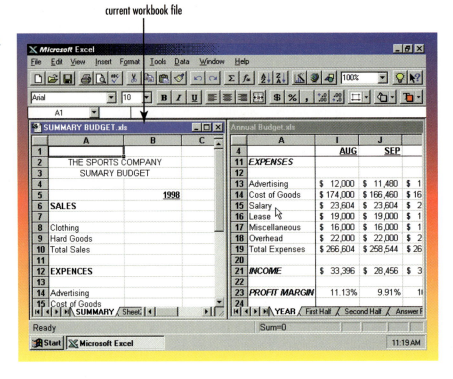

The two workbook file windows appear side by side. The title bar of the current file is highlighted.

Spell-Checking the Worksheet

You notice that in the worksheet title the word Summary is spelled wrong. Just to make sure there are no other spelling errors, you will check the spelling of all text entries in the worksheet.

Concept 5: Spell Check

A spell-checker program locates misspelled words, duplicate words, and capitalization irregularities and proposes the correct spelling. Spell-check programs include a standard dictionary that is used to check the spelling of text entries. If it locates a word that does not match the spelling of a word in this dictionary, a dialog box with a suggested list of replacements is displayed. You can also add your own terms to the dictionary.

Many programs also include a feature that corrects typing errors automatically. The Microsoft Office products call this feature AutoCorrect. You must add the misspelled word and its correct spelling to the list of words and phrases that are corrected automatically before using the feature.

If you have Microsoft Office, the same spelling dictionary and listing of AutoCorrect entries is shared with the other Office applications.

Excel begins checking all worksheet entries from the active cell forward. To begin checking the spelling in the sheet,

Click:  Spelling

> The menu equivalent is **T**ools/**S**pelling or F7.

Your screen should be similar to Figure 3-12.

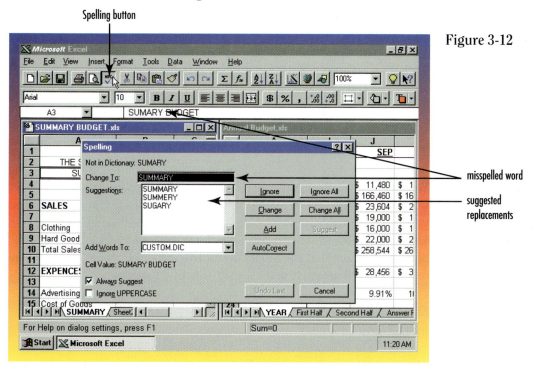

Figure 3-12

Immediately Excel begins checking the worksheet for words that it cannot locate in its standard dictionary. The cell selector moves to the first cell containing a misspelled word, and the Spelling dialog box is displayed. The word it cannot locate in the dictionary is displayed in the first line of the dialog box. The Change To text box displays the suggested replacement. A list of other possible replacements is displayed in the Suggestions list box. If the Change To replacement is not correct, you could select from the suggestions list or type in the correct word in the Change To text box.

The option buttons shown in the table below have the following effects:

Option	Effect
Ignore	Leaves selected word unchanged
Ignore All	Leaves this and all identical words in worksheet unchanged
Change	Changes selected word to word displayed in Change To text box
Change All	Changes this and all identical words in worksheet to word displayed in Change To text box
Add	Adds selected word to a custom dictionary so Excel will not question word during subsequent spell checks

The suggested replacement is correct. To accept the change,

Select: Change

The correction is made in the worksheet and the program continues checking the worksheet and locates another error.

Correct the word.

The program continues checking the worksheet and does not locate any other errors. A dialog box is displayed, indicating that the entire worksheet has been checked. When it reaches the end of the sheet, if the cell selector was not at the beginning of the sheet when checking started, the program will ask if you want to continue checking at the beginning of the sheet. To end spell-checking,

Choose: OK

Linking Workbooks

You need to copy the numbers from the Total column in the ANNUAL BUDGET workbook file into the SUMMARY BUDGET workbook file. However, because you are concerned that more changes may be made to the annual budget, you want to create a link between cells in the two workbook files. Linking the workbooks will ensure that the SUMMARY BUDGET file will be automatically updated if changes are made in the ANNUAL BUDGET workbook.

Concept 6: Link Workbooks

A link creates a connection between workbook files that updates the linked data automatically in one file whenever the data changes in the other file. The link between the workbook files is formed by entering an **external reference formula** in one workbook that refers to a cell in another workbook. When data in a linked cell changes, the workbook that is affected by this change is automatically updated whenever it is opened.

The formula is entered in the workbook that receives the data. This workbook file is called the **dependent workbook**. The workbook that supplies the data is called the **source workbook**. The cell containing the external reference formula (the dependent cell) refers to the cell (the source cell) in the source file that contains the data to be copied.

An external reference formula uses the following format:

=[workbook]file reference!cell reference

The file reference consists of the filename of the source file followed by the name of the sheet. The cell reference of the cell or range of cells containing the number to be copied into the dependent workbook follows the file reference. The two parts of the formula are separated by an exclamation point.

Make the ANNUAL BUDGET workbook window active. If necessary, switch to the Year sheet.

You will create a link between the SUMMARY BUDGET and ANNUAL BUDGET workbooks by entering external reference formulas in the SUMMARY BUDGET workbook that references the cells containing the total numbers in the

ANNUAL BUDGET workbook. The ANNUAL BUDGET workbook is the source workbook, and the SUMMARY BUDGET workbook is the dependent workbook.

The first external reference formula you will enter will link the total clothing sales numbers. To create an external reference formula, you copy the contents of the source cell to the Clipboard, switch to the dependent workbook, and then use the Edit/Paste Link command to create the external reference formula in the specified cell of the dependent workbook. The source cell is cell N7 of the Year sheet in the ANNUAL BUDGET workbook.

Move to: N7

Click: Copy

Make the SUMMARY BUDGET workbook window active and select cell B8.

To create the link in the selected cell,

Choose: Edit/Paste Special/Paste Link

Your screen should be similar to Figure 3-13.

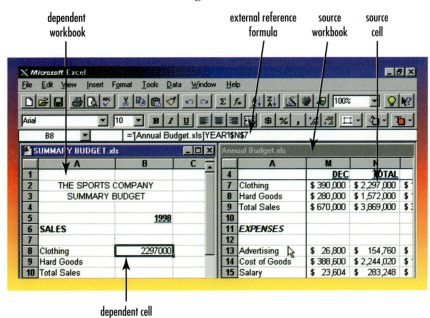

Figure 3-13

The link is created by entering an external reference formula in the selected cell of the dependent workbook. The formula is displayed in the formula bar, and the number in cell N7 of the source workbook is copied into the dependent workbook and displayed in cell B8. Notice that Excel uses absolute references in the external reference formula. Also notice that the cell format was not copied.

Next you want to create a link between the other total numbers in the source workbook. To do this quickly, you can copy the external reference formula down the column. However, you must first change the cell reference in the external reference formula to relative.

To do this, change to Edit mode and position the insertion point on the N7 cell reference.

Press: [F4] **ABS (3 times)**

The cell reference (N7) is now a relative cell reference and will adjust as the formula is copied.

Press: [←Enter]

> You can use [icon] Format Painter to copy the format between workbooks.

You also want to change the cell format to Accounting before copying, so that the format and formula can be copied at the same time.

Format cell B8 to Accounting format with dollar signs and zero decimal places.

Copy the external reference formula down column B through row 24. Clear the formula from any blank cells.

Change the format of the profit margin in cell B24 to Percent style with two decimal places.

Press: [Ctrl] + [Home]

Your screen should be similar to Figure 3-14.

Figure 3-14

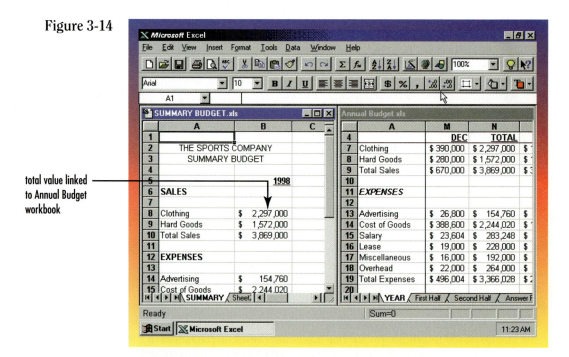

total value linked to Annual Budget workbook

You showed the SUMMARY BUDGET and ANNUAL BUDGET workbook files to the store manager. As you expected, you need to make some changes to the data in the ANNUAL BUDGET workbook. The manager has been told that the lease for the store will increase to $20,000 a month beginning in July.

To reflect this change in the budget, make the ANNUAL BUDGET workbook active and change the lease expense for July through December in the Second Half worksheet to 20000.

All affected formulas are recalculated. The total lease is $120,000 for the Second Half budget. To see the effect on the total profit margin in the Year sheet,

Move to: N23 of the Year sheet

The total profit margin is 12.84 percent. Also notice that the total lease expense has increased to $234,000. The Summary Budget file also reflects the change in data. Because of the change in the lease expense, however, the total profit margin is no longer 13 percent. You need to use the Solver again to adjust the salary values so the profit margin is 13 percent.
Make the Year worksheet active.
The cell pointer should be in cell N23.

> If you do not have Solver installed, follow the directions below to enter the new salary value of $23,104.

Choose: Tools/Solver

The Solver dialog box displays the value and cell references you entered previously. To use Solver,

Choose: Solve

The file has been recalculated using the new data. Solver's analysis shows that the monthly salary expenses will have to be reduced to $23,104 to maintain a 13 percent total profit margin. The total expense, total income, and profit margin in the Year worksheet have been updated to reflect the change of data in the worksheet cells. The SUMMARY BUDGET file has been recalculated using the new data. The total salary expense in cell B16, the total expense in cell B20, and the total income and profit margin have been updated to reflect the change of data in the linked worksheet cells.

You do not want to replace the formulas in the Year worksheet with Solver values.
Restore the original values and create an Answer report of the Solver solution. Enter the value 23104 in the Salary row for both the First and Second Half budgets. Move the Answer Report 2 worksheet after the Answer Report 1 worksheet.

Once an external reference formula is entered in a worksheet, whenever the number(s) in the cell referenced in the source file changes, the dependent file is automatically updated if it is open. However, if the dependent file is not open, it is not updated. To ensure that a dependent file gets updated whenever the source file is opened, an alert message is displayed asking if you want to update references to unopened documents. If you respond Yes, Excel checks the source documents and updates all references to them so that you will have the latest values from the source worksheet.

Make the Year sheet of the ANNUAL BUDGET workbook file current. Unfreeze the panes, and move to cell A1. Update the file Summary information with

> The Window/Unfreeze command is used to unfreeze panes.

the appropriate information. Save the workbook using the filename 1998 ANNUAL BUDGET.

Make the SUMMARY BUDGET workbook file active. Update the Summary Information for the file to display your name as the author, a title, and subject. Move to cell A1 and save this file as 1998 SUMMARY BUDGET.

Note: If you are exiting Excel at the end of Part 1, enter your name in cell A1 of the Summary sheet and print the Summary sheet. When you begin Part 2, load Excel and open the 1998 ANNUAL BUDGET and 1998 SUMMARY BUDGET files.

Part 2

Using Goal Seek

You presented the completed summary worksheet to the store manager. After reviewing the 1998 budget, the manager asks you to add a projected budget for 1999 to the summary budget. The data for the 1999 budget has already been entered for you and saved in a separate file named FUTURE. You want to add this data to your current worksheet file as column C.

Maximize the 1998 SUMMARY BUDGET window.

To copy the contents of the FUTURE.XLS worksheet into the 1998 SUMMARY BUDGET.XLS worksheet,

Choose: File/Open/FUTURE.XLS/Open

Copy the data in cells B4 through B23 of the FUTURE file to cells C5 through C24 in the 1998 SUMMARY BUDGET file. Increase the column width of column C to 12 to fully display the numbers.

To see the rest of the worksheet,

Move to: C24

Your screen should be similar to Figure 3-15.

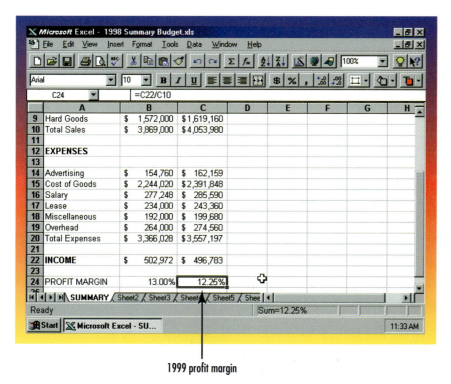

Figure 3-15

1999 profit margin

The profit margin for 1999 is 12.25 percent.

The first change you need to make to the 1999 budget is to adjust the salary expenses so the profit margin is 13 percent for the year. To find this number quickly, you will use the Goal Seek tool.

Concept 7: Goal Seek

The Goal Seek tool is similar to Solver in that it is used to find the value needed in one cell to attain a result you want in another cell. The difference is that the value of only one cell can be changed. Goal Seek varies the value in the cell you specify until a formula that is dependent on that cell returns the desired result.

To use the Goal Seek tool,

Choose: Tools/Goal Seek

The Goal Seek dialog box displays the current cell in the Set Cell text box. This is the correct location of the formula to be solved.

In the To Value text box,

Type: .13

Again you will change the salary expense number to reach a 13 percent profit margin. In the By Changing Cell text box,

> You could also point to cell C16 to enter the cell reference.

Type: C16

To recalculate the formula to meet the specified result,

Choose: OK

Your screen should be similar to Figure 3-16.

Figure 3-16

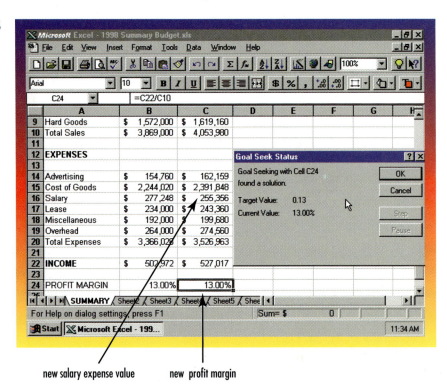

new salary expense value   new profit margin

The Goal Seek Status dialog box is displayed. Goal Seek quickly recalculates the formula and finds that the salary number of 255,356 will make the total profit margin 13 percent. To accept the solution Goal Seek found,

Choose: OK

Using the Goal Seek and Solver tools saves you from performing time-consuming trial-and-error what-if analysis.

Adding Color and Borders

Before sending the SUMMARY BUDGET worksheet to the store manager, you want to enhance its appearance.

Press: Ctrl + Home

Realign the worksheet title so it is centered across columns A through C in rows 2 and 3.

Next you will add color to the title text, add a box around the title, and add color shading within the title box.

If necessary, select the range A2 through C3.

To specify a color for the text contained within the selected range,

Open the ▭▾ Font Color drop-down menu.

Your screen should be similar to Figure 3-17.

> Reminder: To center across columns, use ▭ or the F**o**rmat/C**e**lls/Alignment command.

> The menu equivalent is F**o**rmat/C**e**lls/Font/Color.

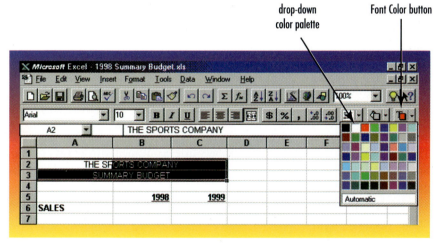

Figure 3-17

A palette of colors is displayed.

Select a color of your choice.

The text appears in the selected color and the button displays the selected color.

Next you will create a box around the title. A box is created using the ▭▾ Borders button, which displays a drop-down list of options. The range A2 through C3 should still be selected.

Open the ▭▾ Borders drop-down list.

The drop-down list box displays 12 border and line styles. More styles are available if you use the menu equivalent. The bottom right option ▭ adds a heavy outline border around the entire cell or range.

> Clicking ▭ applies the color displayed in the button to the selection.

> The menu equivalent is F**o**rmat/C**e**lls/Border/**O**utline.

Click:

The title is surrounded by a box, and the selected border style appears in the button.

> Clicking ▭ applies the border style displayed in the button to the selection.

ss126   Lab 3: Managing a Large Worksheet

> The menu equivalent is **F**ormat/C**e**lls/ **P**atterns.

Finally, you want to add shading to the cells within the box. To do this,

Open the [icon] Color drop-down list box. Select a color of your choice from the palette.

The cells in the selected range are filled with the color you selected.

> Clicking [icon] applies the color displayed in the button to the selection.

Move to: **A1**

Your screen should be similar to Figure 3-18.

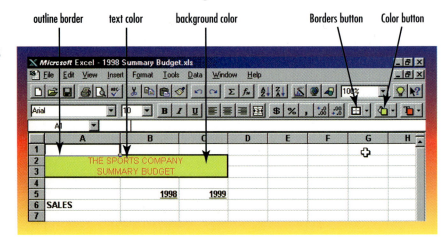

Figure 3-18

The range of cells containing the worksheet title is outlined with a heavy single-line border, the text appears in color, and the range is filled with a color background.

The last formatting change you want to make is to add lines to separate the numbers being summed from the total numbers in the column. To add a single line below the Hard Goods row to separate it from the Total Sales data,

Select: **B9 through C9**

> The menu equivalent is **F**ormat/C**e**lls/ Border/**B**ottom.

Open the [icon] Borders drop-down menu.

Click: [icon]

Press: [Home]

A solid line along the bottom border of the range is displayed. The solid line creates a visual separation between the numbers being summed and the total sales numbers. The border line is different from an underline in that it extends along the entire edge of the cell, whereas an underline would appear under the text within the cell.

Next you want to add the same type of line below the Overhead row to separate it from the Total Expenses row. Rather than reselect the same commands, you can use the Repeat toolbar button to redo the last command you entered. To use this feature,

Select: B19 through C19
Click: Repeat

> The menu equivalent is <u>E</u>dit/<u>R</u>epeat Format Cells or Ctrl + Y.

The solid line is added below the selected range of cells.

Finally, you want to add a double line below the income numbers in cells B22 through C22.

Add a double-line style bottom border below the Income row of data.

Move to: A24

Your screen should be similar to Figure 3-19.

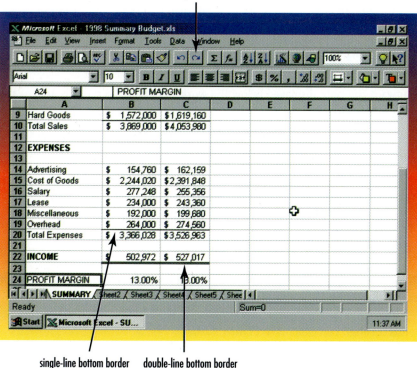

Figure 3-19

Moving Toolbars

The final addition you want to make is to add a note below the worksheet data to explain the data in the worksheet. The Drawing toolbar contains the button to add a text note.

Display the Drawing toolbar.

The Drawing toolbar may be displayed anywhere in the worksheet window. How a toolbar is displayed depends upon its location in the window. A toolbar that is near the edge of the Excel window or above the formula bar has been

> Reminder: Select Drawing from the toolbar Shortcut menu.

placed on a toolbar dock and is called a docked toolbar. A toolbar that is anywhere else within the workspace is a floating toolbar and is displayed in a window with a title bar and Close box.

All toolbars can be moved to any location in the workspace by dragging the toolbar and sizing it. If you change the toolbar height and width, the tool buttons automatically wrap to fit the new shape.

If the Drawing toolbar on your screen is positioned below the Formatting toolbar, point to the background area of the toolbar and drag it to the middle of the workspace.

The toolbar should now be displayed in a window.

Point to the window title bar and drag the Drawing toolbar to the left edge of the window below the Formatting toolbar. Release the mouse button to place the toolbar.

The toolbar no longer displays a title bar, and the border of the toolbar changes from a thick window border to a thin border when the toolbar is in a toolbar dock.

To find out what these buttons do, display the Tooltip and description for each button in the Drawing toolbar.

> Once a toolbar has been moved, it will be displayed at that location each time it is displayed until it is moved again.

Adding Text Boxes

You want the note displayed below the worksheet data. To see this area of the sheet in the window,

Move to: A31

A long note can be easily added to a sheet using the 📄 Text Box button on the Drawing toolbar. To create a text box,

Click: 📄 Text Box

The mouse pointer changes to a +, indicating the program will create a text box as you drag the mouse pointer to specify the size and location of the box.

Move the mouse pointer to cell A27 and drag to create a text box that extends through cell D32 (as in Figure 3-20).

Your screen should be similar to Figure 3-20.

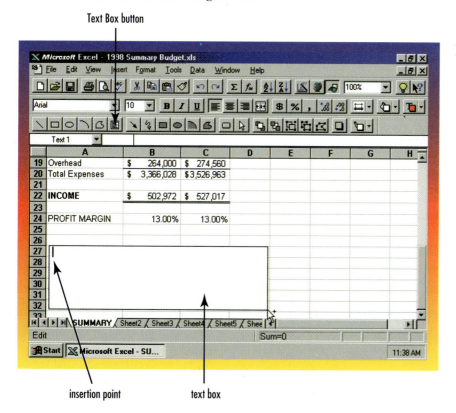

Figure 3-20

The text box displays an insertion point and is waiting for you to enter the text. As you type the text below, do not be concerned if all the text is not visible within the text box. It will scroll in the box as you type to make space for more text. You will adjust the size of the text box as needed after entering the text. In addition, as you type, the text will automatically begin on the next line when the right edge of the text box is reached. You should not press ←Enter to move to the next line. This feature is called **word wrap**.

Type: Above is the proposed budget for 1998 and the projected budget for 1999. The 1998 sales values represent the expected sales based upon an estimated increase from our 1997 sales of 5%.

Press: ←Enter (2 times)

A blank line is inserted. To continue the note,

Type: The 13% total profit margin objective was obtained in both years by reducing salary expenses. This expense will need to be closely monitored in order to maintain this objective.

Now that the note is complete, you want to enlarge the text box to fully display the note. To do this, the text box must first be selected.

ss130 Lab 3: Managing a Large Worksheet

> To delete a selected object, press Delete.

Point to the text box border, and when the mouse pointer appears as ⬚, click on the border.

The text box is now a selected object.

> **Concept 8: Objects**
>
> A text box is one of several different types of elements or **objects** that can be added to a workbook and that can be sized and moved. When an object is selected, it is displayed with eight **selection handles** and a hashed editing border (see Figure 3-21). Handles are the black boxes surrounding the object. They are used to size the object with a mouse.

> You can also move the text box by dragging the border when the mouse pointer is a ⬚.

Now you can adjust the size of the selected text box. The procedure is the same as sizing windows.

> The mouse pointer is a ⬚ when you can size the box.

Using the handles, adjust the size of the box until the text is fully displayed, keeping the box width no larger than column D as in the figure below.

Your screen should be similar to Figure 3-21.

Figure 3-21

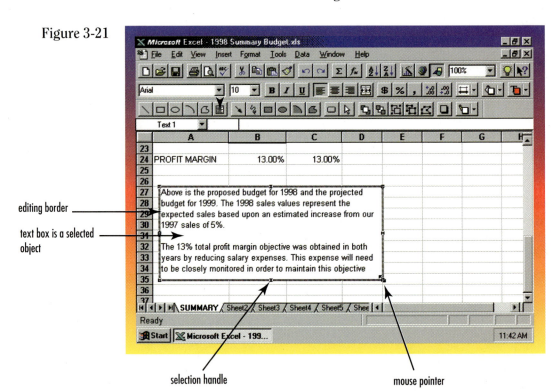

editing border

text box is a selected object

selection handle

mouse pointer

> Pressing Esc also deselects an object.

Now that the text box is the appropriate size, you can deselect the object.

Click anywhere outside the box.

You also no longer need to have the Drawing toolbar displayed.

Hide the Drawing toolbar.

> Reminder: Clear the check from the toolbar Shortcut menu to hide a toolbar.

Using Predefined Headers and Footers

First you will print the SUMMARY BUDGET workbook. To preview how the worksheet will appear,

Click:  Print Preview

> The menu equivalent is File/Print Preview.

You realize that your name and the date are not displayed on the worksheet. Instead of returning to the worksheet and entering the information in a cell, you will add the information to be printed as a header.

> If you entered your name in the worksheet at the end of Part I, delete it.

Concept 9: Headers and Footers

A **header** is a line or several lines of text that appears at the top of each page just below the top margin. A **footer** is a line or several lines of text that appears at the bottom of each page just above the bottom margin. The text can be formatted like any other text. In addition, you can control the placement of the header and footer text by specifying where it should appear; left-aligned, centered, or right-aligned in the header or footer space. Information that is commonly placed in a header or footer is the date and page number.

To add a header and footer,

Choose: Setup/Header/Footer

> File/Page Setup can also be used to modify page layout.

The Header/Footer tab displays the preformatted header and footer, which prints the sheet or workbook name in the header and the page number in the footer. The Header drop-down list box is used to change the predefined text you want displayed in the header.

Open the Header drop-down list box and select the Prepared By [your name] [date], Page 1 option.

The selected header is displayed in the header area of the dialog box.

Footers are entered in the same way as headers. The default footer, which displays the page number, needs to be cleared because the page number is now displayed in the header.

Open the Footer drop-down list box and select the None option.

> None is the first option in the Footer drop-down list box.

To see your changes in the Preview window,

Choose: OK

The changes you made to the header and footer are reflected in the Preview screen (see Figure 3-22).

You would also like to center the worksheet horizontally on the page. To make this change,

Choose: Setup/Margins/Horizontally/OK

Your screen should be similar to Figure 3-22.

Figure 3-22

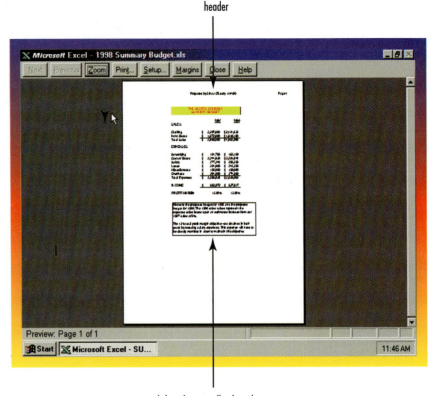

header

worksheet horizontally aligned on page

Again the Preview window reflects the changes, and the worksheet appears the way you want it to appear when printed. To print the worksheet,

Choose: **Print**

If necessary, select the appropriate printer for your system.

Choose: **OK**

The colored text and cell range will appear shaded if you have a black and white printer.

Save the 1998 SUMMARY BUDGET workbook as 1998-1999 SUMMARY BUDGET and close the file. Make the 1998 ANNUAL BUDGET workbook active.

Changing Page Orientation

Next you will print the Year sheet of the 1998 ANNUAL BUDGET workbook.
If necessary, make the Year sheet active. Preview the sheet.
Notice that the entire sheet does not fit across the width of the page. To see the second page,

Click: **Next**

The sheet requires two pages to print using the default settings. To print the entire sheet on a single page, you can change the orientation (layout of the printed worksheet on the paper) so that the worksheet prints across the length of the paper. This type of layout is called **landscape** style. To change the orientation of the worksheet on the page from **portrait** (prints across the width of the page) to landscape,

Choose: Setup/Page/Landscape/OK

> Not all printers can print landscape style. If your printer does not have this capability, skip the instructions on changing the orientation.

The Preview screen is recreated showing how the sheet will appear in landscape orientation. It is still too large to fit on a single page. To adjust the text size to fit the worksheet on a single page,

Choose: Setup/Page/Fit To

By default the Fit To option reduces the worksheet to one page. You also want to display gridlines to make it easier to read along the long lines of data. To do this,

Choose: Sheet/Gridlines/OK

The entire worksheet now fits across the width of the page in landscape orientation.

Creating Custom Headers and Footers

You would also like to add a header to this sheet.

Choose: Setup/Header/Footer

Rather than using one of the predefined headers, you will create a custom header.

Choose: Custom Header

The dialog box on your screen should be similar to Figure 3-23.

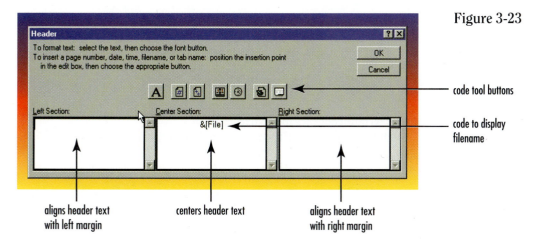

Figure 3-23

The Header edit window is displayed. The Left Section text box will display the header text you entered aligned with the left margin, the Center Section will center the text, and the Right Section will right-align the text. Notice that the Center Section contains the code &[File]. This code instructs Excel to display the filename centered in the header. Excel has five codes that you can use to display information in the header. The tool buttons above the section boxes are used to enter the codes.

Code	Button	Result
&[Page]		Page number
&[Pages]		Total number of pages
&[Date]		Current date
&[Time]		Current time
&[File]		Filename of active document
&[Tab]		Worksheet tab name

The insertion point is currently positioned in the Left Section text box. You want to enter your name, class, and the date in this box.

Type: Created by [your name]

To enter a second line,

Press: ←Enter

Enter the name of your class and the section or time.

Press: ←Enter

On the third line, you will enter the date.

Click: Date Code

The code &[Date] appears in the header box.
  Finally, you want to delete the code that prints the filename from the Center Header text box. To do this,

Press: Tab
Press: Delete

The header is complete.

Choose: OK

The header as you entered it appears in the sample header area of the dialog box.

Choose: OK

Your screen should be similar to Figure 3-24.

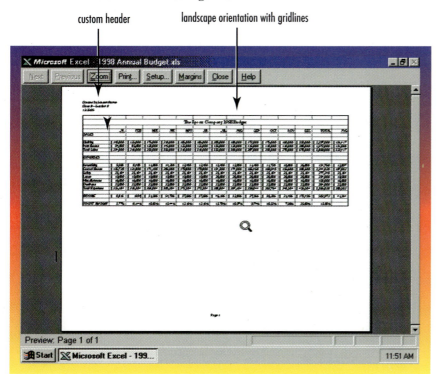

Figure 3-24

The Preview screen reflects the change you made.

Print the worksheet.

Save and close the 1998 ANNUAL BUDGET workbook. Close the Future workbook and exit Excel.

LAB REVIEW

Key Terms

active pane (SS104)
current workbook file (SS115)
dependent workbook (SS118)
docked toolbar (SS128)
external reference formula (SS118)
floating toolbar (SS128)

footer (SS131)
freeze (SS105)
header (SS131)
landscape (SS133)
object (SS130)
pane (SS103)

portrait (SS133)
selection handle (SS130)
source workbook (SS118)
toolbar dock (SS128)
what-if analysis (SS109)
word wrap (SS129)

Command Summary

Command	Shortcut	Toolbar	Action
File/Page Set**u**p/**H**eader/**F**ooter			Adds header and/or footer
File/Page Set**u**p/**L**andscape			Prints worksheet across length of paper
Edit/**R**epeat	Ctrl + Y	◰	Repeats last-used command
Edit/Paste **S**pecial/Paste **L**ink			Creates a link to the source document
Format/C**e**lls/**F**ont/Color		▣	Adds color to text
Format/C**e**lls/Border/**O**utline		▣, ▣	Adds border around selection
Format/C**e**lls/Border/**B**ottom		▣, ▣	Adds border to bottom edge of selection
Format/C**e**lls/Patterns		▣	Adds shading to selection
Tools/**S**pelling	F7	ABC✓	Spell-checks worksheet
Tools/**G**oal Seek			Adjusts value in specified cell until a formula dependent on that cell reaches specified result
Tools/Sol**v**er			Calculates a formula to achieve a given value by changing one of variables that affects formula
Window/**N**ew Window			Creates an additional window for active workbook
Window/**A**rrange/**T**iled			Arranges open windows side by side
Window/Un**f**reeze			Unfreezes window panes
Window/**F**reeze Panes			Freezes top and/or leftmost panes
Window/**S**plit			Divides window into four panes at active cell

Matching

1. =[ANNUAL.XLS] YEAR!$B$12 _____ a. prevents scrolling of information in upper and left panes of a window
2. pane _____ b. spell-checks worksheet
3. freeze _____ c. finds a specific value for a cell by adjusting value of only one other cell
4. landscape _____ d. the sections of a divided window
5. F7 or _____ e. an external reference formula
6. dependent workbook _____ f. worksheet that supplies data in a linking formula
7. current workbook _____ g. worksheet that receives data in a linking formula
8. _____ h. a workbook that is open and available for use
9. goal seek _____ i. prints across length of paper
10. source workbook _____ j. applies color to text

Fill-In Questions

1. Complete the following statements by filling in the blanks with the correct terms.

a. Excel checks spelling by comparing text entries to words in a(n) _____.

b. When a column or row is _____, it is visible in the window all the time.

c. A worksheet window can be divided into four _____.

d. _____ is a what-if tool that changes values in a specified range to attain a result in another cell.

e. The _____ calculates a formula to achieve a given value by changing one of the variables that affect the formula.

f. To view two windows side by side, the Window/ _____ command is used.

g. The link between workbook files is formed by entering a(n) _____ in one file that refers to a cell in another file.

h. The workbook file that receives the data from a link is called the _____ workbook.

i. A(n) _____ is a line of text that appears at the top of each printed page.

j. To print a worksheet across the length of the page, you would change the orientation to _____.

Hands-On Practice Exercises

Step by Step

Rating System
★ Easy
★★ Moderate
★★★ Difficult

★

1. To complete this problem, you must have completed Practice Exercise 3 in Lab 2. Open the file FAT GRAMS from your data disk. In this exercise, you will continue to modify the worksheet.

a. Remove the underlines from the column headings. Draw a bottom border across that row.

b. Draw an outline border around the fat gram counter, including the column headings.

c. Remove your name and the date from below the worksheet.

d. Create a text box and insert the following memo below the worksheet:

To: Laura
From: [your name]
Date: [current date]

Read all food labels carefully. As you can see by the above Fat Gram Counter, foods that are low in calories can be very high in fat. Foods that are high in calories can be very low in fat.

e. Preview the worksheet. Remove the page number footer and center the worksheet horizontally. Print the worksheet. Save and replace the workbook FAT GRAMS.

★★

2. To complete this problem, you must have completed Practice Exercise 5 in Lab 2. In this exercise, you will continue to modify the income statement for Custom Manufacturing. The sales representatives have recently completed an intensive sales seminar. The results seem positive, and the sales manager is confident that a net income of $85,000 is an attainable goal for the first six months.

a. Open the workbook file INCOME STATEMENT on your data disk. Freeze the worksheet panes below the column headings and to the right of the row headings.

b. Use Solver to determine what monthly sales will be required to reach the new net income goal. Keep the Solver solution.

c. Remove your name and the date from the worksheet. Preview the worksheet and replace the default header with a header that displays your name and the date. Print the worksheet centered horizontally on the page and use landscape orientation. Update the documentation to reflect the new sales goal. Save and replace the workbook file. Next, you will link INCOME STATEMENT to the file CUSTOM SALES on your data disk. This file contains the actual sales for the first six-month period.

d. Open the CUSTOM SALES file and sum the columns and rows. Format the values to display commas and two decimals, and change the column widths to accommodate the widest entry. Center the title over the columns. Draw a single bottom border under the column headings and under the Region 4 values. Draw a double-line border under the Total row. Make any other formatting changes you wish.

e. Tile the windows. Make the INCOME STATEMENT file active. Enter an external reference formula to copy the January total sales number from the CUSTOM SALES file into the corresponding cell of the INCOME STATEMENT file. Adjust the formula so it can be copied across the row. Maximize the INCOME STATEMENT file window. Copy the formula. What is the net income?

f. Unfreeze the panes. Add a note to the Sales heading in column A that informs the users that the sales numbers are linked to the total sales numbers in the CUSTOM SALES workbook.

g. Save and replace the workbook file INCOME STATEMENT. Print the worksheet using the previously defined settings. Close the file.

h. Preview the CUSTOM SALES worksheet. Add a header that includes your name and the date. Print the worksheet centered horizontally using landscape orientation. Save and replace the workbook file CUSTOM SALES. Close the file.

3. Kevin O'Neal is a student at Metro Community College. He has just completed his final semester and will graduate with an associate's degree in Information Systems Technology. In this exercise, you will calculate semester and cumulative totals and GPA for each semester.

a. Open the file GRADE REPORT on your data disk. Rename the first four sheet tabs Fall 96, Spring 97, Fall 97, and Spring 98.

b. You can edit several sheets at once by selecting the sheets you want to change and modifying the first sheet in the group. In this portion of the exercise, you will draw an outline border around the first four rows of information on the Fall 96 through Spring 98 sheets.

- Make the Fall 96 sheet active.
- Hold down ⇧Shift as you click the Spring 98 sheet. All four sheets should be selected.
- Select cells A1 through G4 of the Fall 96 sheet.
- Draw an outline border around those cells.
- Change the color of the text and the background.
- Click A1 to clear the highlight.
- Right-click the Fall 96 sheet tab and choose the command Ungroup Sheets. Look at each sheet to see that the formatting was copied.

c. Following the above procedure, draw a bottom border across cells A7 to H7 of the four sheets. While the sheets are still selected, bold the column headings in rows 6 and 7 and bold the Semester Total and Cumulative Total headings in rows 14 and 15. Remember to ungroup the sheets when you are done.

d. In the Fall 96 sheet, multiply the Grade by the Credits Earned to calculate Total Points for Intro to Business. Copy that formula down the column. Sum the Credits Attempted, Credits Earned, and Total Points columns and display the results in the Semester Total row.

e. In cell H14, divide the Semester Total's Total Points by the Semester Total's Credits Earned to calculate the GPA for the semester. Use what-if analysis to see what Kevin's GPA would be if he had earned a 3 instead of a 2 in Western Civ. Change the grade back to a 2.

f. Go to the Spring 97 sheet. Select the Spring 97 through Spring 98 sheets and follow the above procedure to calculate Total Points, Semester Total, and GPA on three sheets at once. When you are finished, click the Fall 96 sheet. Clicking a sheet that is not selected is another way of ungrouping the sheets. Look at each sheet to see that the calculations were performed.

g. Go to cell E15 in the Fall 96 sheet. Enter the reference formula =E14 to copy the Semester Total Credits Attempted number to the Cumulative Total row. Copy the formula to cells F15 and G15 to calculate Credits Earned and Total Points.

h. Go to the Spring 97 sheet and calculate a Cumulative Total for Credits Attempted by summing the Spring 97 Semester Total and the Fall 96 Cumulative Total. *Hint:* You can use pointing to enter the Cumulative Totals formula.

i. Copy that formula to the adjacent cells to calculate Cumulative Totals for Credits Earned and Total Points. Repeat this procedure on the Fall 97 and Spring 98 sheets.

j. Go to the Fall 96 sheet. Select all four sheets. In cell H15, calculate the GPA for the Cumulative Total. Format the Semester Total GPA and the Cumulative Total GPA to display two decimals. look at each sheet to see the GPA for each semester. (*Hint:* Kevin's GPA at the end of the Spring 98 semester is 3.15.) Display the Sheet tab Shortcut menu and ungroup the Sheets.

k. Go to the Fall 96 sheet and preview the workbook. Remove the page number footer. Enter your name in the left footer position and the current date in the right footer position.

l. Document the workbook. Save and replace the workbook file GRADE REPORT. Print all of the sheets.

You will continue this exercise as Practice Exercise 6 in this lab.

4. Marion manages a computer lab at a community college. She has four work-study students to assist her. The students are allowed to earn no more than $900 per semester at $4.75 an hour. Marion has created a worksheet that calculates the amount of money the students have left at the end of each week. By monitoring this amount, she can budget their time so that each student earns enough without exceeding the allotted amount.

a. Open the file WORK STUDY BALANCE on your data disk. The starting amount ($900.00) and hourly rate ($4.75) have been entered in cells B4 and B5 respectively. In cell B10, enter a reference formula that will copy the starting amount for Ed. Keep in mind that you will need to copy that formula to obtain the same starting amount ($900.00) for Carrie Ann,

Molly, and Jason. What formula did you use? Copy that formula to cells B11 through B13.

b. There are 15 weeks in a semester. Week 1 and Week 2 have been entered for you in cells C9 and D9. You can use the AutoFill command to copy a sequence that follows a pattern as long as you start with the first two entries. Select cells C9 through Q9. Choose Edit/Fill/Series/AutoFill/OK. Clear the highlight.

c. Open the file WORK STUDY HOURS on your data disk. This is a report of the number of hours the students have worked each week from the beginning of the semester through the last full week of classes.

d. Use the logic in step b to enter the column headings Week 1 through Week 15 in cells B5 through P5.

e. Tile the windows. In this portion of the exercise, you will enter an external reference formula that will calculate the amount of money each student has left at the end of each week. *Hint:* Since both sheets are visible, you can use pointing to enter the cell references in the formula. Make the WORK STUDY BALANCE file active, and go to cell C10. To calculate the amount of money Ed has left after the first week, subtract his Hours Worked*Rate from his Starting Amount. What is the result? *Note:* It is important that you use cell references and not the numbers they represent in all parts of the formula. Also pay attention to which references should be relative, and which should be absolute.

f. Copy that formula down the column to see how much each student has left at the end of the first week. Maximize the WORK STUDY BALANCE window.

g. Change the numeric format of the new numbers to match the starting amount. Then, copy the Week 1 balances to Week 2 through Week 14, the last week before final exams. Who will be ineligible to work finals week?

h. To keep the row headings in view as you scroll the worksheet, go to column A so you can see all the headings, and then freeze panes at cell C10.

i. What if the students earned $5.00 an hour? Change the rate in cell B5 to $5.00, and scroll to column P. Who will be ineligible to work at the end of the semester? What if the students were allotted $1,000.00 per semester? Change the starting amount in cell B4 to $1,000.00. Will everybody be able work the week of final exams? Do you think they will want to?

j. Molly has a lot of money left over. Use Goal Seek to calculate what the hourly rate would have to be before Molly would run out of money by Week 14 if she worked the same number of hours. What is the result? Use The Undo command to reset the values.

k. Unfreeze the panes. Rename the Sheet1 tab Fall 1996.

l. Center the title across the columns. Select a different font, and increase the font size to 16pt. Draw a bottom border under the column headings in row 9. Draw an outline border around the what-if values and their row labels in cells A4 through B5. Add color to the text and the background within the border. Make whatever other formatting changes you wish using techniques you learned.

m. Preview the worksheet. Add your name and date to the header. Remove the page number footer. Print the worksheet on one page using landscape orientation. Document the workbook. Save and replace the workbook file WORK STUDY BALANCE with the new print settings.

n. Close the workbook. The WORK STUDY HOURS worksheet should be active. Rename the Sheet1 tab Fall 1996. Use whatever formatting techniques you wish to improve the appearance of the worksheet.

o. Preview the worksheet. Add your name and the date to the header. Remove the page number footer. Print the worksheet on one page using landscape orientation. Document the workbook. Save and replace the workbook file WORK STUDY HOURS with the new print settings.

On Your Own

★★★

5. To complete this problem, you must have completed Practice Exercise 6 in Lab 2. Ilsa also wants to create a worksheet to track her earnings using data from the time sheets she maintains each week.

In a new workbook, create the worksheet to track earnings as shown below. Save the workbook file as EARNINGS STATEMENT.

Create a link to calculate the gross pay in the EARNINGS STATEMENT workbook to the total biweekly hours worked from the TIME SHEET workbook. Calculate the gross pay as Rate*Hours.

The statutory deductions will be calculated as follows:
  Federal Income Tax = Gross Pay*15%
  State Income Tax = Gross Pay*3%
  Local Income Tax = Gross Pay*1%
  Medicare Tax = Gross Pay*1.5%
  Social Security Tax = Gross Pay*7%
The voluntary deductions are:
  Union Dues = $10
  Holiday Club = $25

Total the deductions and calculate Net Pay (total deductions – Gross Pay).

Apply appropriate number formats and styles to enhance the appearance of the worksheet. Print the Earnings Statement with a custom header and centered horizontally on the page.

You will continue this exercise as Practice Exercise 1 in Lab 5.

★★

6. To complete this exercise, you must have completed Practice Exercise 3 in this lab. Open the file GRADE REPORT from your disk. Modify this workbook to match your situation. Add or delete sheets as needed. Rename sheet tabs with appropriate semester labels. Save the workbook file as MY GRADE REPORT. Print the workbook.

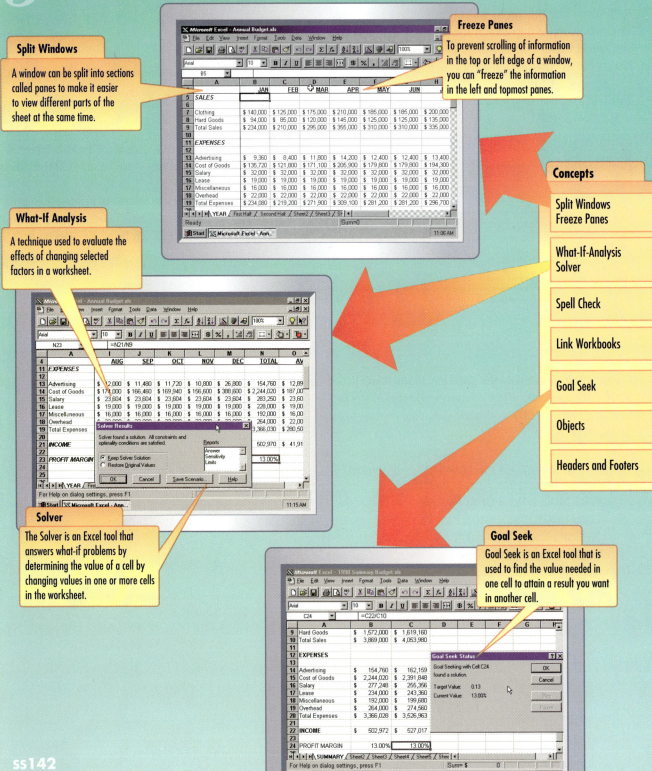

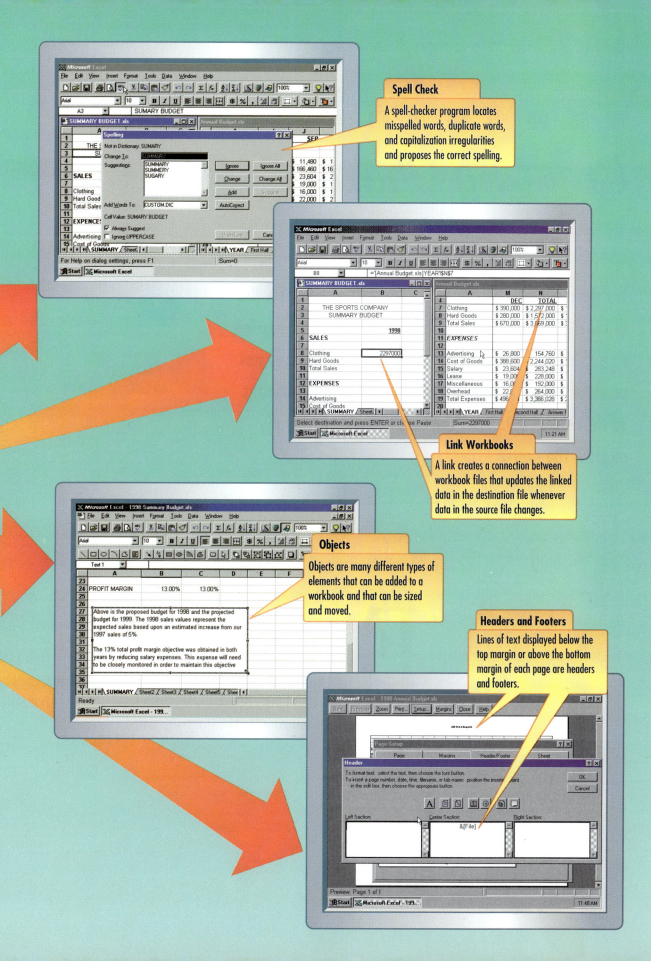

Creating Charts

Try describing an elephant in words. It's not easy. But draw a picture, and the idea is clear. The same applies to numerical data. Looking at the data often does not produce a clear picture of what is actually happening. To clarify the data, you can draw charts to visually explain the data.

> **COMPETENCIES**
>
> After completing this lab, you will know how to:
>
> 1. Use AutoFormat.
> 2. Create several different kinds of charts.
> 3. Select the data to chart.
> 4. Use ChartWizard.
> 5. Size a chart.
> 6. Change the type of chart.
> 7. Activate a chart.
> 8. Move the legend.
> 9. Add patterns, text boxes, and arrows.
> 10. Add data labels.
> 11. Print a chart.

Excel has the capability to create many types of charts from data in a worksheet. The different chart types emphasize data in various ways. You will learn in this lab how to create, modify, and enhance charts using Excel. In addition, you will learn how to select the type of chart that will best represent or emphasize the data you want clarified.

Using Autoformats

> **Concept Overview**
>
> The following concepts will be introduced in this lab:
>
> 1. **Autoformat** — An autoformat is a built-in combination of formats that can be applied to a range.
> 2. **Types of Charts** — Excel can produce 15 basic types of charts with many different formats for each type.
> 3. **Chart Elements** — A chart consists of many parts or elements that are used to graphically display the worksheet data.

CASE STUDY

You have noticed over the past few months while working at The Sports Company that sales are increasing in some sports and declining in others. While looking through the store sales records, you have found sales data by sport for the past several years. You created a worksheet of the data to see if the data supports your observations. Although the data in the worksheet shows the trends in sales, you feel the use of several charts would make it easier to see the trends and growth patterns over the years. You will create several different charts of the sales data.

Part 1

Using Autoformats

Load Excel for Windows. Put your data disk in drive A (or the appropriate drive for your system).

To see the worksheet of sales data, open the workbook file SALES.XLS. If necessary, maximize the worksheet window.

SPREADSHEET

Your screen should be similar to Figure 4-1.

Figure 4-1

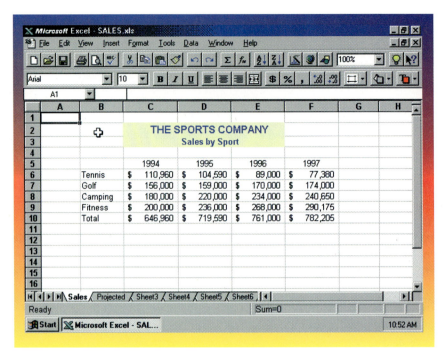

The Sales sheet displays the sales for the years 1994 through 1997. The worksheet lists four sports categories and a total as row labels in column B. The total is the sum of the sales for the four sports categories for each year. The headings for the four years are displayed in row 5.

You also created a worksheet for the projected sales for 1998.

To see this worksheet, make the Projected sheet active.

The data for 1998 projected sales for the four categories is displayed. You will use this worksheet later in this lab.

Make the Sales sheet active again.

Before creating the charts, you would like to improve the appearance of the worksheets by applying an autoformat to the worksheet data.

Concept 1: Autoformat

An **autoformat** is a built-in combination of formats that can be applied to a range of cells. There are 16 autoformats from which you can select. The autoformats consist of a combination of number formats, fonts and attributes, colors, patterns, borders, frames, and alignment settings.

To use an autoformat, you first specify the range you want affected by the formatting. In this case, you want to apply an autoformat to cells B5 through F10. You can select the range or you can let Excel select the range for you. To have Excel automatically select the range, the cell selector must be on any cell in the range. Excel determines that the range you want to autoformat is the range of cells that includes the active cell and is surrounded by blank cells.

Move to: B5
Choose: F**o**rmat/**A**utoFormat

Your screen should be similar to Figure 4-2.

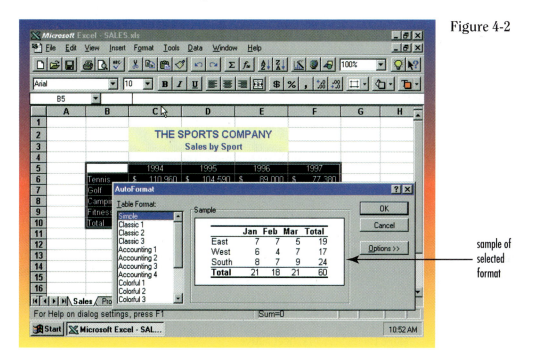

Figure 4-2

sample of selected format

The range B5 through F10 is correctly selected as the range to autoformat, and the AutoFormat dialog box is displayed. The names Excel has assigned each of the 16 different formats are listed in the Table Format list box. The Sample box shows how the selected format will look.

> To preview the autoformats, highlight each name in the Table Format list and look at the table layout in the Sample box.

You think the Accounting 2 format would be appropriate for the data in the Sales sheet. To format the worksheet using this layout,

Select: Accounting 2
Choose: OK

> If necessary, move the dialog box to see the selected range.

> The None autoformat option removes an existing autoformat.

Your screen should be similar to Figure 4-3.

Figure 4-3

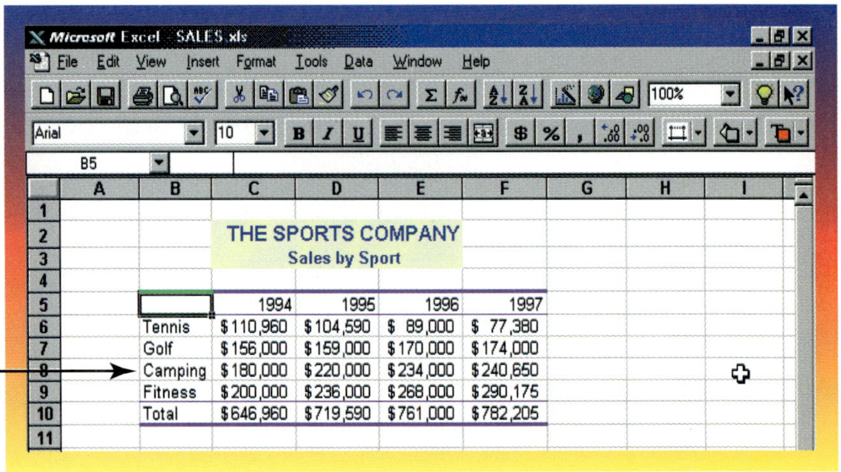

Accounting 2 format style applied to range

The Accounting 2 autoformat has been applied to the selected range. This format includes border lines of different weights, color, accounting number format with two decimal places, and adjustment of column widths to fit the entries in the selected range. You would like to apply this same format to the Projected worksheet.

Make the Projected worksheet active and apply the Accounting 2 autoformat to cells B5 through C10.

Make the Sales worksheet active.

You can use the Repeat button to quickly apply the same autoformat.

About Charts

Although the worksheet shows the sales numbers for each sports category, it is hard to see how the different categories have changed over time. A visual representation of data in the form of a chart would convey that information in an easy-to-understand and attractive manner.

Concept 2: Types of Charts

Excel for Windows can produce 15 basic types of graphs or **charts**, with many different formats for each type. The basic chart types are:

Type   **Description**

 Area charts show the relative importance of a value over time by emphasizing the area under the curve created by each data series.

 Bar charts display data as evenly spaced bars. The categories are displayed along the Y axis and the values are displayed horizontally, placing more emphasis on comparisons and less on time.

 Column charts display data as evenly spaced bars. They are similar to bar charts, except the categories are organized horizontally and values vertically.

 Line charts display data along a line. They are used to show changes in data over time, emphasizing time and rate of change rather than the amount of change.

 Pie charts display data as slices of a circle or "pie." They show the relationship of each value in a data series to the series as a whole. Each slice of the pie represents a single value in the series.

 Doughnut charts are similar to pie charts except they can show more than one data series.

 Radar charts display a line or area chart wrapped around a central point. Each axis represents a set of data points.

 XY (scatter) charts are used to show the relationship between two ranges of numeric data.

 Combination charts display bars and lines in the same chart.

 3-D area charts show areas as solids that display depth as well as height and width.

 3-D bar charts display bars as solids that show depth as well as height.

 3-D column charts display columns as solids that show depth as well as height.

 3-D line charts display lines as ribbons, adding visual interest to simple line charts.

 3-D pie charts display slices as solids that show depth. The front slices of the pie chart are emphasized.

 3-D surface charts display values as what appears to be a rubber sheet stretched over a 3-D column chart. These are useful for finding the best combination between sets of data.

SPREADSHEET

Selecting the Data to Chart

The first chart you want to create will show the total sales pattern over the four years. All charts are drawn from data contained in a worksheet. To create a new chart, you select the worksheet range containing the data you want displayed as a chart plus any row or column headings you want used in the chart. Excel then translates the selected data into a chart based upon the shape and contents of the worksheet selection.

A chart consists of a number of parts or elements, which are important to understand so that you can identify the appropriate data to select in the worksheet.

Concept 3: Chart Elements

The basic elements of a two-dimensional chart are shown in the figure below.

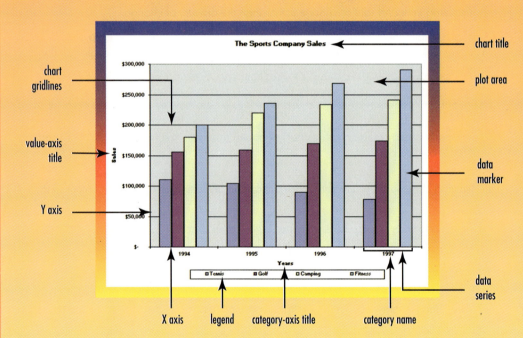

The bottom boundary line of the chart is the **X axis**. It is used to label the data being charted, such as a point in time or a category. The **category names** displayed along the X axis correspond to the headings for the worksheet data that is plotted along the X axis. The left boundary line of the chart is the **Y axis**. This axis is a numbered scale whose numbers are determined by the data used in the chart. Typically the X-axis line is the horizontal line and the Y-axis line is the vertical line.

The selected worksheet data is visually displayed within the X- and Y-axis boundaries. This is called the **plot area**. Each group of related data, such as the numbers in a row or column of the selected area of the worksheet, is called a **data series**. Each number represented in a data series is identified by a **data marker**. A data marker can be a symbol, color, or pattern. To distinguish one data series from another, different data markers are used. In addition, **chart gridlines** are commonly displayed to make it easier to read the chart data. Chart gridlines extend from the Y axis line across the plot area. A **legend** identifies the chart data series names and data markers that correspond to each data series.

A chart can also contain descriptive **titles** that explain the contents of the chart. The chart title is displayed centered above the charted data. Titles can also be used to describe the X and Y axes. The X-axis title line is called the **category-axis title**, and the Y-axis title is called the **value-axis title**.

In pie charts there are no axes. Instead the worksheet data that is charted is displayed as slices in a circle or pie. Each slice is labeled.

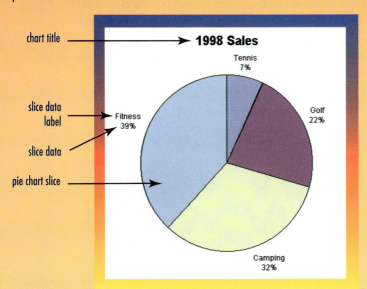

In 3-D charts there can also be an additional axis, called the Z axis, which allows you to compare data within a series more easily. This axis is the vertical axis. The X and Y axes delineate the horizontal surface of the chart.

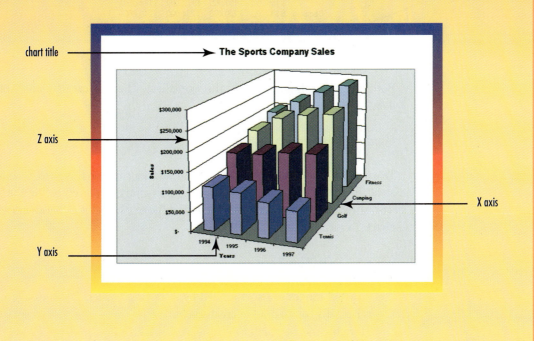

SPREADSHEET

The first chart you will create of the worksheet data will use the year labels in cells C5 through F5 to label the X axis. The numbers to be charted are in cells C10 through F10. In addition, the label "Total" in cell B10 will be used as the chart legend, making the entire range B10 through F10. Notice that the two ranges, C5 through F5 and B10 through F10, are not adjacent and are not the same size. When cells or ranges are not contiguous and you want them to be included in the same selection, it is called a **noncontiguous selection**. When specifying noncontiguous selections to create a chart, the two ranges must be the same size and a rectangular shape. To make the ranges the same size, the blank cell B5 will be included in the selection.

Select: B5 through F5

To add the second range to the selection, press and hold Ctrl while you select the additional range.

Hold down: Ctrl
Select: B10 through F10

Your screen should be similar to Figure 4-4.

Figure 4-4

noncontiguous selection

Both ranges are highlighted in the worksheet. Then, to create a chart of this data,

Choose: Insert/Chart

Two options on the submenu allow you to insert a chart on this sheet or as a new sheet in the workbook. You would like this chart displayed below the Sales worksheet data. A chart that is displayed on the worksheet is called an **embedded chart**. To create an embedded chart,

Choose: On This Sheet

The selected ranges are surrounded by a moving border. The message in the status bar tells you to drag to create a chart.
   Move the mouse pointer into the workspace.

Using ChartWizard **ss153**

The mouse pointer has changed to a +. This indicates Excel is ready for you to specify the location where you want the chart displayed in the worksheet. You can drag the mouse pointer to specify an exact size for the chart. Alternatively you can create a chart using the default size by clicking anywhere on the worksheet. You want to create a default size chart below the worksheet data.

Click: B12

Your screen should be similar to Figure 4-5.

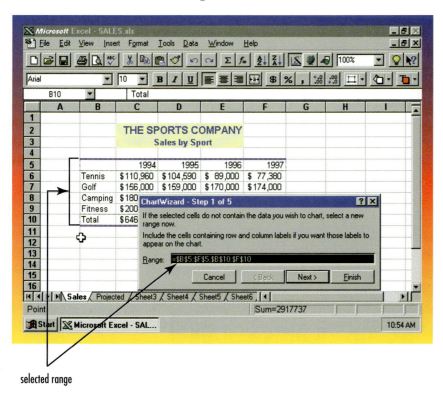

Figure 4-5

selected range

The ChartWizard - Step 1 of 5 dialog box is displayed.

Using ChartWizard

ChartWizard is an interactive program that guides you through the steps required to create a chart. The first dialog box displays the selected range. You can specify another range in the text box or accept the displayed range. To confirm the selected range and go to the second step,

Choose:

SPREADSHEET

The dialog box on your screen should be similar to Figure 4-6.

Figure 4-6

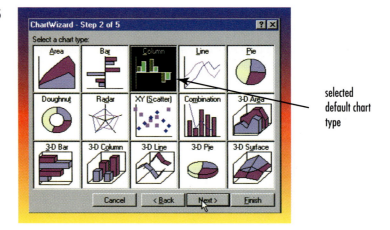

selected default chart type

The Step 2 dialog box displays the 15 types of charts as buttons. The Column Chart button has a dark background, indicating it is selected. A **column chart** displays the values as vertical columns. To accept the default chart type selection,

Choose: Next >

The dialog box on your screen should be similar to Figure 4-7.

Figure 4-7

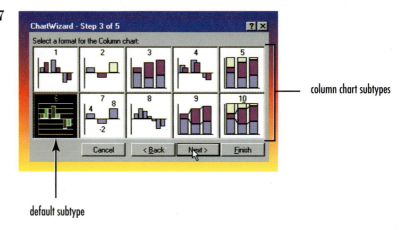

column chart subtypes

default subtype

> Each chart type has at least one subtype.

The Step 3 dialog box displays the 10 different chart subtypes or variations associated with the column chart. The default subtype (option 6) displays each value in the data series as a column with horizontal gridlines. To use the default format,

Choose: Next >

The dialog box on your screen should be similar to Figure 4-8.

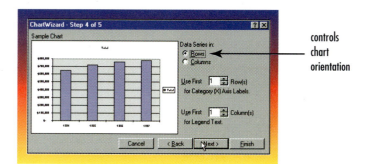

Figure 4-8

controls chart orientation

The ChartWizard - Step 4 dialog box displays a sample of the chart that will be created using the selected worksheet data. The dialog box options allow you to change how Excel interprets the data series. The interpretation varies depending upon the type of chart selected. In a column chart, Excel uses the rows of data as the values and the columns as the categories. This setting, specified by the selection of Rows under the Data Series In option, controls the chart orientation.

The next two options allow you to change how Excel interprets the first row and leftmost column of data. By default Excel uses the first row as the X-axis category labels and the leftmost column as the legend text when the chart orientation is set to Rows. Changing the chart orientation to Columns reverses this, placing the first column of the range along the X axis and the first row of the range as the legend text.

To accept the default settings,

Choose: Next >

In the last step, Step 5, you add a legend and titles to the chart. The Yes button under the Add a Legend option is selected, indicating Excel adds a legend to a column chart by default. The title text boxes, however, are empty. To clarify the chart, you will add a chart title as well as titles along the X and Y axes. To add a chart title,

Choose: Chart Title
Type: THE SPORTS COMPANY SALES

After a few moments, the chart title is displayed centered at the top of the chart in the Sample Chart box.

Next you will add title lines to describe the X and Y axes. The X axis shows the change in sales over the four years, and the Y axis shows the sales in thousands of dollars. To add descriptive titles,

Choose: Category (X)
Type: Years
Choose: Value (Y)
Type: Sales

The Sample Chart box reflects the addition of the two titles. The dialog box on your screen should be similar to Figure 4-9.

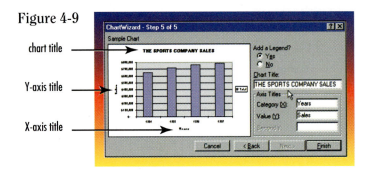

Figure 4-9

chart title
Y-axis title
X-axis title

To complete the chart,

Choose: Finish

The embedded chart with the settings you specified using the ChartWizard is displayed below the worksheet.

To see the entire chart, scroll the window using the scroll bar until rows 10 through 24 are displayed.

Your screen should be similar to Figure 4-10.

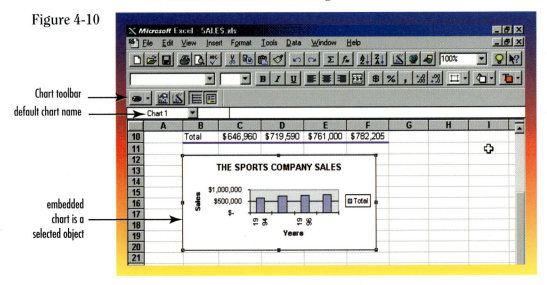

Figure 4-10

Chart toolbar
default chart name

embedded chart is a selected object

Notice that the chart is a selected object. The reference area displays the default chart name, Chart 1. Excel assigns a name to each chart as it is created in the workbook. Also notice that the Chart toolbar is automatically displayed whenever a chart is selected.

If necessary, move the Chart toolbar below the Formatting toolbar. To learn what action the Chart buttons perform, display the Tooltip for each Chart toolbar button.

Sizing a Chart

As you can see, the default chart size is too small to fully display all parts of the chart. A selected chart, like any other selected object, can be sized by dragging the selection handles. It can also be moved and deleted.

   To make the chart larger, adjust the size of the box until it is displayed over cells B12 through G23.

   Your screen should be similar to Figure 4-11.

> Reminder: Select a chart by clicking on it and deselect it by clicking anywhere outside the chart.

Figure 4-11

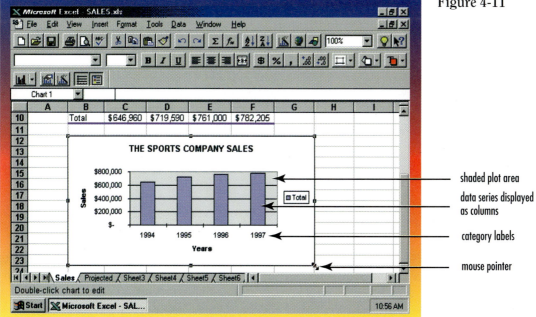

With the chart larger, the X-axis category labels are now fully displayed. Now you can see the years along the X axis and the data series as columns within the chart. Each column represents the total for that year. The chart includes standard formats that are applied to the selected chart subtype, such as a shaded background in the plot area and blue columns.

Changing the Type of Chart

Next you would like to see how the same data displayed in the column chart would look as a line chart. A **line chart** displays data as a line and is used to show trends. This is easily done by changing the chart type using the [icon] Chart Type button on the Chart toolbar. Notice that the currently selected type, Column, is displayed in the Chart Type button.

   Open the [icon] Chart Type drop-down list.

   A palette of the 14 most commonly used chart types and subtypes is displayed. To change the chart type from column to line,

Click: **Line**

Your chart should be similar to Figure 4-12.

Figure 4-12

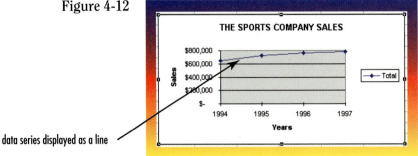

data series displayed as a line

The chart is redrawn as a line chart. The data for the total sales for each year is now displayed as a line. The line chart displays the years along the X axis and the data series as a line within the chart. The line represents the total sales. The Chart Type button also reflects the last selected chart type.

Although the line chart shows the trend in sales over time, because it contains only one data series, it is not as interesting as the column chart.

Change the chart type back to column using the Chart Type button.

Creating a Chart with Multiple Data Series

Now you are ready to continue your analysis of sales trends. You want to create a second chart to display the sales data for each sports category for the four years. You could create a separate chart for each category and then compare the charts; however, to make the comparisons between the categories easier, you will display all the categories on a single chart.

The data for the four years for the four categories is in cells C6 through F9. The year headings (X-axis data series) are in cells C5 through F5, and the legend text is in the range B6 through B9. To specify the chart data series,

Select: B5 through F9

Rather than using the Insert/Chart command, you will use the ChartWizard toolbar button. This button creates an embedded chart and opens ChartWizard.

Click: ChartWizard

To place the chart,

Click: B27

> You could also use Undo or Edit/Undo to change the chart type back to the previous type.

The ChartWizard - Step 1 dialog box is displayed. To confirm the data series range and move to the next box,

Choose: Next >

You think a line chart would be an appropriate chart type. From the Chart Type options in the Step 2 dialog box,

Select:
Choose: Next >

The line chart subtypes are displayed. The default line chart (4) displays the data series with markers and horizontal gridlines. To accept the default,

Choose: Next >

Again Excel selects Rows as the default orientation. To confirm these settings,

Choose: Next >

Finally, in the Chart Title text box,

Type: The Sports Company Sales

As the category-axis title,

Type: Years

As the value-axis title,

Type: Sales
Choose: Finish

Enlarge the chart until it covers cells B27 through G39.

Your screen should be similar to Figure 4-13.

Figure 4-13

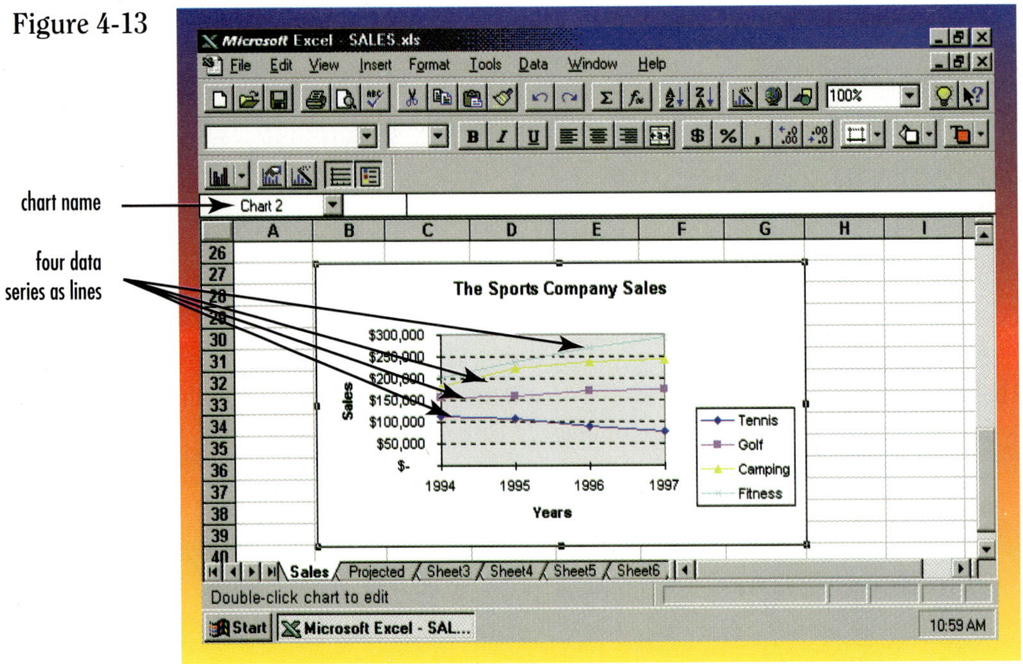

chart name
four data series as lines

The line chart clearly shows that sales in fitness and camping are increasing, sales in tennis are decreasing, and golf sales are steady. The Name box displays "Chart 2," indicating the currently selected chart.

Activating a Chart

Although the line chart shows the sales trends for the four years for the four sports categories, it does not give you a feeling for the magnitude of the change. You feel that a stacked-column chart or an area chart may better represent the data.

First you will change the type to a stacked-column chart. In a **stacked-column chart**, the columns are stacked upon each other rather than displayed side by side. Unfortunately, this type of chart is not an option in the Chart Type palette. To make this and many other types of modifications to a chart, you must first **activate** it.

To activate the chart, double-click on the chart.

The chart is surrounded with an editing border. If your chart is displayed in a separate editing window, it is because the size of your chart is larger than can be displayed in the workbook window. Excel places a chart in its own editing window so you can see the entire chart as you edit it, without scrolling. The Chart Editing window operates the same as if the chart were surrounded with the hashed border.

If your chart is displayed in the Chart Editing window, click on the worksheet to deactivate the chart. Then reduce the size of your chart and activate the chart again.

When a chart is activated, the commands in the Insert and Format menus change to commands that can be used to modify the chart. The command to change the chart type is on the Format menu.

Choose: **F**ormat/Chart **T**ype

> The Format menu options are also available on the Shortcut menu.

Eight types of charts that can be created using the selected data are displayed in the Chart Type dialog box. The current chart type, line, is the preselected option. To select a column chart,

Select: **Column**

Then to change the type of column chart to stacked,

Choose: **O**ptions

The Format Column Group tab dialog box is displayed.
To see the column chart subtypes, if necessary select the Subtype tab.
The Sample box displays the chart as it will appear in the selected chart type. The column chart makes it difficult to see the trends from year to year, although it shows the difference in change quite well. To see how the data will appear as a stacked-column chart,

Select:

The dialog box on your screen should be similar to Figure 4-14.

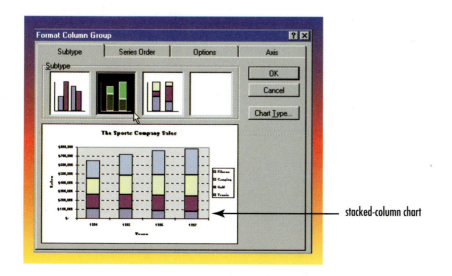

Figure 4-14

The sample chart is redrawn. Rather than a group of columns being displayed side by side, the columns are stacked upon each other. A stacked-column chart shows the proportion of each type of sport to the total sport sales in each year.

The Y-axis scale has changed to reflect the new range of data. The new Y-axis range is the sum of the four categories, or the same as the total number in the worksheet. It is now easy to compare how much each category contributed to the total sales in each year. The stacked-column chart shows the amount of change better, but it is still difficult to see trends. To return to the Chart Type dialog box,

Choose: **Chart Type**

You would like to see the data represented as an area chart. An **area chart** represents data the same as a line chart, but in addition it shades the area below each line to emphasize the degree of change.

Select:

To preview how this chart type will appear,

Choose: **Options**

The Sample box of the Subtype tab displays the data as an area chart. The area chart shows the magnitude of change and the trend from year to year better than the other types of charts. To accept this type,

Choose: **OK**

Your chart should be similar to Figure 4-15.

Figure 4-15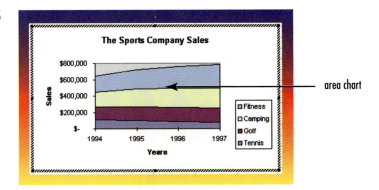

As you can see, it is very easy to change the chart type and format once the data series are specified. The same data can be displayed in many different ways. Depending upon the emphasis you want the chart to make, a different chart style can be selected.

Note: If you are ending your lab session, put your name in cell A1 and print the Sales sheet. Save the file as SALES CHARTS. When you begin Part 2, load Excel, open SALES CHARTS, and activate the area chart.

Part 2

Moving the Legend

After looking at the chart, you decide you also want to modify several other chart features. First you want to move the legend below the X axis.

A chart is an object that is made of many parts or elements that can be individually selected and then formatted or edited. Some of the elements that can be selected are the axis lines, a data series, a data marker, the legend, the entire plot area, or the entire chart.

To select the legend, click on the legend box border.

The legend box is surrounded by selection handles, indicating that it is the selected item and will be affected by any changes you make. In addition, the Name box displays "Legend" as the name of the selected element.

As different elements in the chart are selected, the commands on the Insert and Format menus change to commands that can be used on the selected element.

> If the wrong item is selected, reposition the mouse pointer and click again.

Choose: F**o**rmat/S**e**lected Legend

The Format Legend tab dialog box is used to change the patterns, font, and placement of the legend. To change the legend placement to below the plot area,

Choose: Placement/**B**ottom/OK

The legend entries are displayed on a single line inside the legend box, centered below the chart (see Figure 4-16).

> You can also move the legend by dragging it, and then you can resize it to fit the new location.

Adding Patterns

The next change you would like to make is to add patterns to the chart data series. If you have a color monitor, the data series are automatically displayed in different colors. If you have a monochrome monitor, they are displayed as varying shades of gray. You want to change the default display to black-and-white patterns to make it easier to distinguish one series from the other. Adding black-and-white patterns is particularly important if you do not have a color printer. Without black-and-white patterns, the colors are printed as shades of gray and are very difficult to distinguish.

To add black-and-white patterns, you need to select each data series and use the Format command to change the color and pattern settings. The Shortcut menu also contains a Format option. You can quickly select a chart element and open the related Shortcut menu by right-clicking directly on the element.

Right-click the Fitness area of the chart.
Your screen should be similar to Figure 4-16.

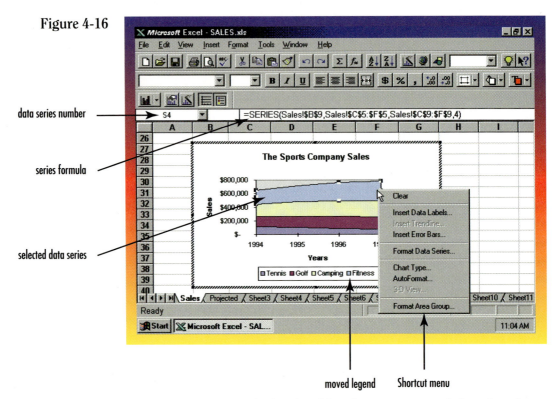

Figure 4-16

The Shortcut menu is displayed and handles appear around the selected area only. Notice that the Name box displays "S4." Each series is automatically assigned a number by the program when the chart is created. The Fitness data series is the fourth series of data that is plotted in the chart.

The formula bar also displays a series formula that links the chart document to the source worksheet document, Sales. The formula contains four arguments: a reference to the cell that includes the data series name (used in the legend), references to the cells that contain the categories (X-axis numbers), references to the numbers plotted, and an integer that specifies the number of data series plotted.

Now you can use the Format menu to change the pattern used in the selected series. From the Shortcut menu,

Choose: Format Data Series

The Format Data Series tab dialog box is displayed.

If necessary, select the Patterns tab.

The options available in the Patterns tab vary depending upon the type of data marker that is selected. In this case, because an area data marker is selected, the options let you change the border and the background area of the selected series. The current setting for each is displayed. To change the area color to black, from the Color palette of options,

> The menu equivalent is Format/Selected Data Series and the shortcut key is Ctrl + 1.

Select: **Black**

The Sample box changes to black.

To add a pattern to the data series, from the Pattern drop-down list box, select a black-and-white pattern of your choice.

The Sample box displays how your selections will appear.

Choose: **OK**

Your chart should be similar to Figure 4-17.

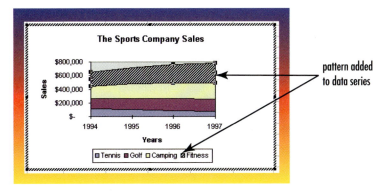

Figure 4-17

The chart is redrawn with the Fitness area of the chart displaying the black-and-white pattern. The legend has also been updated to reflect the new pattern and color selection.

In the same manner, select the other three data series, change the color to black, and select a different black-and-white pattern for each.

The chart displays the selected black-and-white patterns for the four data series.

The last change you would like to make is to remove the shading from the plot area background. The only background visible is above the Fitness data area. From the plot area Shortcut menu,

Choose: **Format Plot Area**

Change the color to white and close the dialog box.

Deselect the plot area. Deactivate the chart by clicking anywhere outside the chart.

Now when you print the chart, it will be printed with black patterns on a white background.

The chart is still selected.

Deselect the chart by clicking anywhere outside the chart.

The Chart toolbar is automatically closed.

Adding a Text Box

The last item you want to add to the area chart is a text box and an arrow pointing to the area of the chart that reflects the increasing sales in fitness. First you will add the text box containing the text "Increasing Sales."

> Right-click the plot area background to display the Shortcut menu.

> Press [Esc] to deselect a chart element.

> You can also press [Esc] to deactivate or deselect a chart.

Display the Drawing toolbar.

Click: **Text Box**

> The text box object can overlap the graphic object.

Move the mouse pointer anywhere in the worksheet and drag to create a text box that is approximately 1/4 inch by 2 inches.

Your screen should be similar to Figure 4-18.

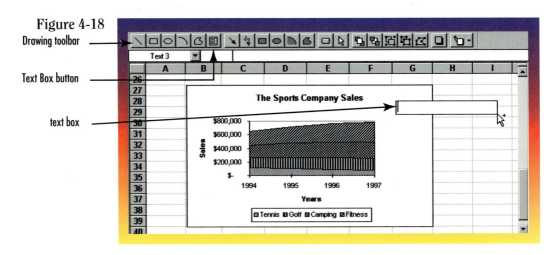

Figure 4-18
Drawing toolbar
Text Box button
text box

The text box displays an insertion point and is waiting for you to enter the text.

> Do not be concerned if the entire text is not displayed in the text box.

Type: **Increasing Sales**

You will move and size the text box next.

Select the text box and adjust the size of the box until it is just large enough to fully display the text on one line. Drag the text box until the box is displayed to the right of the Fitness area.

> The mouse pointer is a ▶ when you can drag the object to move it, or a ↖ when you can size the object.

Your screen should be similar to Figure 4-19.

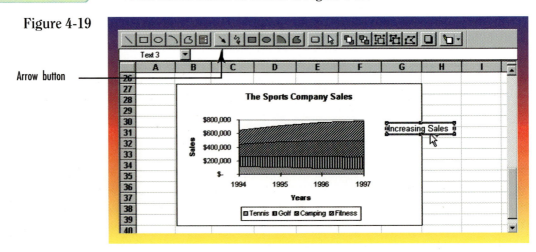

Figure 4-19
Arrow button

Adding Arrows

Next you want to draw an arrow from the text box to the Fitness area of the chart. The Arrow button on the Drawing toolbar is used to create an arrow.

Click: Arrow

The mouse pointer appears as a +.

To draw the arrow, click on the left edge of the text box and drag to the Fitness area.

> If you hold down ⇧Shift while dragging, a straight horizontal line is drawn.

A line with an arrowhead at the end is displayed in the worksheet. The arrow is automatically a selected object. The handles at both ends of the arrow let you adjust its size and location.

If necessary, move and size the arrow to adjust its position as in Figure 4-20. Deselect the arrow.

In the same manner, add a text box with the text "Decreasing Sales" and an arrow pointing to the Tennis area of data.

Your screen should be similar to Figure 4-20.

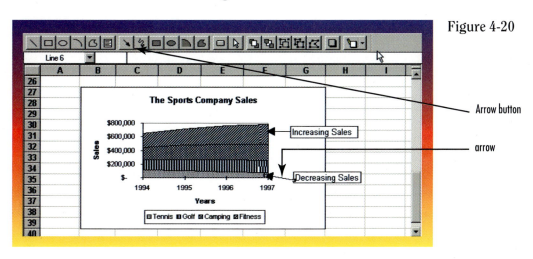

Figure 4-20

Close the Drawing toolbar.

Creating a Combination Chart

The next chart you want to create will show data from both the Sales and Projected sheets. You want to display the past four years' sales numbers as columns and the 1998 projected sales as a line. This type of chart is called a **combination chart**. First you will create a column chart of the sales data for the four years. Then you will add the projected sales data as a line.

Select: B5 through F9

You want to create this chart in its own sheet. To start ChartWizard and place the chart in a new sheet,

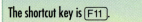

The shortcut key is [F11].

Choose: **Insert/Chart/As New Sheet**

The range displayed in the Step 1 ChartWizard dialog box is correct.

Choose: [Next >]

To accept the default chart type of Column,

Choose: [Next >]

To accept the default subtype for a column chart (option 6),

Choose: [Next >]

The Step 4 dialog box shows that Excel is interpreting the data as rows. You want to change this so the years are the legend text and the categories are the X-axis labels. To change the orientation,

Choose: **Columns**

The Sample box displays the new layout for the chart.

Choose: [Next >]

Finally, add the chart title "Annual vs Projected Sales by [your name]." Enter "Category" as the category-axis title and "Sales" as the value-axis title.

Choose: [Finish]

Your screen should be similar to Figure 4-21.

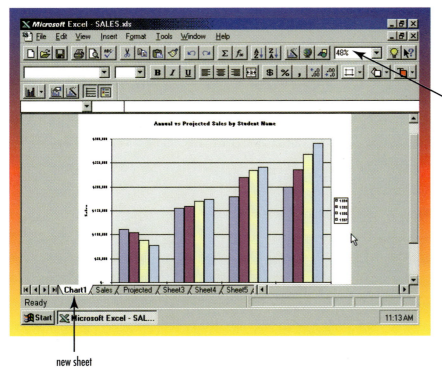

Figure 4-21

zoom percentage displayed in Zoom Control button

new sheet

The column chart is displayed in a new sheet named Chart1. The sheet is inserted to the left of the active sheet. A chart that is not embedded in a worksheet as an object is displayed in a chart sheet. A chart sheet is one of the six types of sheets that can be used in a workbook. Generally, you display a chart in a chart sheet when you want the chart displayed separately from the associated worksheet data. The chart is still automatically linked to the worksheet data from which it was created.

The four data series are displayed as columns grouped by category. The chart in the new chart sheet is sized as it will appear on the printed page. To display the entire chart on the screen, you will reduce the display size of the selection.

Open the [48%] Zoom Control drop-down list.

Select: Selection

> The menu equivalent is **V**iew/**Z**oom/**F**it Selection/OK

The entire chart is now visible in the chart sheet. Excel calculates the zoom percentage based on the current selection in the chart window. In this case the entire chart fits into the current window size.

Next you need to add the projected sales data series to the chart. To add a data series,

Choose: Insert/**N**ew Data

> When a chart is displayed in a chart sheet, the chart does not need to be activated before it is modified.

In the New Data dialog box, you enter the data range to add.

ss170 Lab 4: Creating Charts

> Remember, you can move the dialog box so you can select the worksheet data.

Click: **Projected sheet tab**
Select: **B5 through C9**
Choose: **OK**

The Paste Special dialog box is displayed. By default Excel applies the same orientation, Column, as in the existing chart.

Choose: **OK**

The new data series is added to the chart as a column. To change it to a line,

Select: **1998 data series**

From the [chart] Chart Type drop-down list,

Choose: [icon] **Line**

Your screen should be similar to Figure 4-22.

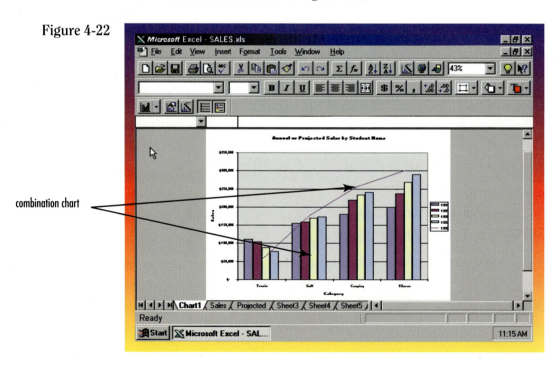

Figure 4-22

combination chart

The selected data series is changed to a line. A combination chart makes it easy to see comparisons between groups of data or to show different types of data in a single chart. In this case you can easily see how the sales for each category are changing compared to projected sales for each category.

Adding Data Labels

You would also like to display on the combination chart the actual numbers plotted for the projected sales. These are called **data labels**. The numbers you want to use as data labels are in cells C6 through C9 in the Projected sheet.

Switch to the Projected worksheet and select cells C6 through C9. Make the Chart 1 sheet active and display the Shortcut menu for the 1998 data series line.

Choose: **Insert Data Labels**

> The menu equivalent is **I**nsert/**D**ata Labels.

In the Data Labels dialog box, you specify how the data labels are to be displayed. You would like to show the values of the data in the projected data series. To do this,

Choose: **Show Value/OK**

Your chart should be similar to Figure 4-23.

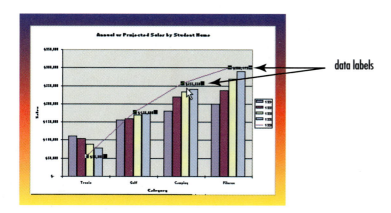

Figure 4-23

The data labels for the 1998 projected sales are displayed next to the data points on the line in the chart. They are selected objects.

Zoom the window to 75 percent to see the data labels better.

The data labels are difficult to see because the numbers are small. To make them more obvious, you will change the font size of the data labels and make them bold.

Display the data labels Shortcut menu.

Choose: **Format Data Labels**

> The menu equivalent is **F**ormat/**Se**lected Data Labels or Ctrl + 1.

Open the Font tab. Select 12 from the Size list box and Bold from the Font Style list box.

> Instead of using the menu, you could use the [10] Font Size and [B] Bold toolbar buttons.

Choose: **OK**

The data labels are now easier to see. Finally, you want the labels to be displayed above their data points on the line.

Select each data label and move it so it is centered above each data point.

Apply different black-and-white patterns to each column data series. Change the plot area background to white.

Creating a Pie Chart

The last chart you will make will use the Projected worksheet data. The sales of fitness items have been increasing and you are particularly interested in next year's sales projections.

Make the Projected sheet active.

You want to see what proportion fitness sales are of all sales for the projected year. The best chart for this purpose is a pie chart. A **pie chart** compares parts to the whole, in a similar manner to a stacked-column chart. However, each value in the range is a slice of the pie displayed as a percentage of the total.

The use of X (category) and data series settings in a pie chart is different from their use in a column or line chart. The X series labels the slices of the pie rather than the X axis. The data series is used to create the slices in the pie. Only one data series can be specified in a pie chart, so you will need to create a new chart.

Select: B6 through C9

Another way to create a chart is to use the Chart Type toolbar button.

Display the Chart toolbar. Select Pie Chart from the Chart Type drop-down list.

To place the chart,

Click: E4

A basic pie chart is drawn in the worksheet. It does not include a chart title or labels to clarify the slices of the pie.

Expand the chart to be displayed over cells E4 through I19.

Your screen should be similar to Figure 4-24.

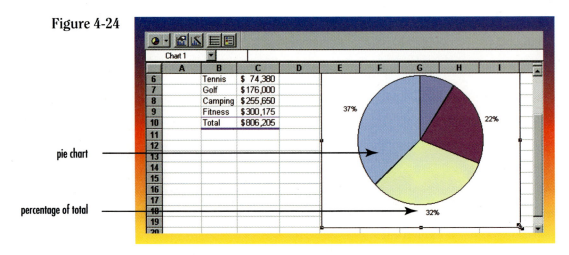

Figure 4-24

pie chart

percentage of total

Each value in the data series is displayed as a wedge of the pie chart, and the percent each wedge is of the total is displayed next to the wedge. However, because the chart does not contain a title or labels, the meaning of the chart is unclear.

> Activate the chart to edit it.

The chart is displayed in its own editing window. To add a chart title,

Choose: Insert/Titles

> You can also choose Insert Titles from the Shortcut menu.

The only title you can add to a pie chart is the main chart title.

Choose: Chart Title/OK

A text box containing the default title placeholder text is displayed above the chart.

> To display the insertion point so you can change the title, click on the text box. Delete the title placeholder.

To enter the new title,

Type: 1998 SALES
Press: ←Enter
Type: By [your name]

The title is displayed centered above the pie chart on two lines.

> To make the title stand out more, select it and increase the font size to 12 points using the [10] Font Size toolbar button. Clear the selection.

> You can also use the Format/Selected Chart Title command.

Unfortunately, the title covers part of the chart. However, before adjusting the title, you want to see if the chart would look better as a three-dimensional pie chart. To change the chart type, from the Chart Type drop-down list,

Choose:

The chart changes to a three-dimensional pie chart, and the title no longer interferes with the chart. Now you want to add labels for the wedges to help clarify the information in the chart.

Choose: Insert/Data Labels

> You can also choose Insert Data Labels from the Shortcut menu.

To display both labels and percents,

Choose: Show Label and Percent/OK

The pie chart is redrawn using the entries in cells B6 through B9 of the selected range as the labels (see Figure 4-25). You would also like to change the format of the category labels to be displayed in italics.

Select: any data label

All the labels are selected because they were entered as a range.

Click: *I* Italic

Your screen should be similar to Figure 4-25.

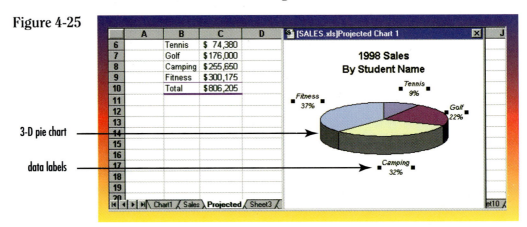

Figure 4-25

Because the category labels were entered as a range, when you changed the format of one label, all the others automatically changed.

Finally, you want to add black-and-white patterns to the wedges.

Select each wedge and use the Format Data Point command on the Shortcut menu to change the color to black and to select a different black-and-white pattern.

Now that the pie chart is formatted as you want it to appear, you want to separate slightly or **explode** the Fitness wedge of the chart to emphasize the data.

Select the Fitness wedge and, to explode the selected wedge, drag it away from the pie.

Your screen should be similar to Figure 4-26.

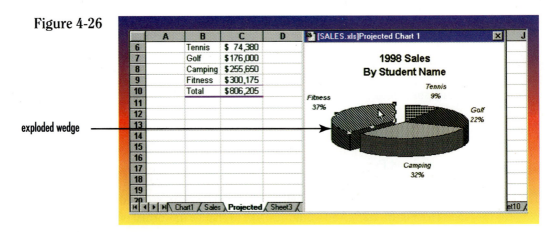

Figure 4-26

The wedge is separated slightly from the other wedges in the pie.

Changing Worksheet Data

As you look at the chart, you notice that the Tennis category represents 9 percent of the total. You think this figure is a little high. To check the data entered in the worksheet for this category,

Move to: C6

The number in cell C6 is 74380. After checking your records, you find that you entered the data incorrectly. It should be 55380.

Type: 55380
Press: ←Enter

The worksheet has been recalculated, and the pie chart has been redrawn to reflect the change in the 1998 data for the Tennis category. Tennis now accounts for 7 percent of total sales for the projected year. Since the chart document is linked to the source data, changes to the source data are automatically reflected in the chart.

Printing Charts

Update the file summary information with your name and applicable comments. Move to cell A1 of the Sales sheet and save the workbook file as SALES CHARTS.

> If you saved the workbook at the end of Part I, clear your name from cell A1 and resave the workbook.

Before printing the charts, you will preview how they will appear when printed. To do this,

Choose: File/Print/Entire Workbook/Preview

Because the combination chart is on a separate sheet, it is displayed on a page by itself. The sheet name is displayed as a header.

Change the header to display your name, page number, and date. Clear the footer.

Preview the Sales sheet containing the column and area charts. Add a header as in the combination chart and clear the footer.

> Choose Next to preview the next sheet.

Your screen should be similar to Figure 4-27.

Figure 4-27

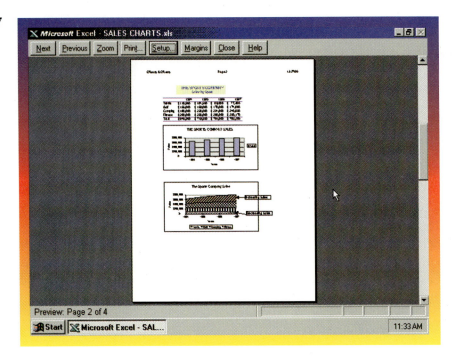

Preview the Projected worksheet containing the pie chart. Add a header as you did with the others and clear the footer.

Printing a worksheet that includes charts requires a printer with graphics capability. However, the actual procedure to print is the same as printing a worksheet that does not include charts.

Choose: **Print**

Close the Chart toolbar. Exit Excel, saving the workbook again if necessary.

LAB REVIEW

Key Terms

activate   (SS160)
area chart   (SS162)
autoformat   (SS146)
category-axis title   (SS151)
category name   (SS150)
chart   (SS149)
chart gridlines   (SS150)
column chart   (SS154)
combination chart   (SS167)
data label   (SS171)
data marker   (SS150)
data series   (SS150)

embedded chart   (SS152)
explode   (SS174)
legend   (SS150)
line chart   (SS157)
noncontiguous selection   (SS152)
pie chart   (SS172)
plot area   (SS150)
stacked-column chart   (SS160)
title   (SS151)
value-axis title   (SS151)
X axis   (SS150)
Y axis   (SS150)

Command Summary

Command	Shortcut	Toolbar	Action
Insert/C**h**art			Inserts chart into worksheet
Insert/**N**ew Data			Inserts new data into chart
Insert/**D**ata Labels			Inserts data labels into chart
Insert/**T**itles			Inserts titles into chart
F**o**rmat/**A**utoFormat			Applies one of 16 built-in table formats to the worksheet range
F**o**rmat/Chart **T**ype			Changes type of chart
F**o**rmat/S**e**lected Legend	Ctrl + 1		Changes legend
F**o**rmat/S**e**lected Data Labels	Ctrl + 1		Changes format of data labels
F**o**rmat/S**e**lected Data Series	Ctrl + 1		Changes format of selected data series

SPREADSHEET

Lab 4: Creating Charts

Matching

1. chart gridlines _____
2. data marker _____
3. stacked-column chart _____
4. X axis _____
5. explode _____
6. plot area _____
7. category-axis title _____
8. Y axis _____
9. legend _____
10. pie chart _____

a. left boundary of chart
b. bottom boundary of chart
c. design or color assigned to each data range in chart
d. area of chart bounded by X and Y axes
e. makes chart data easier to read
f. displays symbols and descriptive labels of data
g. clarifies values displayed along X axis
h. shows proportion of each value
i. to separate wedge slightly from other wedges of pie
j. compares parts to the whole

Fill-In Questions

1. Complete the following statements by filling in the blanks with the correct terms.

   a. A visual representation of data in an easy-to-understand and attractive manner is called a(n) _____.

   b. A(n) _____ describes the symbols used within the chart.

   c. The bottom boundary of a chart is the _____ and the left boundary is the _____.

   d. A chart that is not embedded in a worksheet is displayed in a(n) _____ sheet.

   e. A(n) _____ chart and a(n) _____ chart both display data as a set of evenly spaced bars.

   f. A(n) _____ and a(n) _____ compare parts to the whole.

   g. The _____ toolbar contains commands that let you add text boxes and arrows to a chart.

   h. _____ can be added to a chart to identify the actual data values.

   i. When a chart is printed in black and white, _____ can be added to the data series to make it easier to read.

   j. When a wedge of a pie chart is separated from the other wedges, the wedge has been _____.

Discussion Questions

1. Discuss how the AutoFormat feature can be use to enhance the appearance of a worksheet. What types of formats are associated with autoformats?
2. Discuss how column and bar charts represent data. How do they differ from pie charts?
3. What type of information would best be represented by a line chart?
4. Describe how a 3-D column chart differs from a 2-D column chart.

Hands-On Practice Exercises

Step by Step

Rating System
★ Easy
★★ Moderate
★★★ Difficult

1. WonderWord is a popular word processor available in DOS, Windows, and Macintosh formats. Below is a table that represents sales of this program over the past several years.

	1992	1993	1994	1995	1996	1997
DOS	200000	105330	97350	57830	24560	13687
MAC	94000	75320	64320	74780	74380	84260
WIN	82350	105150	193260	214940	285350	378330

a. Create a worksheet based on this data. Add a title, and use the formatting techniques you learned to enhance the appearance of the worksheet. Make sure that the data you will chart does not contain blank columns or rows. Enter your name and date below the worksheet.

b. Use the ChartWizard to create an embedded 3-D area chart of the data. Use Format 2 from Step 3 of the ChartWizard. At Step 5, turn the legend off, and add appropriate titles. Size the chart so all axis labels are displayed. Center the chart below the worksheet. Enlarge the chart title and choose a different font.

c. Rename the Sheet1 tab Wonderword Sales.

d. Document the workbook. Save the workbook file as WONDERWORD AREA. Print the worksheet with the chart centered horizontally on the page.

e. Change the area chart to a default column chart. Add patterns to the columns, and add titles to the chart. Save the workbook as WONDERWORD COLUMN. Print the worksheet with the chart.

f. Change the column chart to a line chart. Display the legend below the chart. You want to draw attention to increased Windows and declining DOS sales. Add text boxes with appropriate comments, and draw arrows to the Windows and DOS lines. Save the workbook as WONDERWORD LINE. Print the worksheet with the chart.

g. Using the line chart settings, experiment with different chart types, and select one that appeals to you. Format the chart using any techniques you wish. Save the workbook using an appropriate name, and print the worksheet with the chart.

h. Use the three format headings and the corresponding 1997 sales figures to create a 3-D pie chart as a new sheet. Add the title "1997 SALES." Explode the wedge representing the lowest sales value. Add patterns to the wedges. Increase the font size of the wedge labels. Increase the font size of the title, and add a second line that displays your name and the current date.

i. Suppress the header and footer by selecting (none) from the top of both drop-down lists in the Page Setup Header/Footer tab. Document the workbook. Save the workbook as WONDERWORD PIE. Print the Chart sheet.

2. In May of 1995, *Advertising Age* listed the top 100 advertising companies for 1994. The first five are listed in the table below.

Top 5 Advertisers	
Company	**$ Spent**
AT&T Corp.	698.6
Ford Motor Co.	549.3
Sears, Roebuck & Co.	491.7
Kellogg Co.	483.7
McDonald's Corp.	425.8

a. Create a worksheet of this data. Use the formatting techniques you have learned to enhance the appearance of the worksheet.

b. Use the data to create a default 3-D bar chart. Turn the legend off, and add appropriate titles.

c. Size the chart so all axis labels can be displayed. Add a text box below the value axis that displays the comment "In Millions of Dollars." Draw an arrow from the text box to the value axis. Edit the title to include your name and the current date.

d. Document and save the workbook as TOP 5 ADVERTISERS. Print the worksheet with the chart centered horizontally on the page.

3. To complete this exercise, you must have completed Practice Exercise 2 in either Lab 1 or Lab 2. Open the file COOKIE JAR on your data disk.

a. Use the column A row headings and the corresponding first-quarter total values to create an embedded 3-D pie chart. Add an appropriate title. Size the chart so all axis labels can be displayed. Explode the chocolate chip cookie wedge, and add patterns to the slices. Add a text box and an arrow that draws attention to the two wedges that represent the lowest sales.

b. The chart you just created shows a part-to-whole relationship between each cookie type and the total cookie sales for the first quarter. Insert a page break, and create an embedded chart that shows a part-to-whole relationship between each cookie type and each monthly total.

Hint: The data will be in rows, not columns.

c. Add appropriate titles. Size the chart so the legend information can be displayed. Add patterns to each data series, and display the legend below the chart.

d. Document the workbook. Save and replace the workbook file. Print the 1st Quarter Sales worksheet with the charts.

4. As part of a freshman orientation survey, Luzerne University students were asked how many hours a day they expected to spend on school work. The choices were: Less than 1 hour, 1–2 hours, 2–3 hours, and More than 3 hours. Below is a table of the results.

Study Habits	
Choice	**# Responses**
Less than 1 hour	87
1–2 hours	404
2–3 hours	475
More than 3 hours	123

a. Use the table information to create a worksheet, and make any formatting changes you wish.

b. Create an embedded chart that will show a part-to-whole relationship for the four categories of responses. Format the chart as desired.

c. Change the header to display your name and the current date.

d. Document the workbook. Save the workbook file as STUDENT SURVEY. Print the worksheet with the chart centered horizontally on the page.

e. At the end of the first semester, the students were again surveyed. This time, they were asked how may hours a day they actually spent on school work. The table below shows the results from those who responded.

Study Habits	
Choice	**# Responses**
Less than 1 hour	15
1–2 hours	101
2–3 hours	592
More than 3 hours	246

f. Replace the original values with the new values. Save and replace the workbook STUDENT SURVEY. Print the worksheet with the chart. Can you relate to the differences in the results?

On Your Own

5. Sadie Jacobs, owner of Jacobs Furniture Galleries, likes to have her sales staff close a sale with at least 35 percent of the customers with whom they come in contact. The worksheet below displays this month's results.

	A	B	C	D	E	F	G	H
1			Jacobs Furniture Galleries					
2			Monthly Sales Report					
3								
4		Ron	Charmaine	Michael	Polly	Al	Mary Claire	
5	Contacts	113	127	95	129	113	135	
6	Sales	26	49	42	19	43	54	
7	% of Closings							
8								

Create the worksheet shown above and calculate the % of Closings. Create an embedded chart that best compares customer contacts to sales for each employee. Add appropriate titles, and format as desired.

Change the header and footer to include your name and the current date. Print the worksheet with the chart. Document the workbook. Save the workbook file as SALES REPORT.

Use Goal Seek to determine how many sales would be needed to increase the % of Closing to 35 percent for those who do not meet that goal. Save and replace the workbook file SALES REPORT. Print the worksheet with the chart.

6. According to "The College Savings Bank," the 1995 cost of a four-year education was approximately $35,000 and $72,000 respectively for public and private colleges.

	A	B	C	D	E	F	G	H
1		College Costs						
2								
3		1995	1996	1997	1998	1999	2000	
4	Public	35,000						
5	Private	72,000						
6								

Create the worksheet shown above and, using an annual inflation rate of 7.5 percent, complete the worksheet to calculate the cost of a college education for each type of school from 1995 to the year 2000. Add the following comment in a text box below the worksheet:

Note: The above costs include tuition, room, board, books, and other expenses and fees.

Create an embedded chart that will compare private and public school costs annually. Add appropriate titles, and format as desired. Rename the sheet tab.

Create a chart as a new sheet that will show the change in cost from 1995 to 2000. Add appropriate titles, and format as desired. Rename the Chart sheet tab.

Change the header to display your name and the current date. Print the workbook.

Document the workbook. Save the workbook as COLLEGE COSTS.

7. Create a worksheet that tracks your grades. It can be a record of the test scores you received this semester, or it can be a record of your GPA each semester. Create an embedded chart that best represents your grade trends. Use the formatting techniques you learned to change the appearance of the worksheet and the chart. Save the workbook as GRADES. Print the worksheet with the chart.

8. Create a worksheet that displays a list of your monthly expenses (rent, car payment, food, day care, utilities, insurance, credit cards, etc.). Total the expenses. Create a chart that best shows a part-to-whole relationship between each expense and total expenses. Using the formatting techniques you learned, change the appearance of the worksheet and the chart. Save the workbook as EXPENSES. Include your name and the date in a header. Print the worksheet and the chart.

Concept Summary

4 Creating Charts

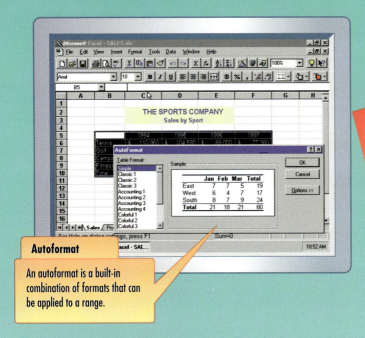

Autoformat
An autoformat is a built-in combination of formats that can be applied to a range.

Concepts
- Autoformat
- Types of Charts
- Chart Elements

Chart Elements
A chart consists of may parts or elements that are used to graphically display the worksheet data.

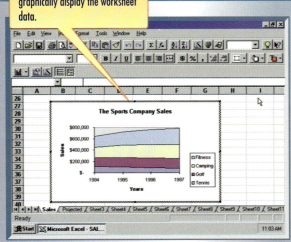

Types of Charts

Excel can produce 15 basic types of charts with many different formats for each type.

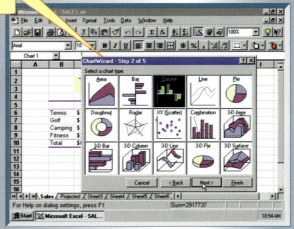

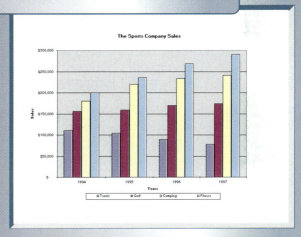

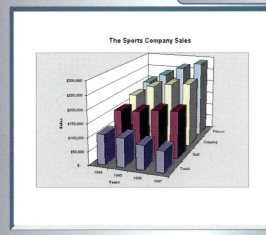

Creating Templates

COMPETENCIES

After completing this lab, you will know how to:

1. Name a range.
2. Use the IF function.
3. Protect a worksheet.
4. Create workbook templates.

You have learned in the first four labs how Excel makes completing your personal, school, or work-related projects much faster, more accurate, neater, and more logical. But Excel can help even more, as you will learn in this lab, by providing advanced features to improve your efficiency and performance.

Among the many advanced features are the hundreds of functions included with Excel that are designed to perform complex financial and statistical analysis of data. In this lab, you will learn about the IF function, an important and useful function that is used to perform conditional tests on data. In addition, you will learn how to create custom templates and to protect your worksheets so that their contents cannot be changed.

Naming a Range   ss185

Concept Overview

The following concepts will be introduced in this lab:

1. **Range Name** — Adding a descriptive range name to a cell or range of cells makes formulas easier to read and understand.
2. **IF Function** — The IF function checks to see if certain conditions are met and then takes action based upon the results of the check.
3. **Worksheet Protection** — Cells can be protected from changes by turning on the worksheet protection feature and including a password.
4. **Workbook Template** — A workbook template is a workbook file that contains predesigned sheets that can be used as a pattern for creating other similar worksheets in new workbooks.

CASE STUDY

The Sports Company has decided to offer its own charge card. As an incentive to apply for a card, customers receive 15 percent off any purchases made using the card the first time. As an incentive to employees to promote the charge card, they earn a bonus for each credit card application they process. The store manager has asked you create a worksheet template to be used to track the monthly new charge card enrollments and employee bonuses.

Naming a Range

The Sports Company is awarding a $1.00 bonus for each credit card application they sign up. Additionally, if during a month a salesperson files 25 applications or more, a bonus of 20 percent on the total is earned. If they file more than 50 applications, a bonus of 30 percent is added to the total amount. Much of the worksheet to be used to enter the weekly charge card enrollment data has already been created for you.

To see what has been done so far, load Excel and open the workbook file CHARGE CARD ENROLLMENT BONUS.XLS. If necessary, maximize the worksheet.

SPREADSHEET

Your screen should be similar to Figure 5-1.

Figure 5-1

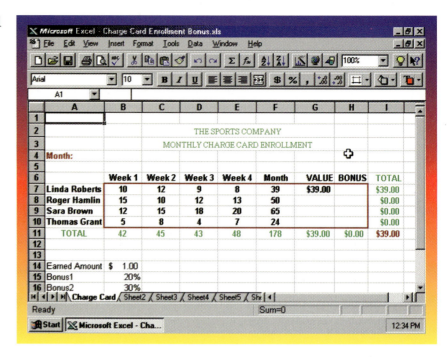

This worksheet displays the names of four salespeople as row headings in column A. The enrollments for each week of the month are entered in columns B through E for each salesperson. The monthly total is displayed in column F. The column labels in cells G6, H6, and I6 define the following:

Value   The number of enrollments times $1.00

Bonus   The Value times 20 percent if 25 or more applications were enrolled in the month, or times 30 percent if 50 or more applications were enrolled in the month.

Total   The sum of Value plus Bonus

The worksheet also contains some sample enrollment data for each salesperson. The sample data for Linda shows that she enrolled ten charge card applicants in week 1, twelve in week 2, nine in week 3, and eight in week 4. To complete this worksheet you need to enter formulas to calculate the Value and Bonus columns.

Move to: G7

Your screen should be similar to Figure 5-2.

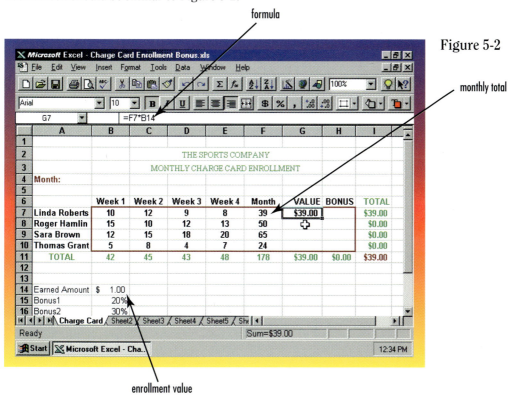

Figure 5-2

The formula in this column will calculate the total enrollment value by multiplying the number in the monthly total cell by $1.00, the amount earned per enrollment value in cell B14. This formula has already been entered to calculate the value for Linda Roberts. To makes the formula easier to read and understand, a descriptive name can be assigned to a cell or range of cells and used in place of the references in the formula.

Concept 1: Range Name

A descriptive **range name** can be assigned to a cell or range of cells and used in place of cell references. The name can be used any time a cell or range is requested as part of a command or in a formula or function.

Excel automatically proposes a name for the cell or range using the contents of the active cell if it contains text, or the cell above or to the left of the active cell if the active cell does not contain text. If the active cell or the cells above or to the left of the active cell do not contain text, or if you do not want to use the proposed name, you can type in a name of your choice. The name can be up to 255 characters. It can include letters, numbers, underlines, periods, backslashes, and question marks. It cannot contain spaces. The first character must be a letter, underline, or backslash. A name that resembles a cell reference is not allowed.

To see how this works, you will assign the name "Earned Amount" to cell B14.

Move to: B14
Choose: Insert/Name/Define

Your screen should be similar to Figure 5-3.

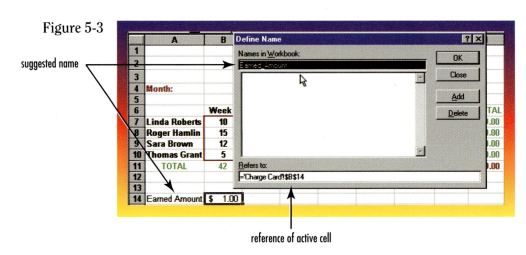

Figure 5-3
suggested name
reference of active cell

In the Names in Workbook text box, Excel has proposed the name Earned_Amount, The proposed name is the contents of the cell to the left of the active cell. Excel replaced the blank space between the words with an underline character because a name cannot contain spaces.

The Refers To text box displays the reference for the active cell. The reference includes the sheet name and cell reference. By default Excel makes cell references absolute. The Names in Workbook list box is empty because this worksheet does not contain any names yet. Since both the name and the cell reference are acceptable, to complete the command,

Choose: OK

In place of the cell reference in the Name box of the formula bar, the name is displayed. Now you can replace the cell reference in the formula in cell G7 with the name. To edit the formula,

Move to: G7

Change to Edit mode and select (highlight) the cell reference B14 in the formula.

To replace the cell reference with the name,

Choose: Insert/Name/Paste

The Paste Name dialog box displays a list of all names. Again, since there are no other names, the only name displayed is Earned_Amount.

Select: Earned_Amount
Choose: OK

Your screen should be similar to Figure 5-4.

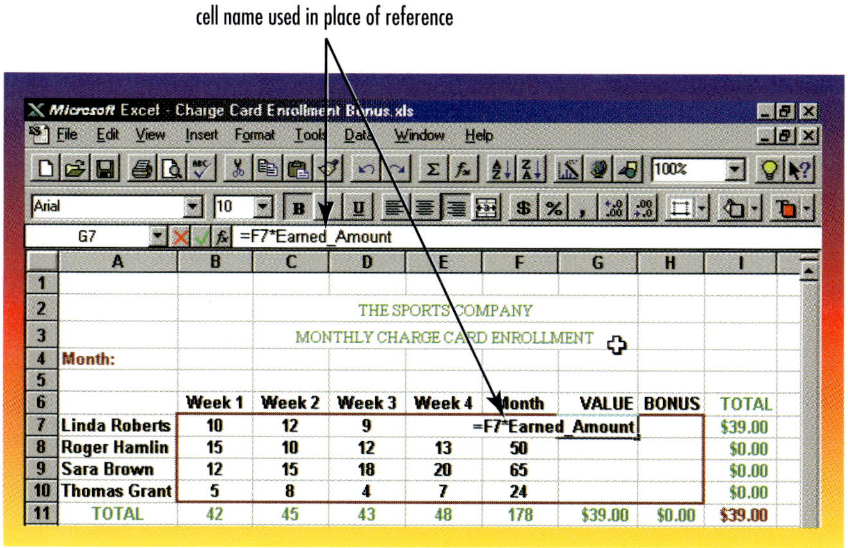

Figure 5-4

cell name used in place of reference

The name Earned_Amount has replaced the reference to cell B14 in the formula. Using a name makes the formula easier to understand.

To complete the edit,

Press: ←Enter

Next, you will name the Bonus percent values in cells B16 and B17 that will be used in the formula to calculate the Bonus. You will name both cells at the same time using the headings in A15 and A16 as the names. To create names using headings in a selected range,

Select: A15 through B16
Choose: Insert/Name/Create

Your screen should be similar to Figure 5-5.

Figure 5-5

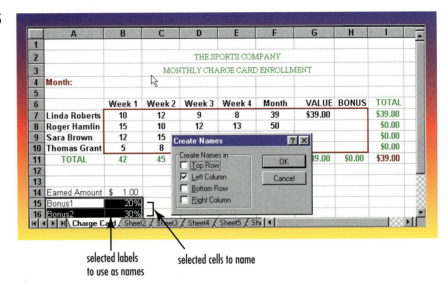

selected labels to use as names

selected cells to name

The Create Names dialog box displays four choices: Top Row, Left Column, Bottom Row, and Right Column. Your selection depends upon the location of the headings in relation to the cells to be named. In this case the headings are located in the column to the left of the cells to be named. This is the selected option. To accept this choice,

Choose: OK

The headings in cells A15 and A16 have been used to name the cells to their right. To confirm this,

Move to: B15

The name assigned to this cell, Bonus1, is displayed in the Name box.

Using the IF Function

Now you are ready to enter a formula in cell H7 to calculate the bonus earned.

Move to: H7

The store gives a 30 percent bonus on total enrollments of 50 or more and a 20 percent bonus on total enrollments of 25 or more. To calculate this value, you will use the IF function.

Concept 2: IF Function

The IF function checks to see if certain conditions are met and then takes action based upon the results of the check. The syntax for this function is:

IF(logical_test,value_if_true,value_if_false)

This function contains three arguments: logical_test, value_if_true, and value_if_false. The logical_test argument is an expression that makes a comparison using logical operators. **Logical operators** are used in formulas and functions that compare numbers in two or more cells or to a constant. The result of the comparison is either true (the conditions are met) or false (the conditions are not met).

The logical operators are:

Symbol	Meaning	Symbol	Meaning
=	Equal to	<>	Not equal to
<	Less than	NOT	Logical NOT
>	Greater than	AND	Logical AND
<=	Less than or equal to	OR	Logical OR
>=	Greater than or equal to		

The logical test argument asks the question, Does the entry in this cell meet the stated conditions? The answer is either True (Yes) or False (No).

The second argument, value-if-true, provides directions for the function to follow if the logical test result is true. The third argument, value-if-false, provides directions for the function to follow if the logical test result is false.

You will enter the IF function using the Function Wizard.

Click:  **Function Wizard**

> The menu equivalent is <u>I</u>nsert/<u>F</u>unction.

The first Function Wizard dialog box is displayed. The IF function is in the Logical category of functions. From the Function Category list box,

Select: **Logical**

The Function Name box now lists only logical functions.

Select: **IF**

> You could also select IF from the Most Recently Used list if it is displayed.

The IF function containing argument placeholders is displayed in the formula bar.

Choose:

The Step 2 dialog box contains three text boxes, one for each IF statement argument. First you will enter the formula to calculate the bonus earned for enrollments of 50 or more. The logical test is whether the total monthly enrollment

(F7) is greater than (>) or equal to (=) 50. The logical_test argument will be F7>=50. In the logical_test text box,

Type: F7>=50
Press: Tab

The function in the formula bar displays the logical test argument you specified.

The value_if_true argument contains the instructions that are executed if the condition is true. In this case if the number in cell F7 is greater than or equal to 50 (true), then G7 is multiplied by 30 percent (G7*30%). To enter the value_if_true argument,

Type: G7*

Instead of entering the bonus amount (30%) to complete the argument, you will reference the named cell, B16, that contains the bonus number. This way, if the bonus changes, the function will not need to be changed. The value_if_true argument then will be: G7*Bonus2. To paste the named range in the argument,

Choose: Insert/Name/Paste
Select: Bonus2
Choose: OK

The cell name is entered in the text box and displayed in the function in the formula bar.

The value_if_false argument contains instructions that are executed if the condition is not true, or false. If the number in cell F7 is less than 50 (false), then the Bonus is 0. To enter the last argument,

Press: Tab
Type: 0

The dialog box on your screen should be similar to Figure 5-6.

Figure 5-6

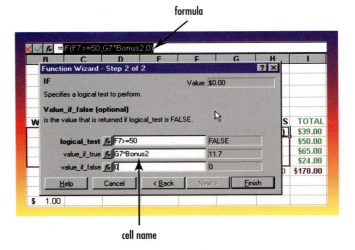

To complete the formula,

Choose: Finish

The Bonus is calculated for Linda using the sample data. The Bonus is $0.00 because the number in cell F7 is less than 50.

Now you need to alter the function to include a second IF statement that will apply the bonus of 20 percent to numbers greater than or equal to 25. The new IF statement will be IF(F7>=25,G7*Bonus1,0). The arguments for the second IF statement are enclosed in their own set of parentheses within the existing formula. This is called a **nested function**. The new function will be:

IF(F7>=50,G7*Bonus2,IF(F7>=25,G7*Bonus1,0)).

> You can use the Function Wizard to add the second IF function.

Edit the formula to include the second IF statement as shown above.

Your screen should be similar to Figure 5-7.

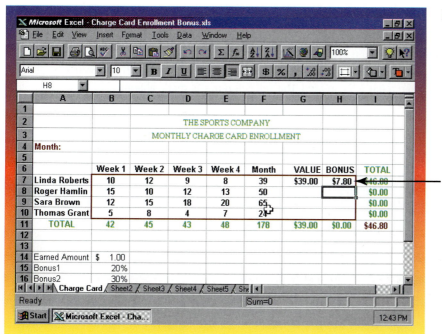

Figure 5-7

bonus earned for enrollment greater than 25

The Bonus for Linda is now $7.80. The formula determined that the number in cell F7 was 25 or more and calculated a 20 percent bonus on the number in cell G7.

Using Paste Special

Next you will copy the formulas used to calculate the Value and Bonus for Linda to calculate these values for the other three salespeople. Notice the border line surrounding the data. So that the top border style that is associated with cells G7 and H7 is not included in the copy, you will use the All Except Borders option in the Paste Special command.

Copy the contents of cells G7 and H7 to the Clipboard. Select the destination range, G8 through H10. Then, to paste the Clipboard contents excluding the border,

Choose: <u>E</u>dit/Paste <u>S</u>pecial/All E<u>x</u>cept Borders/OK

The Value and Bonus formulas are copied to the destination range. All formatting associated with the copied cells is included, except the border. To clear the moving border,

Press: Esc
Move to: G8

The cell name in the copied formula appears exactly as it did in the formula in cell G7. You did not need to change the name to absolute because by default, when a name is created, the cell reference is made absolute.

Move to: H8

Your screen should be similar to Figure 5-8.

Figure 5-8

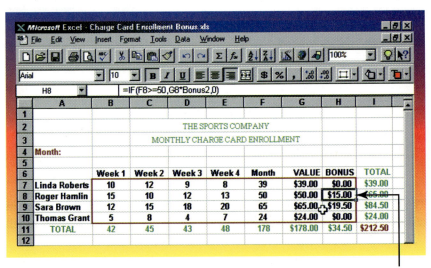

calculated bonus

The calculated Bonus in cell H8 is $15.00. The function calculated the 30 percent bonus because the number in F8 is equal to 50. The calculated Bonus in cell H9 is $19.50 because the number in cell F9 is greater than 50. Finally, the function calculated the Bonus of $0.00 in cell H10 because the number in F10 is less than 25. The IF function is operating correctly.

Protecting a Sheet

Now that the worksheet is complete, you want to prevent changes to the worksheet that would cause headings and formulas in the worksheet to be altered or cleared. To do this, you can protect the worksheet.

> **Concept 3: Worksheet Protection**
>
> To prevent others from changing a sheet's contents, you can **protect** the entire worksheet or specified areas of the worksheet. When you protect a sheet, all cells and graphic objects on the sheet are locked. The contents of a **locked** cell cannot be changed. If you want to leave some cells unlocked for editing, such as in a worksheet you use as an entry form, you can lock cells containing labels and formulas but unlock the entry fields so that others can fill them in. This type of protection prevents you from entering or changing an entry in any locked cells.
>
> An entire workbook can also be protected from unauthorized changes in two ways. The structure of a workbook can be protected so that sheets cannot be moved or deleted or new sheets inserted. A workbook's windows can also be protected. This prevents changes to the size and position of windows and ensures they appear the same way each time the workbook is opened.
>
> In addition, you can include a **password** that prevents any unauthorized person from turning off protection and changing the worksheet. If you use a password, you must remember the password in order to turn protection off in the future. A password can be a maximum of 15 characters and can contain spaces, symbols, numbers, and letters. Excel is case-sensitive for passwords, so you must remember the exact combination of uppercase or lowercase letters you used when you entered the password originally.

Initially, all cells in a worksheet are locked. However, you can enter data in the cells because the worksheet protection feature is not on. When protection is turned on, all locked cells are protected. Therefore, before protecting this sheet, you need to unlock the range of cells where the data will be entered.

Select: B7 through E10
Choose: Format/Cells

> Format Cells is also on the Shortcut menu.

Open the Protection tab in the Format Cells dialog box.

The dialog box on your screen should be similar to Figure 5-9.

Figure 5-9

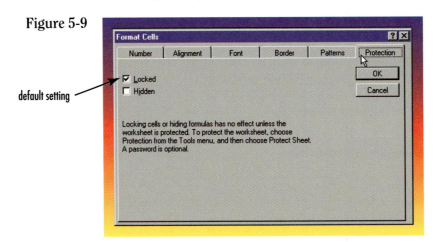

default setting

The Locked option in the Protection tab is checked, indicating the cells are locked. To allow changes to the selected range of cells, clear the Locked option box. Clearing the Locked option unlocks only those cells in the selected range.

Choose: OK

Now you are ready to turn on worksheet protection.

Choose: Tools/Protection/Protect Sheet

The Protect Sheet dialog box shown in Figure 5-10 is displayed.

Figure 5-10

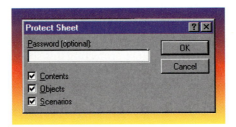

To prevent unauthorized users from removing the sheet protection, you will require a password. A password can be a maximum of 15 characters and can contain any combination of letters, numbers, and symbols. It is also case sensitive, so you must remember the exact combination of uppercase and lowercase letters you used in your password.

To add the password PROTECT,

Type: PROTECT

Asterisks are displayed in place of the characters you typed in the text box to prevent anyone from seeing the password as it is entered.

Choose: OK

To verify the password, in the Reenter Protection Password text box,

Type: PROTECT

Read the Caution in this box.
   To close the dialog box,

Choose: OK

> If the entry you type does not exactly match the original password entry, a warning appears. Choose OK and try again.

Now all locked cells in the worksheet are protected. Any cells you unlocked prior to turning protection on can be changed. To show the effect of trying to enter data into a protected cell, you will try to enter the month in cell A4.
   Move to cell A4 and change to Edit mode.
   A warning dialog box is displayed, informing you that you cannot change entries in locked cells. To clear the message,

Choose: OK

You need to change this cell to unprotected so you can edit it to display the month. To do this, you first need to turn off worksheet protection and then unlock the cell.

Choose: Tools/Protection/Unprotect Sheet

To enter the password,

Type: PROTECT
Choose: OK

> Reminder: Passwords are case sensitive.

Now you can unlock the cell.

Choose: Format/Cells

Clear the Locked option in the Protection folder.

Choose: OK

To turn on protection again,

Choose: Tools/Protection/Protect Sheet

SPREADSHEET

Enter and verify the password, PROTECT.

Choose: OK

Now cell A4 can accept data.

With the cell selector in cell A4, change to Edit mode.

Excel changes to Edit mode, and no warning is displayed. To cancel this action,

Press: [Esc]

Likewise you will be able to enter the data in cells B7 through E10 because they were unlocked before protecting the worksheet.

Creating a Template File

Each time you use this worksheet, you will be entering data for a new month.

To remove the sample data in the worksheet, clear the data in cells B7 through E10.

Move to: A4

Your screen should be similar to Figure 5-11.

Figure 5-11

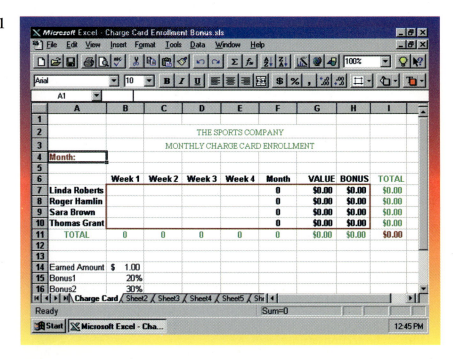

This is how the blank sheet will appear when you use it to enter the charge card enrollment figures. Because this information will be entered in a different workbook file for each month's data, you will save it as a workbook template.

Concept 4: Workbook Template

A workbook **template** is a workbook file that contains predesigned sheets that can be used as a pattern for creating other similar sheets in new workbooks. Templates are useful in any application where input and output are required using the same format. The template saves the user time by not having to redesign the same worksheet form each time the report is needed. The original design can be used repeatedly by saving the workbook containing the data using a different filename than the filename used to save the workbook template.

Excel saves a workbook template using a special file format with the file extension .XLT. Workbook templates are also stored in a special Templates folder. To use a workbook template, you select the template filename from the General tab of the New File dialog box. When you save the workbook after entering data in the template, Excel automatically displays the Save As dialog box so you can specify the new filename. It also changes the file type to an Excel workbook file (.XLS). This ensures that you do not save over the template file unintentionally.

It is good procedure when creating custom workbook templates for others to use to include documentation with the workbook. Template documentation includes:

Template purpose — Should briefly describe what information is needed to complete the template and what output is generated from the template

Template instructions — Should briefly discuss steps for completing the template and how to move to different areas of the worksheet

Template procedures — Should explain how to name and save the workbook file

Update the file summary information with the following template documentation:

Title:	**Monthly Charge Card Enrollment**
Subject:	**Monthly report of charge card enrollments and employee bonuses.**
Author:	**[your name]**
Comments:	**Edit cell A4 to include the report month. Enter the enrollment values in cells B7 through E10. Print the worksheet. Save the workbook as XXX Bonus, replacing XXX with the month.**

Next, you will save the workbook as a template file.

Choose: **File/Save As**

Enter the new filename, CHARGE CARD BONUS, in the File Name text box.

To set the file format to template, you need to specify the type of file from the Save As Type drop-down list box.

Open the Save As Type list box.

A list of file formats is displayed. Your selection from this list determines the way information in a document is stored in a file. Many of the file formats make it easier to use Excel documents with other applications. To store it as a template file,

Select: Template

Notice that the Save In box now displays the Templates folder as the location where the file will be saved.

> If you are prompted to replace a file with the same filename, select Yes.

Choose: Save

Close the CHARGE CARD BONUS template file.

Now you want to create a new workbook file to record the enrollment data for the month of October using the CHARGE CARD BONUS template.

Choose: File/New

> If you save a workbook template to a location other than the Templates folder, the file icon will not appear in the General tab.

If necessary, display the General tab of the New dialog box.

The CHARGE CARD BONUS template appears in the General tab as an icon.

Select: Charge Card Bonus

The preview area displays a portion of the worksheet. To use the template,

Choose: OK

The workbook template is opened and appears just as it did when you saved it.

Each month you will need to enter the name of the month the data represents following the entry in cell A4.

Edit cell A4 by adding "October" following the existing entry. Next, enter the following data for each salesperson:

	Week 1	Week 2	Week 3	Week 4
Linda Roberts	23	15	22	20
Roger Hamlin	12	11	10	13
Sara Brown	14	12	10	10
Thomas Grant	18	25	18	14

When you are done, your screen should be similar to Figure 5-12.

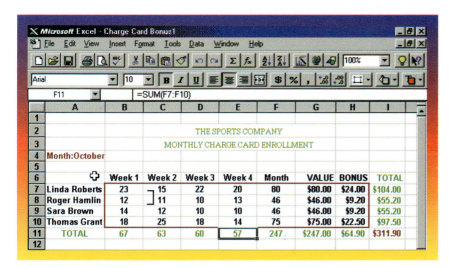

Figure 5-12

Now you are ready to save the workbook. You want to use a filename that reflects the month the data represents.

Choose:

The Save As dialog box is displayed whenever you use a template file. This prevents you from accidentally overwriting the template file with the changes you have made. Excel proposes a filename of Charge Card Bonus1.

Specify the drive containing your data disk as the location to save the file. Change the proposed filename to CHARGE CARD BONUS OCTOBER.

Notice that the Save As Type text box automatically displays "Microsoft Excel Workbook [*.xls]" as the type of file. Again, this prevents you from accidentally creating another template file.

Choose: Save

The workbook is saved using an .XLS filename extension.

Close the CHARGE CARD BONUS OCTOBER file.

LAB REVIEW

Key Terms

locked (SS195)
logical operator (SS191)
nested function (SS193)
password (SS195)

protect (SS195)
range name (SS187)
template (SS199)

SPREADSHEET

ss202 Lab 5: Creating Templates

Command Summary

Command	Action
File/Save As/Save As Type	Sets file format for document
Insert/Name/Define	Assigns a name you specify to a cell or range of cells
Insert/Name/Paste	Places name in formula bar or lists names in worksheet
Insert/Name/Create	Creates names using text in cells
Format/Cells/Protection	Changes protection of selected cells to locked or unlocked
Tools/Protection/Protect Sheet	Turns on protection for all locked cells
Tools/Protection/Unprotect Sheet	Turns off protection for all locked cells

Matching

1. template   _____   a. information supplied to a function for calculation
2. <   _____   b. workbook that contains predesigned sheets to be used as patterns
3. IF   _____   c. keeps worksheet data from being altered
4. protection   _____   d. logical operator
5. arguments   _____   e. evaluates condition and takes one of two actions
6. nested function _____   f. function within another function

Fill-In Questions

1. Complete the following statements by filling in the blanks with the correct terms.

    a. _____ are used in formulas and functions that compare values in two or more cells.

    b. A(n) _____ is a workbook that contains predesigned sheets.

    c. A range _____ can consist of any combination of 255 characters.

    d. The _____ feature is used to keep parts of the worksheet from being accidentally altered or erased.

    e. _____ is important when creating a template so that others will know how the worksheet functions.

Discussion Questions

1. Discuss range names and when it is appropriate to use them. Give some examples.

2. What are logical operators used for? Describe five logical operators and give examples of their use.

3. Discuss why you would want to save a workbook as a template and give several examples of where a template would be useful. Why would you want to protect the cells of a template?

Hands-On Practice Exercises

Step by Step

Rating System
★ Easy
★★ Moderate
★★★ Difficult

★★★
1. To complete this problem, you must have completed Practice Exercise 5 in Lab 3. Open the workbook files EARNINGS STATEMENT and TIME SHEET (in that order) from your data disk. Close both files without saving. Now, open the same files in the reverse order (TIME SHEET first). Is there a difference between the two procedures? What might that be?

In this exercise, you will use an IF function to calculate Regular Hours on the time sheet, and you will protect the worksheets.

- a. Make the TIME SHEET file active. You want to be able to use this workbook over again. Rename the sheet tabs Week 1 and Week 2 so they will apply to any biweekly period.

- b. The Regular Hours column will be calculated by formula, so all you have to do is enter the Total Hours, and the remaining columns will be calculated for you. You will enter an IF function in the cell that displays Monday's Regular Hours in the Week 1 sheet. The function will tell the program that if Monday's Total Hours are greater than or equal to 8, enter the number 8. Otherwise enter Monday's Total Hours. Copy the function down the column and to the corresponding cells in column C of the Week 2 sheet. What was the function you used?

- c. Unlock the Total Hours and cells that display the "Week of" information on both sheets. Protect both sheets.

- d. Make the EARNINGS STATEMENT file active. The formula in B7 has adjusted so that it now refers to the Biweekly Total in the Week 2 sheet of the TIME SHEET file. Erase and unlock the period-ending date and protect the worksheet.

- e. Switch to the TIME SHEET file. Erase the starting dates and total hours from both sheets. Update the documentation, and save the file. Switch to the EARNINGS STATEMENT file. The hours will be zero, and the statutory deductions will be blank. The only values displayed will be the rate and the fixed voluntary deductions. Document the worksheet and save the file.

- f. Enter new starting dates and total hours in both worksheets of the TIME SHEET file. Save the file as CURRENT TIME SHEET and print the worksheets.

- g. Switch to the EARNINGS STATEMENT file. Notice that the hours have changed, and the file is linked to the CURRENT TIME SHEET. Modify the period-ending date. Save the file as CURRENT EARNINGS STATEMENT and print the worksheet.

From now on, if you remember to save the original files with new names when the variable information changes, you can use the originals over and over again. Using templates with linked files is difficult because the dependent worksheet is always looking for the original source template (.XLT file), and you must redefine the link to the temporary copy that the template has loaded.

2. To complete this problem, you must have completed Practice Exercise 4 in Lab 2. Open the workbook file INVOICE on your data disk. In this exercise, you will continue to modify the worksheet.

- a. Draw an outline border around the invoice # and date information. Add color to the text and background. Remove the underlines from the column headings, and replace them with a bottom border. Enhance the appearance of the worksheet by adding lines and/or color in other locations.

- b. The customer wants to purchase an overhead projector, but that model is on backorder. Create a note in a text box below the worksheet stating that the projector is on backorder and the customer will be notified when it arrives in stock.

- c. A 15 percent discount is given to customers who purchase more than 12 items. Insert a column after the Price column and enter the column heading "Discount." In the cell below the heading, enter an IF function that will calculate a 15 percent discount if the quantity for Pentium Computers exceeds 12. Otherwise the cell will display zero. Copy the function down the column. *Note:* When this formula is copied, cells with a zero in them will display "$-" or "-" if the cells are formatted with the Currency or Comma format.

d. Modify the formula in the Total column so the total will be calculated as quantity times the difference between the price and the discount. Copy the new total formula down the column.

e. Save and replace the workbook file INVOICE. Print the workbook.

f. You want to use this invoice over again. Delete the text box. Erase and unlock: the entries for Qty, Description, Price, Invoice #, Date, Customer name and address. Protect the worksheet. Update the documentation. Save the workbook as a template file named INVOICE TEMPLATE.

g. Use the template to enter the following information:

Heading	Entry
Invoice #	12345
Date	Current date
Customer	Your name and address
Qty	20
Description	Highlighters
Price	.99

h. Unprotect the worksheet and delete the blank rows above the Subtotal.

i. Delete your address information at the top of the worksheet.

j. Save the file as an Excel workbook file named MY INVOICE. Print the worksheet.

On Your Own

★★★

3. In this lab you learned to create templates that can be the basis of future workbooks. Excel comes with several workbook templates called Spreadsheet Solutions. Included are an invoice, a loan manager, and a purchase order.

To access the Excel templates, open the Spreadsheet Solutions tab of the New dialog box. The invoice and loan manager operate in much the same way as the templates you created. The purchase order is very similar to the invoice. Select one of these templates.

Once the template you selected is loaded, click the Customize sheet tab once. You can now enter personalized information such as the name of the company, your tax rate, and so on in the form. Add information to complete the template. If you use the invoice or purchase order, you can enter information from the invoice exercise (Practice Exercise 2). If you need help, each template displays a toolbar that contains a Help button .

Note: Once you have customized your template and have returned to the worksheet, the Customize tab will no longer be displayed. However, you can click the Customize button in the upper right corner if you need to return.

Document the workbook. Save the file and print the worksheet.

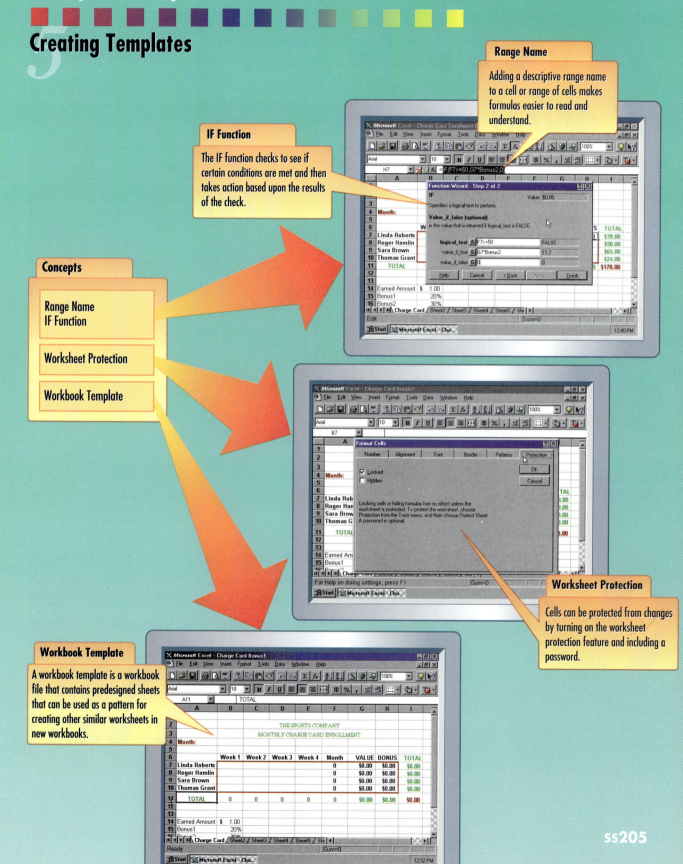

Sharing Data Between Applications

COMPETENCIES

After completing this lab, you will know how to:

1. Paste between applications.
2. Link objects.
3. Embed objects.
4. Update linked and embedded objects.
5. Decide when to use linking or embedding.

Wouldn't it be nice to be able to easily incorporate a spreadsheet you have created using a spreadsheet application into a document you have created using a word processor? Well, you can easily do this using the Microsoft Office applications.

You have probably noticed while using Microsoft Word, Excel, Access, and PowerPoint that the applications have a common user interface such as similar commands and menu structures. In addition to these obvious features, they have been designed to work together, making it easy to share and exchange information between applications.

Concept Overview

The following concepts will be introduced in the lab:

1. Paste Between Applications Information can be copied and pasted between applications. If possible, the pasted information is inserted in the document in a format the document can edit.

2. Linked Object Information can be pasted into another application document as a linked object, which stores a representation of the object and creates a live link to the source document.

3. Embedded Object Information can be pasted into a document created in another application as an embedded object, which stores the object and a reference to the server application in the destination document.

CASE STUDY

Your analysis of sales data for the past four years has shown a steady increase in total sales. However, the analysis of sales in four main categories of sporting goods has shown that sales in fitness and camping are increasing, sales in tennis are decreasing, and golf sales remain steady. You would like to send a memo of these findings to the manager of The Sports Company. In addition, you want to include the worksheet and chart of the Sales analysis in the memo.

Note: This lab assumes that you have completed Lab 2 of *Word 7.0a for Windows 95* and Lab 4 of *Excel 7.0a for Windows 95*. You will need the data file SALES CHARTS you created in Lab 4 of Excel.

Pasting Between Applications

The memo to the manager about the analysis of the sales data has already been created using Word 7.0a. However, you still need to add the Excel worksheet data and charts to the memo.

If necessary, turn on your computer. After Windows 95 is loaded, start the Word 7.0a program. To see the memo to the manager, open the file SALES ANALYSIS MEMO.

Your screen should be similar to Figure 6-1.

Figure 6-1

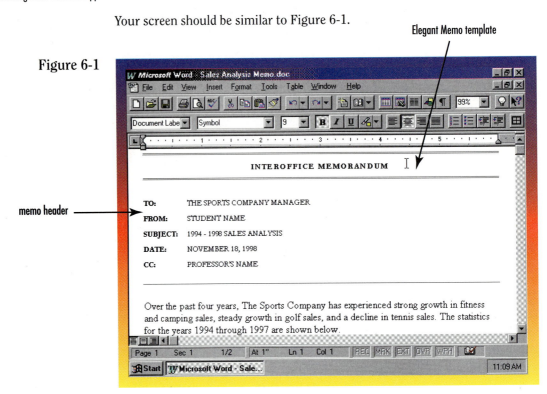

The memo was created using the Elegant Memo template.

In the memo header, replace the Student Name with your name and the Professor's Name with your instructor's name.

The memo consists of three paragraphs.

Scroll the window so you can see the three paragraphs.

Your screen should be similar to Figure 6-2.

Figure 6-2

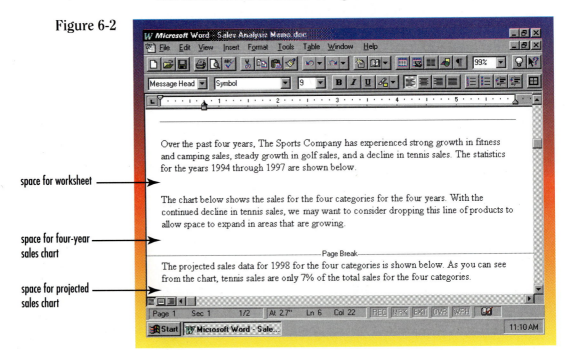

You will insert the data from the Sales sheet of the SALES CHARTS workbook below the first paragraph. Below the second paragraph, you will display a chart of The Sports Company sales. The second page of the memo will display a chart of the projected sales data for 1998 below the paragraph.

Now you are ready to insert the information from the Excel workbook file into the Word memo.

Start the Excel 7.0 application.

There are now two open applications, Word and Excel. Word is open in a window behind the Excel application window. Both application buttons are displayed in the taskbar.

Open the workbook file SALES CHARTS on your data disk. If necessary, move the cell selector to cell A1 of the Sales sheet.

Your screen should be similar to Figure 6-3.

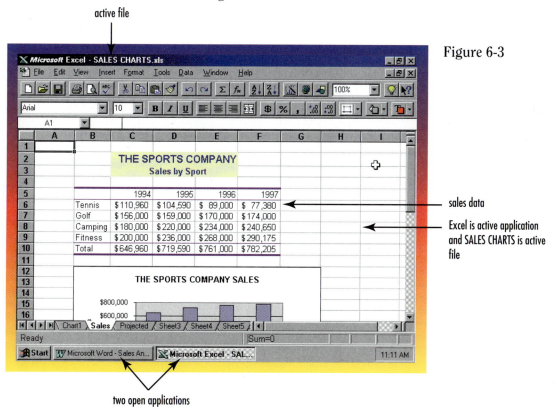

Figure 6-3

Now there are also two open files, SALES CHARTS in Excel and SALES ANALYSIS MEMO in Word. Excel is the active application, and SALES CHARTS is the active file.

First you will copy the worksheet data in the Sales sheet and paste it into the Word memo.

Concept 1: Paste Between Applications

While using the Microsoft applications, you have learned how to use cut, copy, and paste to move or copy information within the same document and between documents in the same application. You can also perform these same operations between applications. For example, you can copy information from a Word document and paste it into an Excel worksheet. The information is pasted in a format that the application can edit, if possible.

> Choose **E**dit/**C**opy or press Ctrl + C or click Copy.

Select and copy the contents of cells B2 through F10.

A copy of the worksheet is stored in the Clipboard. Now you need to specify the location where you want the copied information displayed. To switch to the Word application and make it the active application,

Click: 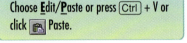 in the taskbar

> Choose **E**dit/**P**aste or press Ctrl + V or click Paste.

You want the worksheet data displayed below the first paragraph.

Move to the second blank line below the first paragraph of the memo. Paste the contents of the Clipboard into the memo.

Your screen should be similar to Figure 6-4.

Figure 6-4

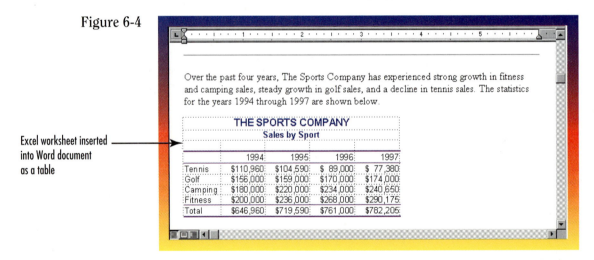

Excel worksheet inserted into Word document as a table

The worksheet data has been copied into the Word document as a table that can be edited and manipulated within Word. Much of the formatting associated with the copied information is also pasted into the document. However, you think the memo would look better if the table was centered between the margins.

Select the entire table.

> Drag or use T**a**ble/Select T**a**ble.

Choose: T**a**ble/Cell Height and **W**idth/Row/Cen**t**er/OK

Clear the selection.

The table is centered between the memo margins.

Linking a Chart to a Word Document

Next you want to display the area chart of sales trends for the four categories in the memo.

Switch to the Excel application and scroll to the bottom of the Sales sheet to view the area chart.

To copy the chart to the Clipboard, you must first select or activate it.

Activate the chart.

Your screen should be similar to Figure 6-5.

> Double-click the chart to activate it.

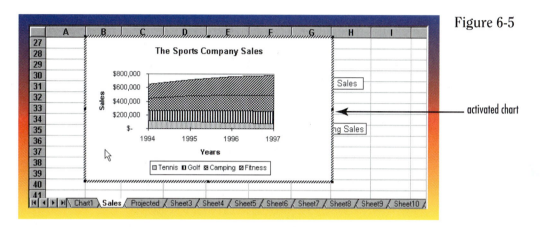

Figure 6-5

— activated chart

The area chart is surrounded by the chart editing border. Notice that the text boxes and arrows are not part of the activated chart. This is because they are separate objects in the worksheet.

Copy the selected chart object to the Clipboard. Switch to the Word application.

You want the chart displayed below the second paragraph.

Move to the second blank line below the second paragraph of the memo.

You will insert the chart object into the memo as a linked object.

Concept 2: Linked Object

Information can also be pasted into another application as a **linked object**. When an object is linked, the data is stored in the **source document** (the document it was created in). A graphic representation or picture of the data is displayed in the **destination document** (the document in which the object is inserted). A connection between the information in the destination document to the source document is established by the creation of a linked **object field code**. This code contains references to the location of the source document and the selection within the document that is linked to the destination document.

When changes are made in the source document that affect the linked object, the changes are automatically reflected in the destination document when it is opened. This is called a **live link**. When you create links, the date and time on your machine should be accurate. This is because the program refers to the date of the source file to determine whether updates are needed when you open the destination document.

SPREADSHEET

By making the chart a linked object, it will be automatically updated if the source document is edited. To create a linked object,

> To link an entire file, use Insert/Object.

Choose: **Edit/Paste Special**

In the Paste Special dialog box, you specify the type of object to create in the destination document. The Paste Link option creates a linked object.

Select: **Paste Link**

The Paste Special dialog box on your screen should be similar to Figure 6-6.

Figure 6-6

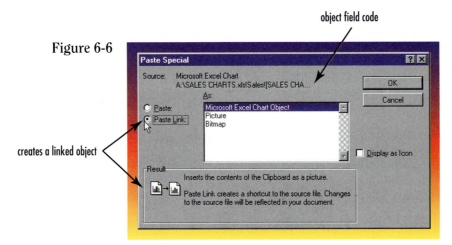

The currently highlighted selection in the As list box, Microsoft Excel Chart Object, will insert the Clipboard contents into the Word document as a picture and create a link to the chart in the source file. The linked object field code is displayed in the Source information area in the dialog box.

Choose: **OK**

If necessary, scroll the window until the entire chart is displayed.

Your screen should be similar to Figure 6-7.

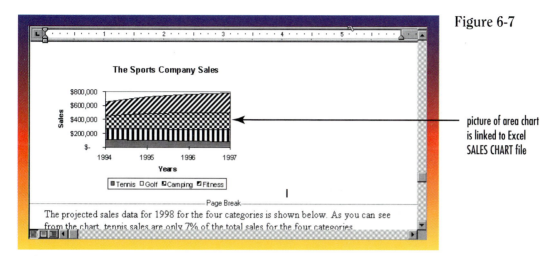

Figure 6-7

picture of area chart is linked to Excel SALES CHART file

A picture of the area chart is displayed in the memo at the location of the insertion point. Word places the left edge of the chart object even with the left margin of the Word document and scales the chart to fit in the document.

Updating a Linked Object

While reading the text and looking at the chart, you decide to change the chart type from an area chart to a line chart. You feel a line chart will show the sales trends more clearly. To change the type of chart, you need to switch to Excel.

Switch to Excel. If necessary, activate the chart.

To change this chart to a line chart,

Click: [📊▼] Chart Type

Click: [📈] Line

> The menu equivalent is **E**dit/Linked Worksheet **O**bject/**E**dit. The object must be selected first. If the application is not open, this command opens the application and associated file. If it is open already, the command switches to the application.

You will also make another change while in Excel. You will change data in the worksheet to verify that the worksheet data that is pasted into the memo is not linked to Excel.

Edit the value in cell F6 to 177380. View the line chart to verify that the chart was automatically updated to reflect this change in data.

To see the changes made in the memo, switch to Word.

Your screen should be similar to Figure 6-8.

Figure 6-8

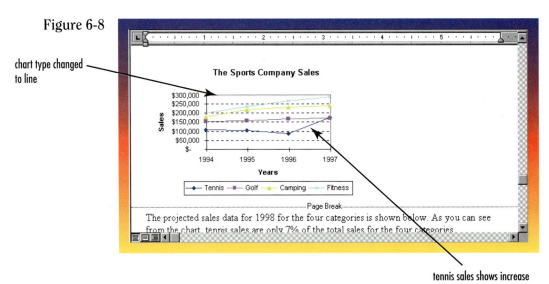

chart type changed to line

tennis sales shows increase

The chart in the memo reflects the change in both chart type and the change in data for the tennis sales. This is because any changes you make in the chart in Excel will be automatically reflected in the linked chart in the Word document.

Next, scroll the memo to view the table.

The table does not reflect the change in data made in Excel. This is because the table is not linked to the worksheet.

Whenever a document is opened that contains links, the application looks for the source file and automatically updates the linked objects. If there are many links, updating can take a lot of time. Additionally, if you move the source file to another location, or perform other operations that may interfere with the link, your link will not work. To help with situations like these, you can edit the settings associated with links. To see how you do this,

Choose: <u>Edit/Links</u>

The dialog box on your screen should be similar to Figure 6-9.

Figure 6-9

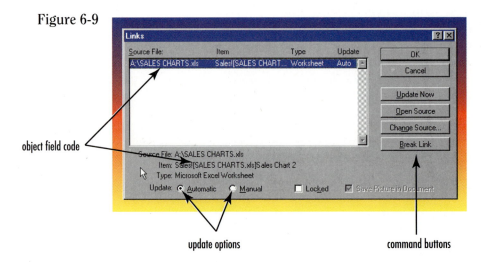

object field code

update options

command buttons

The Links dialog box displays the object field codes for all links in the document in the list box. The field code specifies the path and name of the source file, the range of linked cells or object name, the type of file, and the update status. Below the list box the details for the selected link are displayed. The two update option buttons, Automatic and Manual, are used to change how the object is updated. The default option, Automatic, updates the linked object whenever the destination document is opened or the source file changes. If you change to Manual, the destination document is not automatically updated and you must use the Update Now command button to update the link. The Open Source command button will open the source document for the selected link, and the Change Source button allows you to modify the path to the source document. To return to Excel and change the value in cell F6 back to its original value,

Choose: **Open Source**

Because the workbook and Excel application were already open, using the Open Source command button simply switched to the application window.

Change the value in cell F6 back to 77380. Switch to Word and scroll the memo to view the chart.

The chart is updated automatically again to reflect the change in data.

To see how the chart appears on the page, switch to Page Layout view and set the zoom to 50%. Scroll the memo upward to view both the table and the chart.

Your screen should be similar to Figure 6-10.

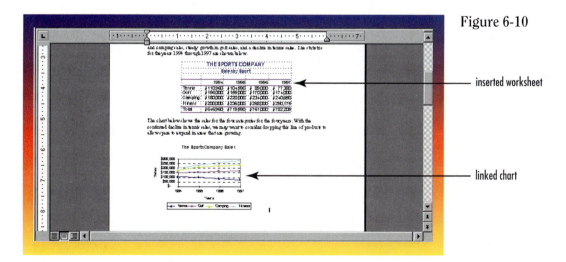

Figure 6-10

— inserted worksheet

— linked chart

You feel the chart would look better if it were surrounded with an outline border and centered. Like the worksheet table object, a linked object can be sized, moved, copied to another location, or deleted like any other object.

Display the Borders toolbar. Select the chart object.

Click:  **Outside Border**

Then, to move the object, you must first enclose the object in a frame.

Choose: **Insert/F̲rame**

> If the border is not completely displayed, it is because the magnification is too small.

Move the chart object so it is centered horizontally on the page. Deselect the chart to see the border line you created.

Your screen should be similar to Figure 6-11.

Figure 6-11

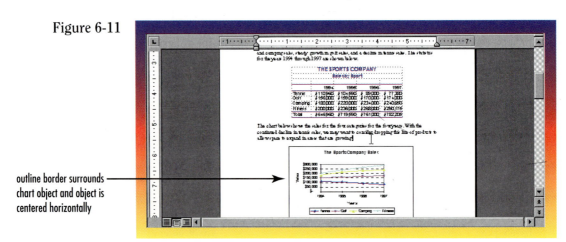

outline border surrounds chart object and object is centered horizontally

> Normal view will not display the linked object in its new position.

Return the zoom back to 100% and the view to Normal.

Embedding Objects

On a second page of the memo, you want to show the projected sales data for 1998.

Move to the second blank line immediately below the paragraph on the second page of the memo.

Switch to Excel. Make the Projected sheet active.

You want to display both the projected worksheet data and pie chart in the memo.

Select the range of cells A1 through I20. Copy the selection to Clipboard and switch to Word.

Because you think the manager may want to change the projected data, you will embed this selection in the memo.

Concept 3: Embedded Object

Information can also be pasted into another application document as an **embedded object**. An object that is embedded is stored in the destination document and becomes part of the document. The entire file, not just the selection that is displayed in the destination document, becomes part of the document. This makes a document containing an embedded object much larger than a document containing the same object using linking.

If the user has access to the application that created the embedded document, called the **server**, the embedded object can be edited or updated from within the destination document. The connection to the server is established by the creation of an embedded object field code. Double-clicking on the embedded object starts the server application within the destination document. Any changes you make to the embedded object are not reflected in the original source file.

Choose: Edit/Paste Special

> To embed an entire file, use Insert/Object.

The Paste Special dialog box on your screen should be similar to Figure 6-12.

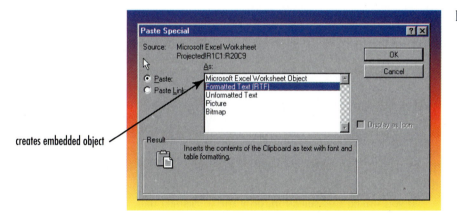

Figure 6-12

creates embedded object

The Paste option creates an embedded object. This is the preselected option. The As list box displays five file format types that can be used to embed the object. To embed the contents of Clipboard into a document so it can be edited using the server application, select the option that displays the server name. Because the Clipboard contents contain an Excel worksheet object, the application name is reflected in the object option.

Select: Microsoft Excel Worksheet Object
Choose: OK

Your screen should be similar to Figure 6-13.

Figure 6-13

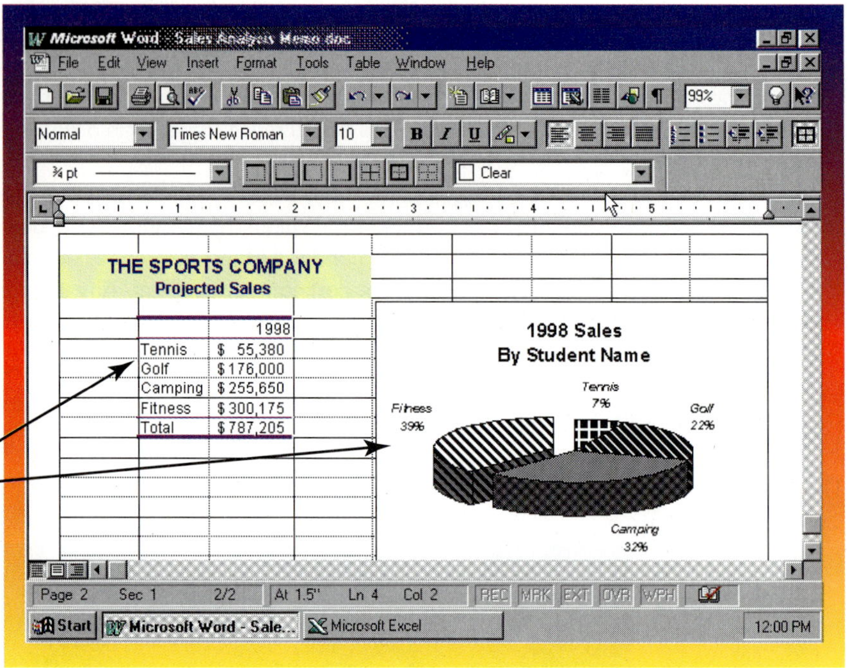

worksheet and chart embedded object

The entire worksheet selection including the chart is displayed in the memo at the location of the insertion point. When an object is embedded, the entire selection is pasted and displayed in the destination document as a single object. The embedded object has an embed object field code that identifies the application type used to create the object.

If you linked this selection, only the worksheet data would appear and be linked in the destination. The chart would not be included in the link. To link the chart, you would need to select the chart object separately and establish a separate link and a separate object.

Select the embedded object and add a border around it. Close the Borders toolbar.

Updating an Embedded Object

To demonstrate how an embedded object works, you will close the source file and application and edit the worksheet from within the Word document. A document that contains a linked or embedded object is called a **container file** or **compound document**.

Switch to Excel. Move to cell A1 of both sheets and save the workbook file as 1994-1998 SALES CHARTS. Exit the program. If Excel asks if you want to save the Clipboard contents to a file, choose No.

The Word application window is displayed.

You show the completed memo to the manager. After looking at it, the manager realizes that the Sales department has recently issued updated sales projections, and asks you to change the memo to reflect this new information.

The server application is used to edit data in an embedded object. To open the server, simply double-click on the embedded object. The embedded object field code identifies the server application to open.

Open the embedded object server application.

Your screen should be similar to Figure 6-14.

> The menu equivalent is **E**dit/Worksheet **O**bject/**E**dit. The object must be selected first.

Figure 6-14

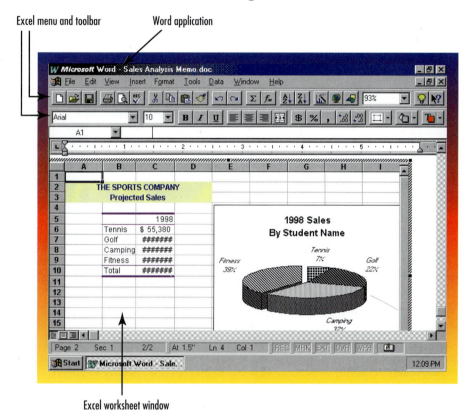

The server application, in this case Excel 7.0, is opened. The Excel menus and toolbars replace some of the menus and toolbars in the Word application window. The selected embedded object is displayed in an editing worksheet window. Now you can use the server commands to edit the object.

If necessary, expand the column width of column C too fully display the values. Edit the tennis projection value to 48,000 and the golf projection to 200,000.

The chart is updated to reflect the change in data. The new projection has decreased the tennis percentage to 6 percent and increased golf to 25 percent. The original Excel file, SALES CHARTS, has not been affected by these changes.

After editing is complete, close the server application by clicking anywhere outside the object.

Edit the lead-in sentence in the memo to reflect the new tennis value (6%). Save the memo as 1994-1998 SALES ANALYSIS. Preview both pages of the memo in the preview screen.

Your screen should be similar to Figure 6-15.

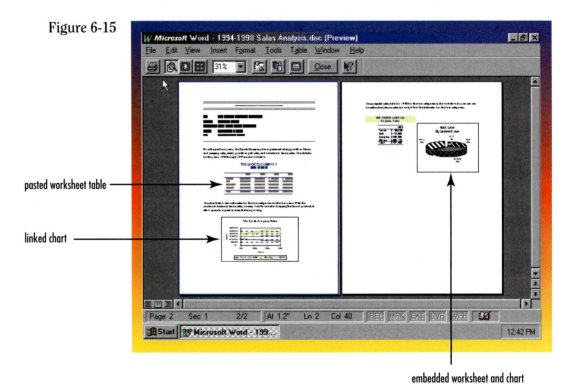

Figure 6-15

pasted worksheet table

linked chart

embedded worksheet and chart

Print the memo.

Note: Do not set the printer to draft quality. If you do, the charts will not print.

Exit Word.

Deciding When to Use Linking or Embedding

Most documents would not include both linked and embedded objects. This is because the reasons for using each are different.

Use linking when:	Use embedding when:
■ File size is important	■ File size is not important
■ Users have access to the source file and application	■ Users have access to the application, but not to the source files
■ The information is updated frequently	■ The data changes infrequently

LAB REVIEW

Key Terms

compound document   (SS218)
container file   (SS218)
destination document   (SS211)
embedded object   (SS217)
linked object   (SS211)
live link   (SS211)
object field code   (SS211)
server   (SS217)
source document   (SS211)

Command Summary

Command	**Action**
Edit/Paste **S**pecial/Paste **L**ink	Links a selection
Edit/Paste **S**pecial/**P**aste	Embeds a selection
Edit/Worksheet **O**bject/**E**dit	Edits an embedded object
Tools/**O**ptions/View/**G**ridlines	Turns on/off display of cell gridlines

SPREADSHEET

Matching

1. linked object   _____   a. a link that automatically updates when the document is opened
2. live link   _____   b. document in which object is inserted
3. source document   _____   c. application that created embedded document
4. compound document   _____   d. an object that is represented in destination document and connected to source
5. embedded object   _____   e. an object that is stored in destination document
6. object field code   _____   f. a document that contains linked and/or embedded objects
7. destination document   _____   g. document in which the linked object was created
8. server   _____   h. code associated with a linked or embedded object.

Hands-On Practice Exercises

Step by Step

Rating System
★ Easy
★★ Moderate
★★★ Difficult

1. Karen works for a large hotel chain in the marketing department. She has recently researched hotel occupancy rates for the Phoenix area and has created a worksheet and stacked-column chart of the data. Now Karen wants to send a memo containing the chart to her supervisor.

a. Open a new Word document using the Professional template.

b. Delete the "Company Name Here" text box. In the header, replace the placeholder information in brackets with the following:

   TO: **Brad Wise**
   FROM: **Karen Howard**
   CC: **[your name]**
   RE: **Hotel Occupancy**

c. Replace the body placeholder text with the following:

   Below is a column chart showing the percent of hotel occupancy rates in the Phoenix area for the years 1990 to 1995.

d. Enter two blank lines below the paragraph.

e. Load Excel and open the workbook file HOTEL. Link the stacked-column chart to below the paragraph in the Word memo.

f. Change the stacked-column chart to a side-by-side column chart.

g. Add a border around the chart object in the memo. Center the chart in the memo.

h. You would like to add another sentence to the memo. Enter the following sentence below the chart:

   The chart shows that the resort occupancy rate is consistently slightly higher than the overall occupancy rate.

i. Save the Word document as HOTEL OCCUPANCY. Preview and print the document. Resave the Excel file.

2. Sean Rees has a summer internship with a local car dealership. He has researched changes in new and used car prices and created a worksheet and line chart of the data. Now Sean wants to send a memo containing the worksheet and chart to his supervisor.

a. Open a new Word document using the Contemporary Memo template. Select and remove the faint gray circle element below and to the left of the How to Use the Memo Template information.

b. Replace the placeholder information in the memo heading with the following information:

TO: **Supervisor**
CC: **[your name]**
FROM: **Sean Rees**
Date: **[current date]**
RE: **Changes in Car Prices**

c. Replace the body placeholder text with the following:

Below is the data you requested showing the percent change in new vs used car prices. I have embedded the Excel worksheet in this Word document file so you can make changes to it if necessary.

d. Enter two blank lines below the paragraph.

e. Enter another paragraph as follows:

I also created a line chart of this data (shown below).

f. Enter two blank lines below the paragraph.

g. Load Excel and open the workbook file CAR ANALYSIS. Below the first paragraph of the Word memo, embed the worksheet and line chart from the workbook CAR ANALYSIS. Add a border around the embedded object. If necessary, adjust the placement of the object so it appears centered under the paragraph.

h. Exit Excel. Do not resave the workbook.

i. The supervisor wants to change the chart to a column chart. Change the embedded line chart to a column chart. Delete the Increasing Cost text box and arrow.

j. Save the Word document as NEW AND USED CAR COMPARISON. Preview and print the document.

3. After completing the first and second half budget for The Sports Company, you want to give the manager the Excel file. You would like to include a memo on a separate sheet of this file to briefly explain the worksheet contents.

a. Open the workbook file 1998 BUDGET that you created at the end of Lab 2. Insert a new sheet before the First Half sheet and change the sheet tab name to Memo.

b. Open Word and create the following memo to the store manager.

TO: **Sports Company Store Manager**
FROM: **[your name]**
DATE: **[current date]**

The 1998 first and second half budget data is contained on the following two sheets. To view the budget worksheets click on the appropriate tab.

If you have any changes or suggestions about the budget, I have scheduled time to work on the budget again next week.

c. Save the memo as BUDGET MEMO. Link the memo to the Memo sheet in the Excel file.

d. After inserting the memo, you decide to add a sentence about the year-to-date income total. Switch back to Word and add the following after the first sentence.

Please note that the second half budget worksheet contains a year-to-date income total in cell H21.

e. Resave the memo and switch to Excel. Save the Excel file as SPORTS COMPANY BUDGET.

f. Print the Word memo document and the Excel Memo sheet only.

On Your Own

4. Dave Robson has gathered population statistics on several Native American tribes for a report and has created a worksheet and pie chart of this data. Now Dave wants to include the worksheet and chart as a separate page in his report. Create a new Word document using the Elegant Report template. Replace the Company Name placeholder with your name. Replace the other placeholder text with an appropriate title and subtitle.

Below the titles, copy and paste the worksheet data from the Excel workbook file TRIBE POPULATIONS.

Box and center the table and remove the gridlines. Copy and link the chart to the document below the table. Box, center, and size the pie chart. Unexplode the Apache slice.

Resave the workbook file. Delete pages 2 and 3 of the template. Save the Word document as Tribal Populations. Preview and print the document.

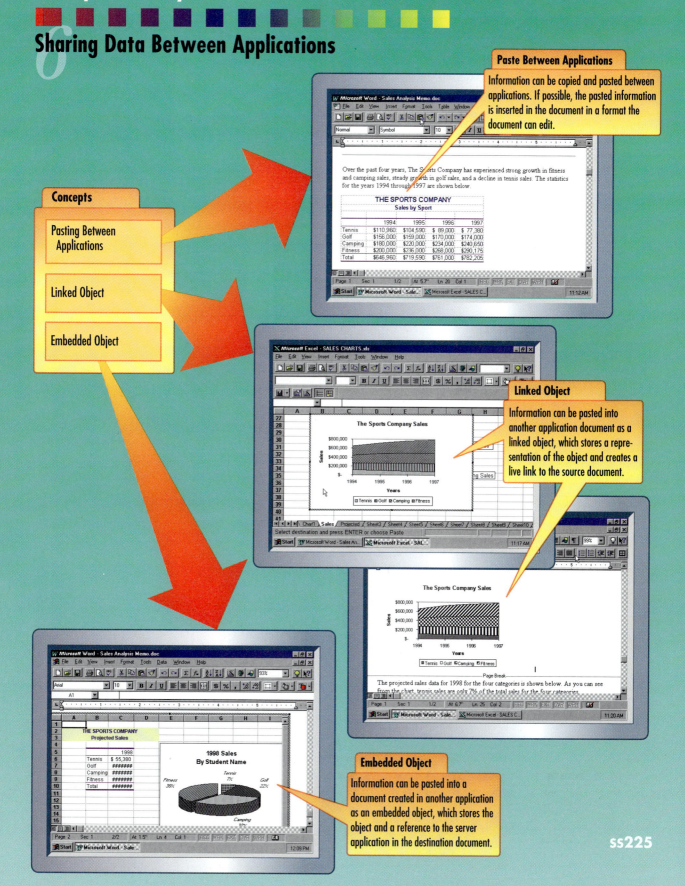

Case Project

Introduction

This project is designed to reinforce your knowledge of the worksheet features used in the Excel labs. You will also be expected to use the Help feature to learn more about advanced features available in Excel.

Case

Marianne Virgili is the Director of the Glenwood Springs Chamber Resort Association. Each quarter the Chamber sends a newsletter called *Trends* to all Chamber members. The Director has asked you to create the end-of-year balance sheet, tables, and graphs to be included in the first-quarter issue of *Trends*. The first-quarter issue will contain the end-of-year balance sheet for the previous year.

Part 1

Open the file GLENWOOD SPRING 1998 BALANCE. This file contains the Glenwood Springs Chamber Resort Association's 1998 balance sheet.

   a. Change the width of columns A and B to fully display the headings. Change the width of column C to 4. Delete column D.

   b. Enter the formulas and functions in column D needed to complete the totals for the balance sheet. The Total Assets number should equal the Total Liabilities plus Capital number.

   c. Format the numbers to be displayed with commas and two decimal places. Format the first number in each group and all totals as currency with two decimal places. If necessary, increase the column widths to fully display the numbers.

   d. Delete all blank rows above each subtotal and grand total.

   e. Add a bottom-line border under the last number in each group above a subtotal and under subtotals immediately above the grand total. Add a double-line border under the grand total of each group.

SPREADSHEET

f. Change the size of the main title to be displayed larger than the rest of the text. Italicize and bold the labels in cells A4 and A22.

g. Insert three blank rows above the main title. Enter your name in cell A1 and the date in a header. Save and replace the workbook.

h. Preview the worksheet before printing. Print the worksheet on one page.

Part 2

This issue of *Trends* will contain two tables. The first table will provide employment information for 1997 to 1998 for Garfield county. The second table will provide information on gross sales.

a. The employment information is shown below. Create a worksheet from this data.

Job Category	1997	1998
Agr., For., Fish.	141	174
Mining	705	813
Construction	856	1171
Manufacturing	284	327
Trans., Comm., Util.	443	504
Wholesale Trade	338	410
Retail Trade	2580	2859
Fin., Ins., Real Est.	522	601
Services	2679	2767
Non-classified	23	15
Government	2234	2328

b. Format the two columns of data to display commas with no decimal places. Add an appropriate title to the worksheet.

c. Add a third column of data to show the percent change from 1997 to 1998. Enter the column heading "% Change" above the new column. Enter the formula to calculate the percent change from 1997 to 1998. Format the column as percent with two decimal places.

d. Add a row to show the total for the two columns of data and the percent change. Enter a row heading and the formulas to make these calculations. Format the data appropriately.

e. Enhance the appearance of the worksheet by adding such features as bold, bottom borders, different fonts, and so on.

f. Put your name and the date in a header. Save and print the worksheet.

The second table will display the percent of gross sales for the second half of 1998 for the five major cities in the county.

g. Open a new worksheet file. Create a worksheet from the following data.

City	Sales	% of Total
Glenwood Springs	165.7	
Silt	3.4	
Rifle	34.7	
Carbondale	19.3	
Parachute	2.3	
Remainder of County	46.1	

h. Add a row to show the total sales. Enter a row heading and formula to make this calculation.

i. Enter the worksheet title "TOTAL GROSS SALES for JUNE-SEPT. 1998 (in millions of dollars)."

j. Enter the formula to calculate the percent of total. Display the numbers as percents with one decimal place.

k. Enhance the appearance of the worksheet using such features as bottom borders, bold, and font changes.

l. Enter your name and the current date in the worksheet.

m. Save and print the worksheet.

Part 3

This issue of *Trends* will also include two charts. The first chart will be a visual representation of the gross sales table you created in Part 2.

a. Open the file you created containing the gross sales data. Create a 3-D pie chart of the gross sales data below the worksheet.

b. Add an appropriate title to the chart. Increase the font size of the title. Display the legend labels next to the percent values.

c. Add patterns and explode the Carbondale wedge of the pie.

d. Save and replace the worksheet. Print the worksheet.

The second chart included in this issue of *Trends* will display the gross sales for each quarter of 1998 and the last two quarters of 1997 for Garfield county and the two surrounding counties, Eagle and Pitkin.

e. Open the file COUNTY GROSS SALES.XLS. Enter your name in cell A1 and the date in cell A2.

f. Create a 3-D column chart of the data displayed in the worksheet in a new sheet.

g. Enter an appropriate title. Add X-axis and Y-axis titles.

h. Add patterns to the columns.

i. Create a header that contains your name and the current date centered over the chart.

j. Save and replace the worksheet. Print the chart only.

Glossary of Key Terms

Absolute reference: Makes the cell reference in a formula remain the same (absolute) when copied. Indicated by a $ character entered before the column letter or row number or both.

Activate: To prepare a chart for editing. Chart appears with a blue hashed border or in a separate window.

Active cell: The cell displaying the cell selector and which will be affected by the next entry or procedure.

Active pane: The pane that contains the cell selector.

Active sheet: A worksheet that is open and that can be modified.

Alignment: The vertical or horizontal placement and orientation of an entry in a cell.

Area chart: A chart that shows trends by emphasizing the area under the curve.

Argument: The data the function can work on. It can be a number, a cell address, a range of cells, or a formula.

AutoCalculate button: A status bar button that shows the sum or average of values or a count of entries in a selected range.

Autoformat: A built-in combination of formats that can be applied to a range.

Automatic recalculation: The recalculation of a formula within the worksheet whenever a value in a referenced cell in the formula changes.

Category-axis title: A label that describes the X axis.

Category name: Labels displayed along the X axis in a chart to identify the data being plotted.

Cell: The space created by the intersection of a vertical column and a horizontal row.

Cell gridlines: The horizontal and vertical lines in a worksheet that create the rows and columns of the table.

Cell selector: The heavy border surrounding a cell in the worksheet that identifies the active cell.

Chart: A visual representation of data in a worksheet.

Chart gridlines: Lines extending from the axis lines across the plot area that make it easier to read and evaluate the chart data.

Column: A vertical block of cells one cell wide in the worksheet.

Column chart: A chart that displays data as vertical columns.

Column letters: The border of letters across the top of the worksheet area that identifies the columns in the worksheet.

Combination chart: A chart that displays data series as columns and lines.

Compound document: A document that contains linked or embedded objects. Also called a container file.

Constant: A value that does not change unless you change it directly by typing in another entry.

Container file: See definition of compound document.

Current workbook file: The workbook that displays the cell selector and that your next procedure will affect.

Data labels: Labels for data points or bars that show the values being plotted on a chart.

Data marker: Represents a data series on a chart. It can be a symbol, color, or pattern, depending upon the type of chart.

Data series: The numbers to be charted.

Date numbers: The integers assigned to the days from January 1, 1900 through December 31, 2099.

Dependent workbook: In an external reference formula, the workbook that receives the data.

Destination: The cell or range of cells that receives the data from the source range.

Destination document: A document in which a linked object is inserted.

Docked toolbar: A toolbar that is attached to a toolbar dock.

Embedded chart: A chart that is inserted into another file.

Embedded object: An object that is stored in the destination document.

Excel application window: The screen that is displayed when the Excel program is started.

Explode: To separate a wedge of a pie chart slightly from the other wedges in the pie.

External reference formula: A formula that creates a link between worksheets.

Fill handle: A small black square located in the lower right corner of the selection that is used to create a series or copy to adjacent cells with a mouse.

Floating toolbar: A toolbar that is displayed in a separate window and is not docked.

Font: The typeface, type size, and style associated with a worksheet entry that can be selected to improve the appearance of the worksheet.

Footer: A line of text printed just above the bottom margin on a page.

Format: The display of entries in the worksheet.

Formatting toolbar: A toolbar that contains buttons used to change the format of a worksheet.

Formula: A mathematical expression that yields a numeric value based on the relationship between two or more cells in the worksheet.

Formula bar: The bar near the top of the Excel window that displays the cell contents.

Freeze: To hold in place on the screen specified rows or columns or both when scrolling.

Function: A built-in formula that performs a calculation automatically.

Header: A line of text printed just below the top margin on a page.

Heading: Row and column entries that are used to create the structure of the worksheet and describe other worksheet entries.

Landscape: The orientation of the printed worksheet so it prints sideways across the length of the page.

Legend: A brief description of the symbols used in a chart that represent the data ranges.

Line chart: A chart that represents data as a set of points along a line.

Link: A relationship created between workbooks by entering an external reference formula. When data in one workbook changes, the other workbook is automatically updated.

Linked object: When an object is linked, the data is stored in the source document and a graphic representation of the data is displayed in the destination document.

Live link: A linked object that automatically reflects in the destination document any changes made in the source document.

Lock: A type of worksheet protection that prevents changes to cells.

Logical operators: Symbols used in formulas that compare values in two or more cells.

Minimal recalculation: The recalculation of only the formulas in a worksheet that are affected by a change of data.

Mixed reference: A cell address that is part absolute and part relative.

Name box: The area located on the left side of the formula bar that is used to display the cell reference of the active cell.

Nested function: A second argument in a function that is enclosed within its own set of parentheses.

Nonadjacent selection: Cells or ranges that are not adjacent but are included in the same selection.

Number: A cell entry that contains any of the digits 0 to 9, and any of the special characters + = ( ) , . / $ % E e.

Object: An element such as a text box that can be added to a workbook and that can be selected.

Object field code: A code that references the location of the source document for both linked and embedded objects.

Operands: The values on which a numeric formula performs a calculation.

Pane: A division of the worksheet window, either horizontal or vertical, through which different areas of the worksheet can be viewed at the same time.

Password: Prevents unauthorized users form entering data in a worksheet.

Pie chart: A chart that compares parts to the whole. Each value in the data range is a wedge of the pie (circle).

Plot area: The area of the chart bounded by the axes.

Portrait: The orientation of the printed worksheet so it prints across the width of a page.

Protection: A worksheet feature that prevents changes to data and formats.

Range: A rectangular block of adjoining cells in the worksheet.

Range name: A descriptive name assigned to a cell or range of cells.

Reference: The column letter and row number of a cell.

Relative reference: A cell reference that automatically adjusts the cell references in a formula to the new location in the worksheet when the formula is copied or moved.

Row: A horizontal block of cells one cell high in the worksheet.

Row number: The border of numbers along the left side of the worksheet area that identifies the rows in the worksheet.

Save: Places the contents of a document in a file on a disk, preventing you from losing your work due to a power failure or other mishap.

Selection handle: Small boxes surrounding a selected object that are used to size the object.

Server: The application in which an embedded object is created.

Sheet: A division of a workbook that is used to display different types of information in Excel.

Sheet tab: On the bottom of the workbook window, the tabs where the sheet names appear.

Source: The cell or range of cells whose contents you want to copy.

Source document: The document that stores the data for the linked object.

Source workbook: In an external reference formula, the workbook that supplies the data.

Stacked-column chart: A chart that displays the data values as columns stacked upon each other.

Standard toolbar: A toolbar that contains buttons used to complete the most frequently used menu commands.

Style: A named combination of formats that can be applied to a selection.

Tab scroll buttons: Located to the left of the sheet tabs, they are used to scroll sheet tabs right or left.

Template: A predesigned worksheet that contains blank spaces for entry of data.

Text: A cell entry that contains text, numbers, or any other special characters.

3D reference: A reference for a cell or range in another sheet or sheets in the same workbook.

Title: In a chart, descriptive text that explains the contents of the chart.

Toolbar dock: The region around the edge of the worksheet window where toolbars can be placed.

Typeface: The appearance and shape of characters. Some common typefaces are Roman and Courier.

Value-axis title: A label that describes the values on the Y axis.

Variable: A value that changes if the data it depends on changes.

What-if analysis: A technique used to evaluate what effect changing one or more values in formulas has on other values in the worksheet.

Word wrap: Feature that automatically determines when to begin the next line of text.

Workbook: The file in which you work and store sheets created in Excel.

Workbook window: A window that displays an open workbook file.

Worksheet: Similar to a financial spreadsheet in that it is a rectangular grid of rows and columns used to enter data.

Workspace: The area of the Excel application window where workbook windows are displayed.

X axis: The horizontal axis of a graph.

Y axis: The vertical axis of a graph.

Command Summary

Command	Shortcut	Toolbar	Action
File/**O**pen <filename>	Ctrl + O	🗁	Opens an existing workbook file
File/**C**lose			Closes open workbook file
File/**S**ave <filename>	Ctrl + S	💾	Saves current file on disk using same file name
File/Save **A**s <filename>			Saves current file on disk using a new file name
File/Save **A**s/Save File As Type			Sets file format for document
File/Proper**t**ies			Displays information about a file
File/**P**rint	Ctrl + P	🖨	Prints a sheet
File/**P**rint/Page Set**u**p/**L**andscape			Prints worksheet across length of paper
File/**P**rint/Page Set**u**p/Header/Footer			Adds header and/or footer
File/E**x**it		✕	Exits Excel
Edit/**U**ndo	Ctrl + Z	↶	Undoes last editing or formatting change
Edit/**R**epeat	Ctrl + Y	↷	Repeats last-used command
Edit/**C**opy	Ctrl + C	📋	Copies selected data to Clipboard
Edit/**P**aste	Ctrl + V	📋	Pastes selected data from Clipboard
Edit/Paste **S**pecial/**P**aste			Embeds a selection
Edit/Paste **S**pecial/Paste L**in**k			Links a selection
Edit/F**i**ll			Fills selected cells with contents of source cell
Edit/F**i**ll/**S**eries/AutoF**i**ll			Automatically extends data and alphanumeric headings
Edit/**D**elete/Entire **R**ow			Deletes selected rows
Edit/**D**elete/Entire **C**olumn			Deletes selected columns
Edit/**M**ove or Copy Sheet			Moves or copies current sheet
Edit/Worksheet **O**bject/**E**dit			Edits an embedded object

SPREADSHEET

ss236 Excel 7.0a

Command	Shortcut	Toolbar	Action
View/Toolbars			Displays or hides toolbars
View/Zoom		100%	Changes magnification of window
Insert/Rows			Inserts blank row above insertion point
Insert/Columns			Inserts a blank column
Insert/Worksheet			Inserts a new, blank worksheet in workbook
Insert/Chart		[icon]	Inserts chart into worksheet
Insert/Function	Shift + F3	f_x	Inserts a function
Insert/Data Labels			Inserts data labels into chart
Insert/Titles			Inserts titles into chart
Insert/Name/Define			Assigns name to a cell or range of cells
Insert/Name/Paste			Places name in formula bar or lists names in worksheet
Insert/Name/Create			Creates names using text in cells
Insert/Note			Inserts a note to a cell
Insert/New Data			Inserts new data into chart
Format/Cells/Protection			Changes protection of selected cells to locked or unlocked
Format/Cells	Ctrl + 1		Applies formats to selection
Format/Cells/Number/Currency			Applies Currency format to selection
Format/Cells/Numbering/Accounting			Applies Accounting format to selection
Format/Cells/Font			Changes font and attributes of cell contents
Format/Cells/Font/Color		[icon]	Adds color to text
Format/Cells/Alignment		[icons]	Aligns data left, center, or right in cell space
Format/Cells/Alignment/Center across selection		[icon]	Centers cell contents across selected cells
Format/Cells/Border/Outline			Adds border around selection
Format/Cells/Border/Bottom			Adds border to bottom edge of selection
Format/Cells/Patterns		[icon]	Adds shading to selection
Format/Column/Width			Changes width of columns
Format/Column/Autofit Selection			Changes column width to match widest cell entry
Format/Sheet/Rename			Renames sheet
Format/Style			Changes attributes of cell entries
Format/AutoFormat			Applies one of 16 built-in table formats to worksheet range
Format/Chart Type		[icon]	Changes type of chart
Format/Selected Legend	Ctrl + 1		Changes legend

Command	Shortcut	Toolbar	Action
F**o**rmat/S**e**lected Data Labels	Ctrl + 1		Changes format of data labels
F**o**rmat/S**e**lected Data Series	Ctrl + 1		Changes format of selected data series
Tools/**S**pelling	F7	ABC✓	Spell-checks worksheet
Tools/**G**oal Seek			Adjusts value in specified cell until a formula dependent on that cell reaches specified result
Tools/Sol**v**er			Calculates a formula to achieve a given value by changing one of variables that affects formula
Tools/**P**rotection/**P**rotect Sheet			Turns on protection for all locked cells
Tools/**P**rotection/**U**nprotect Sheet			Turns off protection for all locked cells
Window/**N**ew Window			Creates an additional window for active workbook
Window/**A**rrange/**T**iled			Arranges open windows side by side
Window/**S**plit			Divides window into four panes at active cell
Window/**F**reeze Panes			Freezes panes to top and left of active cell

SPREADSHEET

Windows 95 Review

The following is an alphabetical arrangement of the most common Windows 95 features. The features are described in general. Wherever applicable, a How To section discusses how to perform the task.

Arranging Windows: There are two ways to arrange windows: cascade and tile.

    Cascade   Layers open windows, displaying the active window fully and only the title bars of all other open windows behind it.

    Tile   Resizes each open window and arranges the windows vertically or horizontally on the desktop

Cascading windows is useful if you want to work primarily in one window but you want to see the title of other open windows. Tiling is most useful when you want to work in several applications simultaneously, because it allows you to quickly see the contents of all open windows and move between them. However, the more windows that are open, the smaller the space available to display the tiled window contents.

    The commands to tile windows on the Windows 95 desktop are displayed in the taskbar shortcut menu. In most Windows 95 applications, the commands are found in the Window menu.

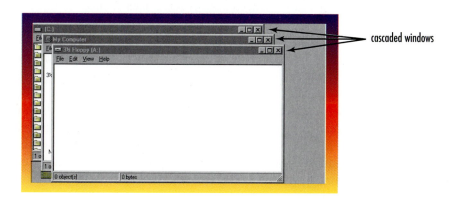

cascaded windows

SPREADSHEET

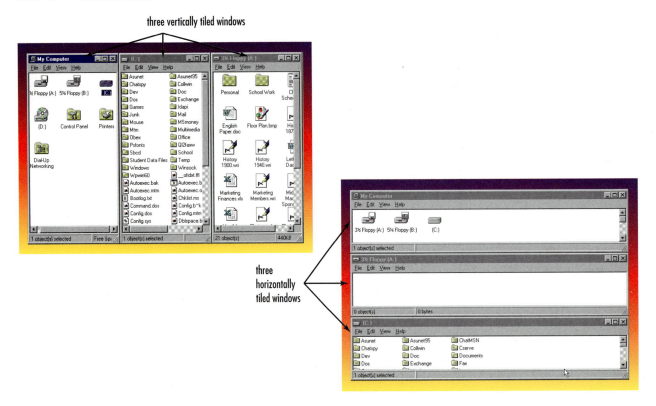

Cut, Copy, and Paste: All Windows applications include features that allow you to remove (cut), duplicate (copy) and insert (paste) information from one location to another. The location that contains the information you want to cut or copy is called the source. Then the command to cut or copy the selection is used, and the selection is stored in a temporary storage area in your computer's memory called the Clipboard. Finally, you select the location, called the destination, where you want to insert a copy of the information stored in the Clipboard and use the Paste command.

How To: The commands to perform these tasks are found in the Edit menu. The toolbar equivalents are ✂ Cut, ▣ Copy, ▣ Paste, and the keyboard shortcuts are Ctrl + X to Cut, Ctrl + C to Copy and Ctrl + V to Paste. The information must be selected before it is copied or cut.

Desktop: The Windows 95 screen is called a desktop. It displays icons that represent various tools and features. Like your own desk at home, you can add and remove items from the desktop, rearrange items, or you can get rid of them by throwing them away in the "trash." You can also open items and, much like a drawer in your desk, find other tools or materials you have stored. You can place these items on the desktop or take items off the desktop and place them in the "drawer." Just like your own desk, your most frequently used items should be on the desktop so you can quickly begin work, while those items that you use less frequently should be put away for easy access as needed.

Dialog Box: A dialog box is how Windows programs provide and request information from you in order to complete a task. All dialog boxes have a title bar at the top of the box that displays a name identifying the contents of the dialog box. Inside the dialog box are areas to select or specify the needed information and command buttons.

How To: Select an item in a dialog box by clicking on the item, by pressing [Alt] and the underlined letter, or by tabbing to the item. Type information in a text box. Select (highlight) an item in a list box. Click on option buttons and check boxes to turn on/off the item.

Tab dialog box: Many dialog boxes include tabs that open to display options related to the feature in the tab. The tab names appear across the top of the dialog box and indicate the different categories of tabs. The tab name of the active tab is displayed in bold. The options displayed in the open tab are the available options for the feature.

How To: To select and open a tab in a tab dialog box, click on it with the mouse or move to the tab using [Ctrl] + [Tab] to select the tab to the right or [Ctrl] + [Shift] + [Tab] to select the tab to the left.

Dialog Box features: The features shown in the table below are found in dialog boxes. However, not all features are found in every dialog box.

Feature	Description
text box	An area where you type in the requested information.
option buttons	An option preceded with a circle. The selected option displays a black dot. Only one option can be selected from a list of option buttons.
list box	A box displaying a list of information from which you can select.
drop-down list box	A box that displays the currently selected item and a ▼ button. Clicking the ▼ button displays a drop-down list of items from which you can select.
check box	An option preceded with a square. The selected options display a ☑. More than one check box option can be selected at a time.
sliding controls	Dragging the lever in the control increases or decreases the related setting, such as volume.
command buttons	Instruct Windows to carry out the instructions on the button. The two most common command buttons are OK and Cancel. Other buttons you will see are Close, Help, Options, Setup, Display, and Settings.

Drag and Drop: Common to all Windows applications is the ability to copy or move selections by dragging and dropping. This feature is most convenient for copying or moving short distances or when the place you want to drag and drop to is visible onscreen. Using drag and drop does not copy to the Clipboard.

How To: First select the item to be copied or moved. Then point to the selection and drag. A drag-and-drop insertion point + appears while dragging to show where the selection will be pasted. When you release the mouse button, the selection is copied or moved to the new location. To copy, hold down [Ctrl] while dragging. The mouse pointer displays a + when you copy.

Editing: Making changes to or correcting existing entries is called editing. Editing is commonly performed in all applications as well as within text boxes used in dialog boxes or Wizards.

How To: Generally, editing is performed by moving the insertion point to the location of the error, deleting the text that needs to be modified, and retyping the entry correctly. Two frequently used keys to delete entries are the [Backspace] key (removes characters to the left of the insertion point) and the [Delete] key (removes characters to the right of the insertion point). You can also select the text to be removed and replace it with existing text as you type.

Files and Folders: The information your computer uses is stored in files. The instructions used to run a program are stored in program files. For example, the word processing program on your computer consists of many files that contain the program statements required to use the program. The information you create while using a program is stored in data files. For example, if you write a letter to a friend using the word processing program, the contents of the letter are stored as a data file.

In addition, you can create folders and subfolders in which you store files that are related. Storing related files in folders keeps the disk organized and makes it much easier to locate files. Both files and folders are identified by names that are descriptive of the contents of the file or folder.

The organization of folders, subfolders, and files on your disk is called a hierarchy or tree. The top-level folder of the disk is the main or root folder. This folder is created when the disk is formatted. All folders are branches from the main folder. Subfolders are branches under a folder. Files can be stored in the root folder, a folder, or a subfolder. The figure in (left) is a graphical representation of folders and subfolders.

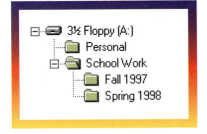

Help: The Windows Help facility is a quick way to find out information about commands or features. The Help menu is always the last menu in the menu bar and always contains a Help Topics command. This command opens the Help Topics tab dialog box. The three tabs, Contents, Index, and Find, provide different methods of getting help information. The Find tab allows you to select a word from a list that you need help on and then locates and displays all topics containing the word. The Contents tab displays broad Help categories preceded with book icons. Clicking on the book opens the book and displays additional books or specific Help topics. Topics are preceded with a ? icon, and when selected open the related Help window. The Index tab area allows you to select a topic from a list that you need help on. Windows Help can also display brief screen tips.

How To: Select Help Topics from the Help menu to open the Help dialog box. Clicking [?] What's this? in a dialog box and then clicking on the area in the box that you want Help information on displays a Screen Tip for the item. Clicking the [?] button in the toolbar displays Help Screen Tips on toolbar buttons, commands, or other items on the screen.

Insertion Point: The insertion point appears in a text entry area to show your location within the text. It appears as a vertical blinking bar.

How To: The insertion point is moved using the directional keys or by clicking in the text at the location you want the insertion point to appear. The mouse pointer appears as an I-beam when positioned in text, to make it easy to indicate where to move the insertion point.

Menus: A menu is one of many methods you can use to tell the program what you want it to do.

Start menu: The Start menu is a special Windows 95 menu that is used to access and begin all activities you want to perform on the computer.

How To: Click the Start button on the taskbar to open the Start menu.

Menus bars: Most menus are displayed in the menu bar immediately below the title bar of the window. When opened, a menu displays a list of commands, called a drop-down menu. Horizontal lines within many menus divide the commands into related groups.

How To: Most menu bar menus can be opened simply by clicking on the menu name. Using the keyboard, you need to press [Alt] or [F10] and type the underlined letter of the menu name. To clear a menu without making a selection, click anywhere outside the menu or press [Esc].

Shortcut menus: Other menus, called Shortcut menus, pop up when you right-click on an item. They contain commands related to the object you were pointing to when you right-clicked.

How To: Right-click an item to display its Shortcut menu.

SPREADSHEET

Selecting and Choosing commands: Once a menu is open, you can select and choose commands from the menu. Selecting indicates a command is "ready" to be used. Choosing a command performs the action associated with the command.

How To: You select a command by moving the highlight bar, called the selection cursor, to the command. Simply pointing to the command moves the selection cursor to it. (You can also move the selection cursor with the directional keys on your keyboard if it is more convenient.) You choose the selected command by clicking on it, or by typing the underlined command letter, or by pressing ⏎Enter. When the command is chosen, the associated action is performed.

Menu features: The features shown in the tables below are found on menus. However, not all features are found on every menu.

Feature	Description
ellipses (...)	Indicates that a dialog box will be displayed for you to specify additional information needed to carry out the command.
▶	Indicates a submenu of commands will be displayed.
dimmed command	Indicates that the command is not available for selection until certain other conditions are met.
shortcut key	A key or key combination that can be used to execute a command without using the menu.
checkmark (✔)	Indicates a toggle type command. Selecting it turns the feature on and off. The checkmark indicates the feature is on.
Bullet (•)	Indicates that the commands in that group are mutually exclusive: only one can be selected. The bullet indicates the currently selected feature.

A mouse

Mouse: The mouse is a hand-held hardware device that is attached to your computer. It controls an arrow called the mouse pointer that appears on your screen. The pointer movement is controlled by the rubber-coated ball on the bottom of the mouse. This ball must move within its socket in order for the pointer to move on the screen. The ball's movement is translated into signals that tell the computer how to move the onscreen pointer. Some computers use a track ball to move the mouse pointer. The direction the ball moves controls the direction the pointer moves.

The mouse pointer changes shape on the screen depending on what it is pointing to. Some of the most common shapes are shown in the table on the next page (right).

How To: Moving the mouse across your desktop moves the pointer in the direction you are moving the mouse. The mouse is held in the palm of your hand with your fingers resting on the buttons. If you pick up the mouse and move it to another location on your work surface, the pointer will not move on the screen.

On top of the mouse are two buttons. You use these buttons to choose items on the screen. The mouse actions and descriptions are shown in the next table.

Action	Description
Point	Move the mouse so the mouse pointer is positioned on the item you want to use.
Click	Quickly press and release the left mouse button.
Double-click	Quickly press and release the mouse button twice.
Drag	Move the mouse while holding down a mouse button.
Right-click	Quickly press and release the right mouse button.

Pointer Shape	Meaning
▶	Select
↔	Horizontal Resize
↕	Vertical Resize
↘	Diagonal Resize
✥	Move
▶?	Help Select
⊘	Unavailable
⌛	Wait
I	Text Select

Moving Windows: When open, windows may appear in different locations on your desktop. Sometimes the location of the window is inconvenient. Moving a window simply displays the window at another location on the desktop. It does not change the size of the window.

How To: A window is moved by clicking on the title bar and dragging an outline of the window to the new location on the desktop.

Naming Files: To save your work as a file on the disk, you must assign it a filename. The filename should be descriptive of the contents of the file. Windows 95 applications allow you to use long filenames of up to 255 characters. A filename can contain the letters A to Z, the numbers 0 to 9, spaces, and any of the following special characters: underscore (_), caret (^), dollar sign ($), tilde (~), exclamation point (!), number sign (#), percent sign (%), ampersand (&), hyphen (-), braces ({}), parentheses (), "at" sign (@), apostrophe ('), and the grave accent (`). Filenames cannot contain commas, backslashes, periods or any the following characters: \ / : * ? " < > |.

In addition to a filename, a filename extension can be added. A filename extension is up to three characters and is separated from the filename by a period. Generally a filename extension is used to identify the type of file. It is not always necessary to enter a filename extension, because most application programs automatically add an identifying filename extension to any files created using the program. For example, Word 7.0 files have a filename extension of .doc. The parts of a file name are shown below:

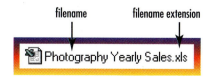

Properties: Properties are the settings associated with objects and files.

How To: An object's properties can be viewed using the View/Properties command or the Shortcut menu. A file's properties are viewed and changed using the File/Properties command. The Properties command is also commonly located on the Shortcut menu. The Property sheet displays the property settings.

Saving Files: While using any application, the document you are creating is stored in your computer's temporary memory as you work. It is lost if you do not save your work to a file on a disk. The file is a permanent copy of your document that is named and can be accessed at a later time. Although many programs create automatic backup files if your work is accidentally interrupted, it is still a good idea to save your work frequently.

How To: Two commands on the File menu of all Windows programs can be used to save a file: Save and Save As. The Save command saves a document using the same path and filename by replacing the contents of the existing disk file with the changes you have made. The Save As command allows you to select the path and provide a different filename. This command lets you save both an original version of a document and a revised document as two separate files. When you save a file for the first time, either command can be used.

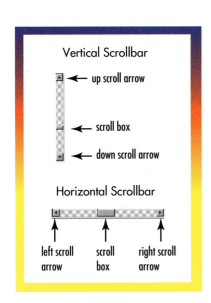

Scroll Bar: Whenever there is more information than can be displayed in a window or list box, a scroll bar is displayed. It is used with a mouse to bring additional lines of information into view. The vertical scroll bar is used to move vertically, and the horizontal scroll bar moves horizontally in the space. All scroll bars have scroll arrows and a scroll box. The location of the scroll box on the scroll bar shows your relative position within the area of available information. In many scroll bars, the size of the scroll box also indicates the relative amount of the information that is available. For example, a small box indicates that only a small amount of the total available information is displayed, whereas a large box indicates that almost all or a large portion of the total amount of available information is displayed.

How To: Clicking the scroll arrows in the vertical scroll bar scrolls the information in the window line by line vertically in the direction of the arrows. Clicking the scroll arrows in the horizontal scroll bar moves the information in the window horizontally. Dragging the scroll box moves vertically or horizontally to a general location within the area. Clicking above or below the scroll box moves information by screenfuls within the window.

Selecting: When an item is selected, it is highlighted and will be affected by the next action that is performed.

> **How To:** Clicking an item on the screen selects the item. The keyboard can also be used to select items. Generally, pressing [Tab] moves the highlight forward to the next item and [Shift] + [Tab] moves it backward.

Selecting Text: Selecting text expands the highlight to cover the area of text that will be affected by your next action. Selecting text is commonly used to modify existing entries in a dialog box and in most applications.

> **How To:** There are many methods you can use to select an area of text. The most common method is to drag the mouse across the text. You can drag in any direction in the document to extend the highlight. You can drag diagonally across text to extend the highlight from the character the insertion point is on to the last character in the selection. You can also drag in the opposite direction to deselect text. Additionally, you can use the keyboard to select text by holding down [Shift] while pressing a directional key. Either method requires that you move the insertion point to the beginning or end of the area to be selected before you select it. You can also select the entire document using the Select All command on the Edit menu in all Windows 95 applications. Pressing [Delete] removes all selected text. Typing new text automatically replaces all selected text.

Sizing Windows: A window may appear on the desktop in different sizes, and sometimes the current size is too small or too large. A window can be changed to just about any size you want.

> **How To:** Clicking the ▢ Maximize button enlarges a window to its largest possible size, and clicking the ▬ Minimize button reduces a window to a button. A window can be custom sized by pointing to the window border and dragging the border. Dragging inward decreases the size, and dragging outward increases the size. Dragging a corner increases or decreases the size of the two adjoining borders at the same time.

Status Bar: A status bar at the bottom of the window displays information about program settings you are using and the task being performed.

Toolbar: The toolbar is a bar of button icons displayed below the menu bar. Toolbar buttons replace menu selections for many of the most common commands. The icons graphically represent the feature that is activated when selected.

> **How To:** Click on the button to activate the command. A Tooltip consisting of the button name and a brief description displayed in the status bar can be displayed for each toolbar button by pointing to the button.

SPREADSHEET

Undo: Common to all Windows applications is the ability to undo the effects of last action or command. However, some actions you perform cannot be undone. If the Undo command is unavailable, it appears dimmed and you cannot cancel your last action. Some programs allow you to undo multiple actions, up to a certain limit.

How To: Choose the Undo command from the Edit menu. The keyboard shortcut is Ctrl + Z, and the toolbar button equivalent is ↶ Undo. If the Undo button displays a ▼, clicking it displays a drop-down list of the most recently performed actions that can be undone. Selecting from the list reverses the selected action as well as all subsequent actions.

Window: A window is a rectangular section of the screen that is dedicated to a specific activity or application. The window border outlines the window. All windows have the basic parts shown below:

Feature	Description
title bar	A bar located at the top of the window that displays the application name.
Control-menu box	An icon located on the left end of the title bar that when opened displays the Control menu. This menu consists of a list of commands that are used to move, size and otherwise control the window.
Minimize button ▭	Used to reduce a window to a button.
Maximize ▢	Used to enlarge a window to its maximum size.
Restore button ▣	Returns the window to its previous size.
Close button ☒	Used to exit the application running in the window and close the window.
menu bar	Displays a list of menus that can be used within the application displayed in the window.
scroll bar	Whenever the window cannot fully display the information, a scroll bar is displayed.

Windows 95: Windows 95 is an operating system program that controls all the parts of your computer. It uses a graphical user interface (GUI, pronounced "gooey") that displays pictures called icons representing the items you use. The icons are buttons that when "pushed" activate the item.

All Windows programs have a common user interface, which makes it easy to learn and use all types of programs that run under Windows. A common user interface means that programs have common features, such as menu commands and toolbars. For example, a command such as Save in a spreadsheet program is also found on the same menu (File), has the same toolbar button, and performs the same action as it does in a word processing program.

Index

Absolute references, SS65-67
Accounting format for numbers, SS73-74, SS147-148
Activating charts, SS160-161
Active cell, SS14
Active pane, SS104
Active sheet, SS14, SS82
Addition, in formulas, SS37-38
Alignment:
    changing, in cells, SS39-41
    defined, SS7
    right-aligning, SS39-42
Application window, Excel, SS12-13
Area charts, SS149, SS162-167
Arguments:
    for functions, SS60
    for IF functions, SS191
Arithmetic operators, SS37
Arrows, adding to charts, SS156
AutoCalculate, SS12-13, SS35
AutoFill, using, SS85-86
Autoformats, using, SS145-148
Automatic recalculation, SS38
AutoSum, using, SS60-63, SS87
AVG function, SS60

Bar charts, SS149
Bold, formatting as, SS80-82
Borders, adding to worksheets, SS125-126

Buttons:
    Align Left, Align Right, SS41
    Arrow, SS167
    AutoCalculate, SS12-13, SS35
    AutoSum, SS60
    Bold, SS80-82
    Borders, SS125
    Cancel, SS21
    Center, SS41
    Center Across Columns, SS79
    Close, SS12-13
    Control-menu, SS12
    Copy, SS32
    Date Code, SS134
    Enter, SS21
    Font Color, SS125
    Format Painter, SS81
    Function, SS21
    Function Wizard, SS64, SS191
    Help, SS15
    Italic, SS81
    Minimize, SS12-13
    Open, SS30
    Paste, SS33, SS35
    Repeat, SS127
    Restore, SS12-13
    Spelling, SS117
    tab scroll, SS14
    Text Box, SS128
    TipWizard, SS15-16
    Underline, SS82
    Undo, SS71

Category-axis title, SS151
Category names, on charts, SS150
Cell notes, adding, SS67-68
Cell selector, SS14
Cells:
    active, SS14
    clearing data from, SS22, SS63
    defined, SS7, SS14
    deleting, SS77
    destination, SS33
    inserting, SS77
    locking, SS195
    moving contents of, SS78
    selecting, SS20
    source, SS32
Centering:
    across columns, SS79
    cell contents, SS41
    worksheets on page, SS131-132
Chart toolbar, SS156
Charts:
    activating, SS160-161
    adding arrows to, SS167
    adding patterns to, SS163-165
    adding text boxes to, SS165-166
    area, SS149, SS162-167
    changing type of, SS157-158
    column, SS149, SS154-157
    combination, SS149, SS167-170
    data labels on, SS171, SS173
    elements of, SS150-151
    embedded, SS152, SS156

Charts (continued):
- gridlines on, SS150
- legends on, SS150, SS163
- line charts, SS149, SS157-160
- with multiple data series, SS158-160
- pie, SS149, SS172-174
- printing, SS175-176
- redrawing with new data, SS175
- sizing, SS157
- stacked-column, SS160-162
- titles on, SS150-151, SS173
- types of, SS149

ChartWizard, using, SS153-156
Clicking with mouse, SS18
Clipboard, SS32-33
Color, adding to text, SS125-127
Column charts, SS149, SS154-157
Column letters, SS14
Columns:
- centering across, SS79
- changing width of, SS69-70
- defined, SS7, SS14
- deleting, SS77
- inserting, SS77

Combination charts, SS149, SS167-170
Comma format for numbers, SS72
Commands:
- Edit/Clear/Contents, SS22
- Edit/Copy, SS32, SS36, SS210
- Edit/Delete/Entire Column, SS77
- Edit/Delete/Entire Row, SS77
- Edit/Fill, SS35, SS36
- Edit/Fill/Series/AutoFill, SS85
- Edit/Linked Worksheet Object/Edit, SS213
- Edit/Links, SS214
- Edit/Move or Copy Sheet, SS83
- Edit/Paste, SS33, SS36, SS210
- Edit/Paste Special/All Except Borders, SS194
- Edit/Paste Special/Paste, SS217
- Edit/Paste Special/Paste Link, SS119, SS212
- Edit/Repeat Format Cells, SS127

Commands (continued):
- Edit/Undo, SS158
- Edit/Undo Column Width, SS71
- File/Close, SS29
- File/Exit, SS45
- File/New, SS200
- File/Open, SS30
- File/Page Setup, SS131
- File/Page Setup/Fit To, SS133
- File/Page Setup/Header/Footer, SS133
- File/Page Setup/Landscape, SS133
- File/Page Setup/Margins/Horizontally, SS131
- File/Page Setup/Portrait, SS133
- File/Print, SS44, SS88
- File/Print/Entire Workbook, SS175
- File/Print Preview, SS131
- File/Properties, SS41
- File/Properties/Summary, SS88
- File/Save, SS42
- File/Save As, SS42, SS199
- File/Save As/Save As Type, SS199
- Format/AutoFormat, SS147
- Format/Cells, SS39, SS73, SS195
- Format/Cells/Alignment, SS125
- Format/Cells/Border/Bottom, SS126
- Format/Cells/Border/Outline, SS125
- Format/Cells/Font, SS80
- Format/Cells/Font/Color, SS125
- Format/Cells/Patterns, SS126
- Format/Cells/Protection, SS195
- Format/Chart Type, SS161
- Format/Column/Width, SS69
- Format/Selected Chart Title, SS173
- Format/Selected Data Labels, SS171
- Format/Selected Data Series, SS164

Commands (continued):
- Format/Selected Legend, SS163
- Format/Sheet/Rename, SS84
- Format/Style, SS75
- Insert/Chart, SS152
- Insert/Chart/As New Sheet, SS168
- Insert/Columns, SS77
- Insert/Data Labels, SS171, SS173
- Insert/Function, SS64, SS191
- Insert/Name/Create, SS189
- Insert/Name/Define, SS188
- Insert/Name/Paste, SS188, SS192
- Insert/New Data, SS169
- Insert/Note, SS68
- Insert/Object, SS212
- Insert/Rows, SS77
- Insert/Titles, SS173
- Insert/Worksheet, SS83
- repeating, SS127
- Tools/Goal Seek, SS123
- Tools/Options/View/Gridlines, SS219-220
- Tools/Protection/Protect Sheet, SS196
- Tools/Protection/Unprotect Sheet, SS197
- Tools/Solver, SS112, SS121
- Tools/Spelling, SS117
- View/Toolbars, SS16
- View/Zoom, SS71
- View/Zoom/Fit Selection, SS169
- Window/Arrange/Tiled, SS108, SS115
- Window/Freeze Panes, SS105
- Window/New Window, SS108
- Window/Remove Split, SS104
- Window/Split, SS103
- Window/Unfreeze, SS121

Compound documents, SS218
Constant values, SS20
Container file, and embedded objects, SS218
Control-menu buttons, SS12

Index

Copying:
  with AutoFill, SS85-86
  data, SS32-36
  defined, SS7
  external reference formulas, SS119
  formats, SS81
  formulas, SS57-59
  to a range, SS34-36, SS110-111
  sheets, SS82-83, SS122
  worksheets to Word documents, SS207-210
COUNT function, SS60
Currency format for numbers, SS72-73
Current workbook file, SS115

Data:
  changing, SS175
  clearing from cell, SS22, SS63
  copying, SS32-36
  entering, SS20-22
  moving, SS78
  numbers as, SS27-28
  sharing between applications, SS207-221
  text as, SS20
Data labels, on charts, SS171
Data markers, on charts, SS150
Data series, on charts, SS150
Date numbers, SS41, SS72
Dates:
  adding to headers and footers, SS134
  entering current in cell, SS41
  formatting, SS72
Decimals, increasing and decreasing, SS74-75
Deleting:
  cell contents, SS22, SS63
  cells, rows, columns, SS77
Dependent workbook, in linking, SS118
Designing worksheets, SS19
Destination cells, SS33
Destination document, SS211

Dialog boxes:
  ChartWizard, SS153-156
  Define Name, SS188
  Format Cells, SS40, SS196
  Format Column Group, SS161
  Goal Seek Status, SS124
  Links, SS214
  Open, SS30
  Paste Special, SS212, SS217
  Print, SS44
  Protect Sheet, SS196
  Solver Parameters, SS112
  Solver Results, SS113
  Style, SS76
Division, in formulas, SS37
Docked toolbar, SS128
Documenting:
  with cell notes, SS67
  templates, SS199
  workbooks, SS41-42
  worksheets, SS19
Doughnut charts, SS149
Dragging with mouse, SS18
Drawing toolbar, SS127-128, SS166

Editing entries in cells, SS23-25
Electronic spreadsheets. *See* Spreadsheets, Worksheets
Embedding:
  charts, SS152, SS156
  linking vs., SS221
  objects, SS216-221
  updating embedded objects, SS218-220
Entering:
  data, SS20-22
  formulas, SS37-38, SS55-57
  functions, SS59-65
  numbers as, SS27-28
  text as long entries, SS25-27
Equal to, logical operator, SS191
Excel 7.0a for Windows 95:
  application window for, SS12-13
  exiting, SS45
  filenames in, SS43
  loading, SS12

Excel 7.0a for Windows 95 (cont.):
  sharing data with Word application, SS207-221
  window elements of, SS12-13
Exploding slice on pie charts, SS174
Exponentiation, in formulas, SS37
External reference formula, SS118

Files:
  closing, SS29
  current workbook, SS115
  linking, SS7, SS86-88
  naming, SS43
  opening, SS30
  printing, SS44-45
  renaming, SS42-43
  saving, SS42-43
Fill handle, SS35
Filling a range, SS35
Fit To option for printing, SS90
Floating toolbar, SS128
Fonts:
  changing, SS79-82
  defined, SS80
Footers:
  custom, SS133-134
  predefined, SS131-132
Formatting:
  as bold, SS80-82
  copying, SS81
  defined, SS7, SS39
  as italic, SS81
  numbers, SS72-75
  as underlined, SS82
Formatting toolbar, SS12-13, SS14, SS41
Formula bar, SS12-13
Formulas:
  copying, SS57-59
  defined, SS7
  entering, SS37-38, SS55-57
  external reference, SS118
Freezing window panes, SS105-107, SS121

SPREADSHEET

Function keys:
   ABS [F4], SS67, SS120
   Edit [F2], SS23
   Spelling [F7], SS117
Function Wizard, using, SS64-65
Functions:
   defined, SS7, SS60
   entering, SS59-63
   entering with Function Wizard, SS64-65
   IF, SS190-193
   nested, SS193
   syntax for, SS60, SS191

Goal Seek, using, SS1220124
Graphs, SS7. *See* Charts
Greater than, logical operator, SS191
Gridlines:
   on charts, SS150
   printing with, SS90

Handle, fill, SS35
Handles, selection, SS130
Headers:
   custom, SS133-135
   predefined, SS131-132
Headings, row and column, SS20
Help for Excel, SS15

IF function, SS190-193
Inserting and overwriting, SS24
Insertion point, moving, SS23
Italic, formatting as, SS81

Keys:
   arrow, SS18
   [←Backspace], SS21, SS23
   [Caps Lock], SS23
   [Delete], SS22, SS23
   [End], SS18, SS23
   [←Enter], SS21-22
   [Esc], SS21
   [Home], SS23, SS70
   [Insert], SS24
   [Num Lock], SS16
   [Page Down], [Page Up], SS17, SS18

Labels, defined, SS7
Landscape style, printing, SS133
Left-aligning cell contents, SS41
Legends on charts, SS150
   moving, SS163
Less than, logical operator, SS191
Line charts, SS149, SS157-160
Linked objects, SS211
Linking:
   charts to documents in Word, SS211-216
   files, SS7, SS86-88
   updating linked objects, SS213-216
   vs. embedding, SS221
   workbooks, SS118-122
Live link, SS211
Locking cells, SS195
Logical operators, SS191

MAX function, SS60
Menu bar, SS12-13
MIN function, SS60
Minimal recalculation, SS38
Mixed references, SS66
Mode indicator, SS12
Modes:
   Edit, SS23
   Point, SS55-57
   Ready, SS12-13
Mouse:
   moving around worksheet with, SS18
   selecting a range with, SS34
Mouse pointer, SS12, SS13
Moving:
   cell contents, SS78
   defined, SS7
   legends in charts, SS163
   sheets, SS115
   toolbars, SS127-128
Multiplication, in formulas, SS37

Name box, SS12-13, SS14
Naming:
   ranges, SS185-190
   sheets, SS84
Nested functions, SS193
Noncontiguous selections, SS152
Notes, cell, SS67-68
Number signs in cells, SS70
Numbers:
   entering, SS27-28
   formatting, SS72-75

Object field code, SS211
Objects:
   embedding, SS216-221
   linking, SS211-216
   text boxes as, SS130
   updating linked, SS213-216
Office, Microsoft, and Shortcut Bar, SS9
Operands, SS37
Operators:
   arithmetic, SS37
   logical, SS191
Overwriting and inserting, SS24

Page numbers, adding, SS134
Panes:
   active, SS104
   freezing, SS105-107
   splitting windows into, SS103
   unfreezing, SS121
Passwords for worksheets, SS196-197
Pasting:
   between applications, SS207-210
   contents of Clipboard, SS33, SS35
Percent format for numbers, SS72, SS76-77
Pie charts, SS149, SS172-174
Plot area, SS150
Portrait style, printing, SS133
Previewing workbooks, SS88-91

Index

Printing:
    charts, SS175-176
    with Fit To option, SS90
    with gridlines, SS90
    landscape or portrait, SS133
    workbooks, SS44-45
    worksheets, SS131
Protecting worksheets, SS195-198

Radar charts, SS149
Ranges:
    copying to, SS34-36
    defined, SS34
    filling with data, SS35
    naming, SS185-190
    selecting, SS34, SS41
Recalculating worksheets, SS38
References, SS14
    absolute, SS65-67
    mixed, SS66
    relative, SS58, SS66
    3D, SS86
Relative references, SS58, SS66
Right-aligning cell contents, SS39-41
Row numbers, SS14
Rows:
    defined, SS7, SS14
    deleting, SS77
    inserting, SS77-78

Saving:
    template files, SS199-200
    workbooks, SS42-43
Scatter charts (XY), SS149
Scrolling worksheets, SS17-18
Selection handles, SS130
Server application, SS217
Sheet tabs, SS14
Sheets:
    active, SS14, SS82
    copying, SS82-83
    defined, SS14
    moving, SS115
    moving between, SS83
    naming, SS84

Shortcut Bar, SS9
Solver, using, SS111-115
Source cells, SS32
Source document, SS211
Source workbook, SS118
Spell-checking workbooks, SS116-118
Split box, SS103
Splitting windows, SS103-104
Spreadsheets:
    advantages of using, SS6-7
    defined, SS5
    terminology for, SS7
    3D, SS6
    See also Worksheets
Stacked-column charts, SS160-162
Standard toolbar, SS12-13, SS14
Status bar, SS12-13
Styles, applying, SS75-77
Subtraction, in formulas, SS37
SUM function, SS60-63
Syntax:
    for functions, SS60
    for IF functions, SS191

Tab scroll buttons, SS14
Tables, Excel data as, SS210
Tabs:
    Alignment, SS40
    formatting, SS40
    sheet, SS14
    Summary, SS42
Templates:
    creating, SS198-201
    defined, SS199
    documenting, SS199
    Elegant Memo (Word), SS208
    saving, SS199-200
Testing worksheets, SS19
Text boxes:
    adding to charts, SS165-166
    adding to worksheets, SS128-130
Text entries, defined, SS20
3D charts, SS149

3D references, SS86
Tiling windows, SS108
Time:
    adding to headers and footers, SS134
    format, SS72
TipWizard toolbar, SS15-16
Title bar, SS12-13
Titles, on charts, SS150-151, SS173
Toolbar dock, SS136
Toolbars:
    Chart, SS156
    displaying, SS16
    docked, SS128
    Drawing, SS127-128, SS166
    floating, SS128
    Formatting, SS12-13, SS14, SS41
    moving, SS127-128
    Standard, SS12-13, SS14
    TipWizard, SS15-16, SS45
    using, SS15-16
True type fonts, SS80
Typefaces, SS80

Undo, using, SS71

Value-axis title, SS151
Values:
    defined, SS7
    variable and constant, SS20
Variable values, SS20

What-if analysis:
    defined, SS7, SS109
    with Goal Seek, SS123-124
    with Solver, SS111-115
    using, SS109-111
Windows, Excel:
    elements of, SS12-13
    splitting, SS103-104
    tiling, SS108
    viewing multiple, SS107-108
Windows 95, review of, SS239-248

SPREADSHEET

Word (Microsoft):
    copying Excel data to, SS207-210
    linking charts to documents in, SS211-216
Word wrap, SS129
Workbook window, SS13
Workbooks:
    closing, SS28-29
    current, SS115
    defined, SS13
    dependent, for linking, SS118
    documenting, SS41-42
    linking, SS118-122
    opening, SS29-31
    opening a second, SS115-116
    previewing, SS88-91
    saving, SS42-43
    source, for linking, SS118
Worksheets:
    adding borders to, SS125-126
    adding color to, SS125-127
    adding text boxes to, SS128-130
    and AutoFormat, SS145-148
    centering on page, SS131-132
    changing data on, SS175
    copying data to Word documents, SS207-210
    designing, SS19
    documenting, SS19

Worksheets (continued):
    elements of, SS14
    entering data in, SS20-22
    formatting, SS145-148
    headers and footers in, SS131-132
    linking, SS86-88
    moving around, SS16-18
    passwords for, SS196-197
    protecting, SS195-198
    recalculating, SS38
    scrolling, SS17-18
    spell-checking, SS116-118
    styles, applying to, SS75-76
    testing, SS19
    title for, entering, SS25-26
    zooming, SS71-72
Workspace, window, SS12-13
WYSIWYG, SS6, SS7

X axis, SS150-151
XY charts, SS149

Y axis, SS150-151

Z axis, on 3D charts, SS151
Zooming:
    charts, SS169
    worksheet, SS71-72

Notes

ss255

SPREADSHEET

Notes